THE COMPLETE IDIOT'S GUIDE® TO

Auto Repair

by Vyvyan Lynn with Tony Molla

ALPHA
A member of Penguin Group (USA)

To those closest to my heart: my children, my friend, and my sister.

ALPHA BOOKS

Published by the Penguin Group

Penguin Group (USA) Inc., 375 Hudson Street, New York, New York 10014, USA

Penguin Group (Canada), 90 Eglinton Avenue East, Suite 700, Toronto, Ontario M4P 2Y3, Canada (a division of Pearson Penguin Canada Inc.)

Penguin Books Ltd., 80 Strand, London WC2R 0RL, England

Penguin Ireland, 25 St. Stephen's Green, Dublin 2, Ireland (a division of Penguin Books Ltd.)

Penguin Group (Australia), 250 Camberwell Road, Camberwell, Victoria 3124, Australia (a division of Pearson Australia Group Pty. Ltd.)

Penguin Books India Pvt. Ltd., 11 Community Centre, Panchsheel Park, New Delhi—110 017, India

Penguin Group (NZ), 67 Apollo Drive, Rosedale, North Shore, Auckland 1311, New Zealand (a division of Pearson New Zealand Ltd.)

Penguin Books (South Africa) (Pty.) Ltd., 24 Sturdee Avenue, Rosebank, Johannesburg 2196, South Africa

Penguin Books Ltd., Registered Offices: 80 Strand, London WC2R 0RL, England

Copyright © 2007 by Vyvyan Lynn

International Standard Book Number: 978-1-59257-495-7
Library of Congress Catalog Card Number: 2006938595

09 08 07   8 7 6 5 4 3 2 1

Interpretation of the printing code: The rightmost number of the first series of numbers is the year of the book's printing; the rightmost number of the second series of numbers is the number of the book's printing. For example, a printing code of 07-1 shows that the first printing occurred in 2007.

Printed in the United States of America

Note: This publication contains the opinions and ideas of its authors. It is intended to provide helpful and informative material on the subject matter covered. It is sold with the understanding that the authors and publisher are not engaged in rendering professional services in the book. If the reader requires personal assistance or advice, a competent professional should be consulted.

The authors and publisher specifically disclaim any responsibility for any liability, loss, or risk, personal or otherwise, which is incurred as a consequence, directly or indirectly, of the use and application of any of the contents of this book.

Most Alpha books are available at special quantity discounts for bulk purchases for sales promotions, premiums, fund-raising, or educational use. Special books, or book excerpts, can also be created to fit specific needs.

For details, write: Special Markets, Alpha Books, 375 Hudson Street, New York, NY 10014.

Publisher: *Marie Butler-Knight*
Editorial Director/Acquiring Editor: *Mike Sanders*
Managing Editor: *Billy Fields*
Development Editor: *Lynn Northrup*
Senior Production Editor: *Janette Lynn*
Copy Editor: *Michael Dietsch*

Cartoonist: *Shannon Wheeler*
Cover Designer: *Bill Thomas*
Book Designer: *Trina Wurst*
Indexer: *Tonya Heard*
Layout: *Chad Dressler, Eric S. Miller*
Proofreader: *John Etchison*

Contents at a Glance

Contents

Introduction

I've written on many topics, from natural disasters to how to pick a great Easter bonnet. Research is part of a writer's life, and topics of great interest spark the curiosity factor, causing a rapid firing of questions. This book is just that for me, a rapid firing of questions about a topic that can and will save my readers money, time, anxious moments by the side of the road, and yes, maybe even lives. Car maintenance that makes vehicles safer on our highways can be incorporated into a busy schedule. It's all a matter of learning what to do, when to do it, and how to do it. Then it just becomes part of your life.

Everything you want to learn, but would rather learn on your own, will be covered in this book. How do you get your hood to release after you pop the switch inside the car? How do you check your fluid levels? How do you know what fluids go where and how much fluid should be added? You will learn these basics and more. You will also learn how to work on your vehicle safely. Yes, you can work on your vehicle with no problems if you pay attention to safety rules, learn and follow each repair step, and never start a job you don't have adequate time to finish.

Cars fascinate, intrigue, and excite me. They grant a trip to the grocery store or a brief respite from the rest of the world. However, the freedom of driving comes with extreme responsibility. My son will tell you that the advice I gave and still give him is "Focus." When you are in the driver's seat, your job is the road no matter what your passengers are doing.

So accept extreme responsibility each time you get behind the wheel. However, if you take a few moments and get into a regular routine of keeping your car in the best possible condition, your focus will most likely become a pleasure.

While you may or may not want to do your own repairs, this book will give you a critical basic knowledge base. This knowledge base enables you to speak with a technician with confidence. Just imagine—instead of saying, "I hear a strange wurrrrRRRRrrrrwuRRRrrr noise when I try to start my car," you can say, "I'm hearing a noise that most probably indicates a need to check the charge on my battery." Auto knowledge is auto empowerment. And this knowledge is appreciated by technicians.

What You'll Find in This Book

The book is set up in three parts, with four appendixes. Let's take a look at what you'll be learning.

Part 1, "Deciding to Learn About Your Car," gives you car basics, information about extended warranties, what tools you will need for basic repairs, and a chapter that tells you how to incorporate a regular maintenance routine.

Part 2, "Identifying and Troubleshooting Your Car's Systems," shows and explains the systems that make up your car as well as gives you information on how to maintain your systems and troubleshoot problems.

Part 3, "Showing Off Your Vehicle," tells you when and how to keep the outside of your car sparkling and the inside clean. This part also aids you in basic body and interior repairs.

I took great care with the appendixes. This is where you go to look up a problem quickly, find a term or great car resource, and find handy maintenance checklists and a vehicle fact sheet.

The aim of this book is to make this job a part of your life. It takes about three weeks to create a habit. So read at least the first part of this book and begin creating habits like checking the oil and tires and cleaning the windshield while your car is filling up with gas. Then go on to the other jobs. Once you know what to do and begin to see positive results, you'll be hooked on your new regular car-maintenance routine.

Extras

Inside every chapter you will find valuable sidebars:

CarLogic
These sidebars give you great insights into everything auto: how it works and how to keep it working.

Speedbumps
These sidebars tell you when—and why—you need to use caution.

Auto-Biography
Here you'll find background information as it relates to cars today, as well as miscellaneous tidbits.

Drive Time
Every term you'll need for your new auto-repair vocabulary is included in these sidebars.

Acknowledgments

I would like to thank Robert and Theresa Russell for their wonderful helpful natures and auto-care know-how. I'd also like to thank Lynn Northrup for her hard work on this manuscript.

Special Thanks to the Technical Reviewer

The Complete Idiot's Guide to Auto Repair was reviewed by an expert who double-checked the accuracy of what you'll learn here, to help us ensure that this book gives you everything you need to know about auto repair. Special thanks are extended to Tony Molla.

Tony Molla is the vice president of communications for the National Institute for Automotive Service Excellence (ASE) in Leesburg, Virginia. With over 40 years of experience in the automotive service industry, Tony is an ASE-certified automotive technician, author of more than a dozen technical and car-care manuals, and recipient of several Outstanding Editorial Achievement awards.

Trademarks

All terms mentioned in this book that are known to be or are suspected of being trademarks or service marks have been appropriately capitalized. Alpha Books and Penguin Group (USA) Inc. cannot attest to the accuracy of this information. Use of a term in this book should not be regarded as affecting the validity of any trademark or service mark.

Part 1

Deciding to Learn About Your Car

Congratulations! You are embarking on a mission. On this mission you will develop a newfound intimacy with your vehicle that may just turn into a love affair. If you aren't already enamored, just give us a few pages. We'll begin with the most important information: safety guidelines for working on your vehicle. Then you'll learn how to open the hood and change a tire. This is knowledge that will make you feel more confident while driving. We'll also chat a bit about octane levels before moving on to information you'll feel better knowing before you buy a vehicle. We'll tell you about extended warranties and give information about car dealership service departments and how to get your technician in your corner. Next we move on to what tools you'll need to have in your car in case of a roadside emergency and the tools you'll need for basic repairs and regular vehicle maintenance. The last chapter equips you with a regular maintenance routine for your vehicle. We'll tell you what you need to do to what and when you'll need to perform basic maintenance.

Chapter 1

Car Basics: What You Need to Know

In This Chapter

♦ Staying safe while you work

♦ Gas pump basics

♦ Fuel economy for your car

♦ Changing a flat tire and checking tire pressure

♦ Raising the hood

♦ A look at how power doors and locks work

With all the jobs you already have, why would you want to add auto maintenance and auto repair to your "to-do" list? That's a good question. And one easily answered. Learning how your car works and how to keep it working can save you time, money, and maybe even your life. And believe it or not—please do believe it—these jobs can be learned and implemented painlessly. Just repeat after me: "I do not have to be a specially trained auto mechanic to do routine maintenance and repair."

You may not harbor even a remote passion for tinkering with cars, but everyone feels more in control with basic knowledge of the elements that make up their lives. Your car is clearly a basic element. You rely on it to carry you and your family safely from point A to point B on a daily basis.

Vyv remembers her dad's routine of getting the family car ready for trips. He checked the fluid levels, the tire pressure, and the mileage. The mileage check was one she grew to hate as she became a teenager and cruised farther than she was supposed to. He also cleaned the windshield, the windows, headlights, and taillights. Yes, he could have had this done at a full-service station. They were plentiful then, but he felt better checking on the car himself. When the family went on vacations and it was time to fill up the gas tank, he checked the car again or had the service-station attendant do so. He developed a routine and stuck to it.

As soon as you learn a few basics about your automobile, you can develop your own car-checkup routine and feel confident about how to do those little jobs that keep you from encountering the bigger, more expensive jobs.

Safety First

If you are motivated to do a repair job, are ready to learn the basics, and have time and the right tools, you will do just fine. However, some repairs should be left to your mechanic or technician, and we'll let you know what they are as we troubleshoot your car's systems. Newer-model cars come with electronic systems that may require special tools and computers to do some repairs. It's always worth the effort to read your owner's manual to learn how your vehicle is designed, and to get an idea of which repair jobs an owner can tackle and which are best left to a technician.

When considering whether you can do a repair, also keep in mind your body's abilities. If you avoid muscle shirts because your biceps and triceps are no-shows, some jobs that require arm strength are going to be hard. Also, some jobs call for a strong back. *Jacking up your car* and trying to get a tool into a tight angle may be called for when attempting certain jobs. Toolmakers realize car owners have physical limitations and are inventing new tools to aid the mechanic every day. If you have physical limitations or a disability, check to see whether there is a tool that might make the job easier for you. (Refer to the list of inventive tool manufacturers in Appendix C.) But if not, it would probably be best to have your technician do the repair.

Drive Time _____

Jacking up your car is the process of lifting all or part of your car off ground level with a jack. You can use many different kinds of jacks to do this. Check your owner's manual to see what kind is in your car. Some common ones are different varieties of hydraulic jacks and the mechanical scissor jack (both are pictured later in the chapter).

Keep these safety rules in mind while working on your car:

- Do not begin a repair or maintenance job on your car if you are not feeling well, if you are tired or are taking medicine that makes you drowsy, or if you've been drinking.

- Never smoke while doing repair or maintenance work.

- Keep a charged "BC" fire extinguisher ("B" for liquid fires and "C" for electrical fires) near your work area.

- Do not crawl under a vehicle supported by *just* a jack. Always use a pair of jack (support) stands positioned underneath the vehicle to keep your vehicle from falling on you. (These are pictured in Chapter 3.)

- Disconnect the negative battery cable when doing electrical-repair work.

- Make sure you are fully clothed in work clothes. Be aware that anything that dangles, such as long hair, loose clothing, scarves, or jewelry, can become caught in moving parts under the car hood and cause you serious injury.

- If the engine is running or the vehicle has been driven within the past half hour or so, the engine, radiator, exhaust, muffler, and other parts beneath the hood will be very hot. Don't touch!

- Never open the radiator cap on a hot engine. The engine should cool for at least a half hour before you attempt to open the cap. Even then, use extreme caution.

- Wear eye protection when working on your vehicle. Wearing a breathing mask is also a good idea to avoid inhaling chemicals under the hood.

- Focus on the job at hand when working on your vehicle and don't allow yourself to become distracted. Why? To avoid injury. Even when the vehicle is turned off there are all sorts of mishaps that can occur—not the least of which is having a wrench slip and banging your knuckles (ouch!).

- Always let a family member or neighbor know when you are going to be working on your car, especially if you will be crawling underneath your vehicle.

- Beware of toxic chemicals like coolant and battery acid. Read the directions on the label (coolant) and follow directions on how to clean (rid the battery posts of acid) a battery in Chapter 4.

- Work in a space that allows you fresh air.

- Never store gasoline in your garage, basement, or anywhere in your home. Gasoline and gasoline vapors are highly flammable.

- Don't use gasoline for any purpose but to fuel a vehicle.

- Always purchase and store gasoline in a UL-approved safety container that is vented to release pressure that builds up inside the container. Remember to open the vent!

Auto work, just like any other job you undertake, will require you to pay attention to safety rules. Just think what would happen if you didn't know to keep your hand off a hot stove! These rules are not to frighten, but to educate. Life is ordered by common sense, and auto repair is no different. So don't be afraid to pop the hood latch and explore. Your car won't blow up just by popping the hood latch unless there's some sort of fluke accident waiting to happen.

Pumping Your Own Gas

Today, full-service gas stations are the exception rather than the rule. That's not good for at least a couple of reasons. Full service meant each time you filled up your gas tank, an attendant checked your oil and tire pressure and cleaned your windshield all while the gas went into your tank. It also meant you didn't have to worry about smelling like gas when you breezed into work.

Self-service means just that: you maneuver your car up to a pump and figure out whether to pay before you pump or after, not to mention figuring out how to operate the gas pump. In the long run, full-service stations would be cheaper on your pocketbook even though the gas price might be a few cents more, if that was the only way routine maintenance was being performed on your car. But since that option is no longer widely available, here's a step-by-step primer to get the gas from the pump into your car's gas tank:

1. Check to see which side of the car your gas tank is on. Drive up to the pump with the gas-tank side of the car facing the pump. Stop and turn off your car.

2. Pull the latch (inside the vehicle) or press the button to open your gas-tank door (it usually has a picture of a gas pump on it), or open the door (if outside the vehicle) to the gas tank manually. Unscrew the gas cap and place it where it won't roll off your car. (Some gas caps are attached.)

3. Payment methods vary. Some stations have a "pay before you pump" requirement, especially after dark, so check notes on the pump before attempting to fill your tank. If you're paying with a credit card and the pump is credit card accessible, swipe the card and watch the monitor for the correct way to complete your transaction. If the pump doesn't offer payment by credit card, you'll need to go inside and let a cashier take your credit-card information.

4. There are usually three types of octane levels of gas offered at the pump: regular, premium, and super (see the following section for more on types of fuel). Check your owner's manual for the recommended fuel for your car.

5. Slide your fingers around the handle of the gas hose and lift it off the pump. Then insert the nozzle into the tank of your car. You may or may not have to push a button on the pump to choose the type gas you want. Sometimes you have to pull up the part of the pump that was holding the nozzle in order to activate the pump.

6. Place your index finger around the trigger and pull back. You'll notice the gallons of gas pumped as well as the amount of money spent as the gas flows into your tank. If you're filling up the tank, you can set the trigger on the gas hose to run and continue to fill your car while you wash your windshield, check the oil, and check the tires. When your tank is full, the gas will shut off.

> **Speedbumps**
>
> If your vehicle has a diesel engine, it runs on diesel fuel. The diesel you buy at a pump—which is usually located away from gasoline pumps—is generally obtained from petroleum or crude oil. Never pump diesel fuel in a car that doesn't have a diesel engine (or vice versa).

7. When you're done pumping gas into your vehicle, remove the nozzle. Keep baby wipes or some type of hand-cleaning towelettes in your car to clean gas off your hands.

8. Screw the gas cap back on and close the door. Make sure you don't leave the gas cap loose. This can cause a check-engine warning light to come on in some vehicles.

Commonsense safety measures like not smoking while at a service station or while pumping gas are also good rules to follow. Also, you must shut the vehicle off before you attempt to put fuel in the tank. And bear in mind what makes gasoline a great fuel also makes it deadly. Keep these qualities of gasoline in mind:

◆ Gasoline vaporizes easily, which makes the vapor that rises above the liquid ignite as well as the liquid. Inhaling the vapor for an extended period of time can cause sickness.

◆ Gasoline is easily ignited, meaning striking a match, smoking, or static electricity too close to gasoline or the vapors can cause the substance to ignite or explode.

◆ Gasoline in even small amounts can cause a potent explosion.

What Fuel Is Best for Your Car?

You pull in to get gas, but what type should you buy? Are the high-*octane* fuels better for your car? No. High octane, which equals out to a higher-price gas, doesn't guarantee better performance. Your car may be built to run regular low-octane fuel—most are. Check your owner's manual to see what the most effective octane level is for your car. Buying higher-octane gasoline is a waste of your hard-earned money unless your owner's manual advises it or your engine is knocking.

You may not know about engine knock, so here is a bit of history. Fact or fiction: Detergents in regular gasoline aren't sufficient to keep an engine clean. Fiction! Pre-1970s, before leaded gasoline was retired, cars needed premium gas to control octane-related engine knocking. Combustion-knocking occurs in the power stroke (combustion) of a four-stroke internal combustion engine if combustion is interrupted by a detonation of unburned air/gas mixture. Today most cars are equipped with electronic "knock sensors." These sensors adjust engines to accommodate different fuel grades. While high-compression engines could get better fuel efficiency with the higher-octane gas, it's a good bet it's not enough difference to make up for the expenditure for the higher-priced gas. But, as always, check your owner's manual.

Here are some tips for getting the most from the gas you purchase:

Drive Time

Octane is a part of gasoline that can keep an internal combustion engine from knocking. An engine with high compression may require higher octane, which means the fuel won't autoignite as quickly as lower-octane fuel.

- Gas mileage decreases at high speeds, so be mindful of the speed limit.

- Drive gently in stop-and-go traffic. Fast acceleration when taking off from stoplights or from stops in traffic jams, etc. eats into your gas mileage.

- Turn off the engine if you know you will have a wait.

- Use your cruise control when driving on the open road.

- Clean out your trunk to lighten your vehicle's load and increase gas mileage. (Having a clean trunk is always a good plan so you can get to your jack and tool-box when needed.)

- Don't pack items in a roof rack. The wind drag can make your ride less fuel efficient.

- Remember your maintenance routines as outlined in this book and in your owner's manual!

Keeping your engine tuned; maintaining your tires at the right air pressure, in good condition, and in alignment; using the motor oil recommended by your car's manufacturer; changing the oil at the correct intervals; and changing the air filter as recommended will also make your vehicle more fuel efficient.

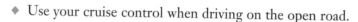

Auto-Biography

Trying to decide whether running the air-conditioning is worth the extra fuel expenditure? According to the *Consumer Reports* auto-test department, it is more fuel efficient to drive with windows down and the air-conditioning off in stop-and-go traffic; *however*, when reaching speeds over 45 mph, it is actually more fuel efficient to drive with windows up and the air-conditioning on. Why? Wind drag comes into play at higher speeds. Drag is what you would imagine—it slows down or impedes progress.

Changing a Flat Tire

Flat tires happen to everyone sooner or later. There are many reasons why a tire may become defective. We'll discuss them in Chapter 7. But no matter the reason or location, whether you are out on the road or at home, you either have to change it yourself or have it changed. (It's always a good idea to practice changing a tire *before* you have to!) Here is a guide to help you get back in the driver's seat and rolling on down the road.

Before changing a tire, make sure that you are on level ground and away from traffic. Do not attempt to change a tire in an unsafe location—for example, if you are on a busy road or interstate highway and too close to traffic, or if you're in a dark or unsafe location. If you decide to change the tire yourself, you need to make sure the car is in park or, if you have a manual transmission, that the car is in first gear. Before you get out of the car, set the parking brake and put your keys in your pocket where you won't lose them. (Vyv always puts her keys in her pocket and then touches her pocket to take herself off autopilot—it's just a mental check habit when life gets busy and she's multitasking.) Keep something like bricks or wooden blocks in your car to block the tires on the opposite end of the car of where your flat occurred. Or buy wheel chocks, shown in the following illustration. They work as well as bricks and blocks, are inexpensive, and can be purchased in bright yellow. If you're changing a tire on the side of the road, bright colors will make others notice you, especially on cloudy days, during twilight, or after dark.

Be sure to brace both wheels on the opposite end of the car from the tire you are working on. For example, if you are working on a tire on the front of your vehicle, both back tires should be braced.

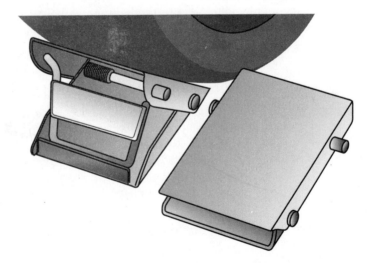

You will need to have the following tools in your car at all times. (For a more complete list of the tools you need to keep in your car and information on jack stands, refer to Chapter 3.)

- ◆ Spare tire

- ◆ Car jack (scissor jack or hydraulic jack)

- ◆ Can of WD-40

- ◆ Lug wrench

- ◆ Wheel chocks (or bricks or wooden blocks)

- ◆ Emergency triangles

- ◆ Flashlight with fresh batteries

- ◆ Nonflammable sealant

- ◆ Battery-operated air compressor (optional)

Speedbumps

Never drive on a flat tire unless you are in danger. Doing so will damage the wheel and call for a more costly repair.

Emergency triangles alert motorists that a roadside emergency has occurred. Triangles are safer than flares unless you buy battery-operated flares.

Scissor jack.

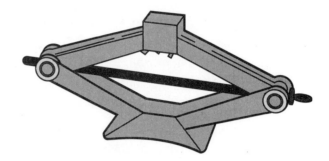

Hydraulic bottle jack.

Lug wrenches come in different styles. Some are designed to make the job much easier. Ask the auto-parts salesperson what is available and make your decision based on how much muscle you have to put into the job.

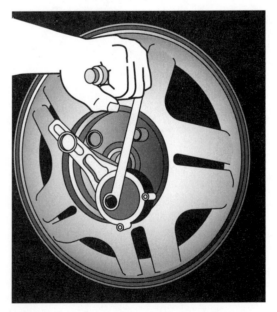

If you get a flat tire while you're driving, follow these steps to pull over:

1. Keep a cool head. Do not stomp the brake pedal; instead, remove your foot from the accelerator and allow the vehicle to slow down gradually. But be ever mindful of traffic. You will have to factor in how to stay safe as you maneuver around other motorists and inch closer to the side of the road or exit.

2. Grasp your steering wheel firmly and slowly move to a safe place on the side of the road, as far away from traffic as you can.

3. Park on a level spot, turn off your ignition, set the parking brake, turn on your hazard flashers, safely exit your car on the nontraffic side of the road, and set out your emergency triangles. You'll need to set up a triangle in the front and rear of your vehicle.

Once you've safely pulled your car over, you're ready to change the flat. (It's always a good idea to practice changing a tire *before* you have to!) The following illustrations show the sequence of steps involved in changing a flat.

Step 1: If your wheel has a wheel cover, carefully remove the cover with the flat end of the lug wrench or per directions in your owner's manual.

Step 2: Loosen the lug nuts in a counterclockwise direction, but don't remove them yet. If the lug nuts are hard to turn by hand, try spraying them with WD-40.

Step 3: Place the jack according to the directions in your owner's manual. Make sure you follow these directions for jack placement so that you don't damage your vehicle.

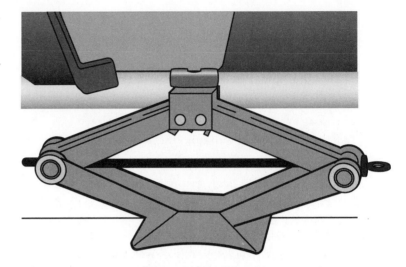

Step 4: Raise the tire approximately 2 inches off the ground. To be safe, keep your hands out from under your car when raising the car off the ground during a tire change.

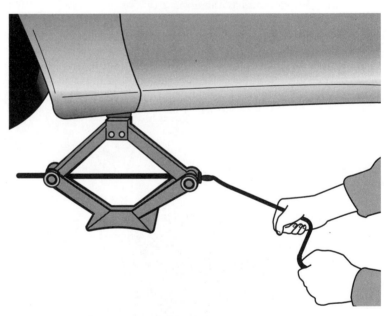

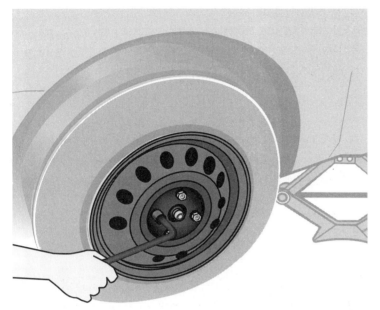

Step 5: When you have the tire jacked up off the ground, remove the lug nuts. Be sure to put the lug nuts in a safe place—your pocket or cap, for example—so you won't lose them.

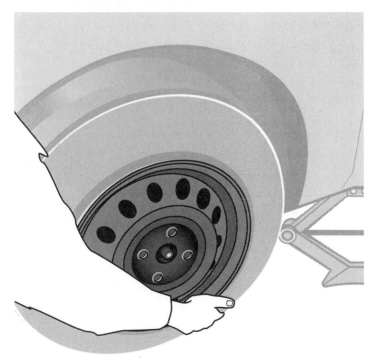

Step 6: Remove the tire, placing it on the ground out of your way. Make sure it does not end up rolling out into traffic!

Step 7: Put your spare tire on the exposed wheel studs, and then place the lug nuts on by hand.

Step 8: Use the lug wrench to tighten the lug nuts in an X (crisscross pattern). This makes the wheel adhere evenly to the hub.

Step 9: Lower the vehicle and check lug-nut tightness again. You may need to have your mechanic check the lug-nut tightness if you aren't sure you tightened the lug nuts to specification (this information is in your owner's manual).

When you're done, put the lug wrench, flat tire, jack, and wheel cover back into the trunk. If necessary, get the tire fixed or replaced as soon as possible. You should always have a full-size spare tire in your trunk. The temporary-use tires that come with many vehicles are for just that: temporary use (basically, just to get you to a repair station). Also, you should not drive faster than 45 to 50 mph when using a temporary tire.

CarLogic _____

If your tire has a puncture and there is no way to change the tire, you can use a foam sealant. Just remember you want a sealant that is *nonflammable*. Flammable sealants have caused fatalities. And remember if you use a sealant for a puncture you still have to have the puncture fixed ASAP. Also, many technicians are hesitant to work on tires that sealants have been used on because it makes for a messy job. If you have a tire that is leaking slowly and have a battery-operated air compressor in your trunk, this is also a good way to get back on the road and to a place you can change or have the tire changed.

How to Check Tire Pressure and Add Air to Tires

It's amazing how something so easily checked as tire pressure can cause so much trouble if left undone. Improperly inflated tires can cause everything from auto crashes to poor gas mileage to poor handling, and it makes your tires wear out too soon. The correct amount of air pressure for your vehicle's tires is noted in your owner's manual and may also be listed on a tire-pressure decal on the driver's side of the car in the doorjamb or in the glove-box lid.

Here's how to check tire pressure:

1. Find and take the cap off the air-pressure valve. Put it in a safe place.

2. Put the air-pressure gauge onto the valve. (You will have to press it down to keep air from escaping). Check the reading on your air-pressure gauge.

Check the reading on the measuring stick that extends from the bottom of your air-pressure gauge.

Putting air in tire through air valve.

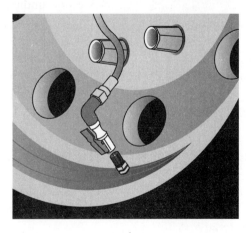

3. If you are low, add air until you reach the recommended pressure (per your owner's manual.)

4. If you overfill the tire, release air by pushing on the metal stem in the center of the valve.

5. Replace the valve cap.

Repeat these steps with each tire. Don't forget to check the spare, too. You will need it one day!

CarLogic _____

For a more accurate reading, always check tire pressure after your vehicle has been idle for a while, when the tires are cool. Why? The temperature of the tire affects the reading. A hot tire will show more air pressure than is available.

Raising the Hood

If you've never attempted any maintenance jobs on your car, raising the hood may be one of the first jobs you need to learn. It's not difficult.

First, find the hood release located inside your car. (It's on the driver's left side and normally labeled HOOD.) Pull that lever or push that button.

Now stroll around to the front of the car. Look for the safety latch, the part that keeps the hood down while you are driving should the hood release be pulled by mistake. You will usually find the safety latch behind the grill. If you can't find the safety latch, check your owner's manual to find out where your vehicle's safety latch is located.

It may take you a few minutes to find the release switch, but feel around until you do. Pull or push the switch until it unlatches. (When first finding this latch, it helps to squat down to grill level and slide your fingers around inside the grill in search of the latch.) Raise the hood. If there is a rod to help steady the hood, put it in place. Some vehicles have them; others have hoods that stay up on their own. You'll be able to tell which you have when you open the hood, but the best avenue is to look in your owner's manual before you are balancing a heavy hood with one hand and searching for a hood stabilizer with the other.

Locking and Unlocking Your Car

Do you need a tutorial before you can lock and unlock your car doors? Cars today can have four or five different ways to unlock the doors, including keypads, keyless entry systems, and conventional locks.

The two basic ways to unlock your car doors are …

♦ Manually with a car key or, if you are inside, with your fingers.

♦ By using the actuator located inside the car door.

Drive Time

A **body controller** is a computer that is responsible for many qualities that make your car smarter and safer, such as alerting you when you leave your lights on and telling you to take your keys out of the ignition. It also tells your car which method you are using to unlock your car doors.

Locking and unlocking your vehicle manually is a no-brainer, so we won't tarry long on that subject. The next way is by actuator. The actuator's job is to move the lock up and down upon your request. And because today's cars may have different ways to lock/unlock, a *body controller* in your car recognizes the way you are attempting to unlock your vehicle and acts according to your command.

Car designers continue to update vehicles to ensure drivers are as safe as possible. Your keyless entry touchpad operates with your safety in mind; however, when you purchase a new vehicle with new locking and unlocking technology, be sure to have the salesperson explain exactly how to work the keypad, and what each command is for so your safety equipment doesn't put you in danger. For example, you need to know how to work this accessory so you don't accidentally lock yourself out of the car. This information will be in your owner's manual, but it's a good idea to have a little hands-on instruction as well.

The Least You Need to Know

♦ You will save time and money by learning to do routine maintenance jobs on your car.

♦ Always pay attention to safety guidelines before beginning any repair.

♦ Most cars can run on lower-octane gasoline; check your owner's manual to be sure.

♦ Learn how to change a tire before you are stranded and *have* to learn on the side of the road.

♦ Raising your hood isn't hard after the first time.

♦ The body controller, or computer, makes your car smarter and safer by sending a message to open your car door upon command.

Chapter 2

Before You Buy

In This Chapter

- ◆ Should you purchase an extended warranty?
- ◆ Warranties for used cars
- ◆ Inspecting the car before you buy
- ◆ Pick a great technician—within or outside of the dealership
- ◆ Choosing a body shop
- ◆ How to get great service from your technician

You've probably noticed cars are becoming more high-tech each year. Technology can be both good and bad. All those gadgets, gizmos, and computer chips are great until they malfunction and your warranty has expired. And until the auto industry and all satellite auto businesses are on board with the special equipment and software to diagnose and do all repairs, you may be left with fewer auto-repair shop choices. Although cars today don't need repairs as often as did autos of previous generations, when your car does need repairs, your pocketbook may become anorexic. Why?

Presently, many independent mechanics do not have the tools to work on repair problems that have to be computer scanned. The equipment is expensive, more expensive for the independent than for dealerships. Added to that handicap, scanning equipment and software aren't always available to independents because dealerships get preferential treatment. When an independent purchases the equipment, repair prices are forced up. This problem normally affects cars at least three years old that are no longer covered under warranty. Because this is a problem that has persisted over the past decade, lawmakers are now getting involved and the Federal Trade Commission (FTC) will play a big role in leveling the auto-repair playing field.

But what does this mean for your pocketbook? Should you buy an extended warranty? We'll give you the lowdown on extended warranties as well as tell you what your manufacturer warranty should cover. Manufacturer warranties usually cover bumper to bumper on new cars. (Car systems are usually covered by a general manufacturer and powertrain warranty. Find out what is covered before you buy. The warranty information should also be in the owner's manual. Routine maintenance such as an oil change isn't usually covered.) We'll also go over what to consider when taking your car to a dealership for repairs and how to find an independent technician. Let's get busy!

Understanding Extended Warranties

When it comes to extended warranties, *buyer beware!* Do not purchase an extended warranty without reading the terms carefully. And be prepared to do more than scan the warranty, because what is and is not covered may be hazy on some contracts. When purchasing a new vehicle, make an educated decision, not a spur-of-the-moment decision, about manufacturer extended warranties. They can add as much as $2,000 more to what you are financing.

Extended warranties are usually sold by car dealers, but you need to be aware that the dealership probably makes a tidy profit on the sale of these warranties. If you know where to shop, you can find the same or better warranty coverage directly from a warranty company and at a lower cost. To find a good company, do an online search on extended warranty companies. One site that offers a buyer's guide is www.extended-warranty.info. Another source for this information is consumer watchdog Clark Howard, www.clarkhoward.com.

CarLogic _____

If you have a problem with a new car and your new car cannot be repaired after many attempts, you may be able to invoke the Lemon Law—consumer-friendly legislation that holds manufacturers responsible for the quality of the vehicles they sell. If you purchase a new vehicle (and in some states lease a vehicle) and the vehicle proves to be defective, the manufacturer is liable for repairing the vehicle or, if repairs don't prove successful, replacing the vehicle. Check with the attorney general in your state to see how the law is applied in your state, or type "Lemon Law" into an online search engine for information.

Here are a few tips to help you in your search:

♦ Once you find a warranty company that interests you (by word of mouth, the Internet, or phone book), check it out with the Better Business Bureau (BBB). The warranty company should have sound insurance coverage and be financially sound.

♦ A good warranty company will be able to do business in all 50 states. Why is this a good sign? Well, some states set high standards for warranty companies to meet in order to be granted a license.

♦ The company should offer a contract in language that is easily understood by a layperson. The warranty should state what is and is not covered, who is allowed to do the repairs, whether you can choose your own technician, how and in what time period claims will be paid, and how much this warranty is going to cost you.

♦ You want a warranty company that will make billing simple. You take the car in and the company pays for the repairs at time of service. That's the plan you want!

The bottom line is to determine how long you intend to keep your vehicle. If it's less time than your manufacturer's warranty is good for, you certainly won't need an extended warranty. If you think you'll keep the car longer and want to invest in a good warranty, you will need to research the best extended warranties. Usually the best ones are, of course, the more expensive ones.

While weighing your decision about extended warranties, you might check into auto clubs as another option. Auto clubs are good for roadside problems. My favorite is affordable and full of services for its membership. Automobile Association of America (AAA) is well worth the annual $60 fee. AAA will send out a tow truck, jump-start your vehicle, and unlock your car should you lock your keys inside. AAA always offers many other goodies with the membership, like traveler's checks, motel discounts, discounts on eyeglasses, and more.

CarLogic

Sometimes you'll find the newer the vehicle, the less the extended warranty costs, because the company you buy the warranty from is hoping you won't keep the car past the manufacturer's warranty. So it's a toss-up. It is sometimes (not always) cheaper to buy an extended warranty when the car is newer, but unnecessary if you don't intend to keep the car past the factory warranty. Do your homework to see what fits your personal situation and pocketbook best.

Extended warranties usually don't cover every single little thing that needs replacing on your vehicle. Cosmetics like outside trims, paint, upholstery, and carpeting usually aren't covered. You may also have to foot the bill for vehicle lights, batteries, tires, and brake repairs that come from wear. Regular maintenance like changing the oil, tuning up the vehicle, and keeping coolant in your vehicle is also at your expense. Warranty companies usually ask you to keep your maintenance receipts showing you observed the owner's manual guidelines for routine maintenance. This proves you made the effort to keep your vehicle maintained and that your repair claim should be paid.

It's a good idea to let your technician look over the extended warranty before you choose to buy. Read the fine print in the warranty contract, making sure you can use any repair shop you choose. Based on the type of vehicle you have and the repairs your technician foresees, ask him what deductible you should choose. This could be a very important decision for your pocketbook. Find out whether you have to pay a deductible for each part being repaired and each time that same part is repaired. Also find out if you have to pay a deductible for "each repair visit" to a repair shop or if you are charged a deductible for "each repair done" during that visit.

Warranties for Used Vehicles

The FTC requires dealerships (or anyone selling more than six cars yearly) to post a Buyer's Guide in all used vehicles. The Buyer's Guide is a consumer-friendly document that gives the consumer information such as possible repairs anticipated for this type vehicle and what warranty protection is available, if any. Review this document carefully. If the Buyer's Guide says a warranty is still in effect, it will override a sales contract that offers no warranty.

Cars bought new are covered under a manufacturer warranty. If you purchase a used car that is still under the manufacturer warranty—which is usually for three years or 36,000 miles—you are entitled to the remaining time on that warranty. (But warranty coverage is becoming a selling tool, so negotiate a longer period of time if possible.)

You will find warranty coverage information under the "systems covered/duration" section of the Buyer's Guide. You will also need to obtain the vehicle's written warranty. Your next step is to find out what is still covered and for how long. To find out this information, phone the vehicle manufacturer's office. Have the Vehicle Identification Number (VIN) written down when you call so the manufacturer can ID your vehicle and give you the information you require.

 **Speedbumps**

Before buying a used car, you may want to check to see whether any parts on the vehicle have been recalled. Call the U.S. Department of Transportation Auto Safety Hotline (1-800-424-9393).

There are also warranties called powertrain warranties on new cars that can last up to 10 years. The average is around 5 years or 60,000 miles, but in today's competitive car-selling arena, warranties have become good marketing tools. This can work out well for you, the buyer. Ask your car dealer about the powertrain warranty before you buy. Ask what is covered and for how long. Powertrain warranties usually cover the engine, transmission, transaxle, and drive system. (We'll take a closer look at the drive train system in Chapters 16 and 17.)

Manufacturer and powertrain warranties cover just about everything on the vehicle except normal wear and tear. These warranties are in effect until the predetermined date of expiration no matter how many owners the car may have. Demonstrator, executive, or program cars are categorized as used just like a car that has been purchased before, and the warranty period begins the first day it is driven. Remember, different manufacturers offer different types of warranties, so read your warranty information and call the manufacturer if you have any questions.

As Is – No Warranty

If the "as is – no warranty" box on the Buyer's Guide is checked, but the dealer promises to repair the vehicle or take the car back if you're not satisfied, make sure the promise is written in the Buyer's Guide. Don't get in a hurry and forget this step. If you do, you have no recourse should the car fall apart the moment you drive away. Some states have a policy on "as is" sales for used vehicles. You can find out what the

"No-Warranty" laws are in your particular state by contacting your state's attorney general. "As is" cars are a consumer risk. There may be times when you decide to take a vehicle on these terms, especially if this is an older vehicle, but make sure you have the vehicle checked out before you buy.

In-House Warranty

If you buy a car from an independent dealer, you may get an in-house warranty. These warranties cover various repair jobs. The big drawback on these warranties is you must have the repairs done only at that dealership. The best defense is always a good offense, so by all means ask to see the vehicle warranty being offered by the dealer. Find out what company is backing up the warranty. Sometimes it will be a warranty company. It's in your best interest to check this company out with the Better Business Bureau to make sure the company is legitimate. Find out how long it has been in business. Also, it never hurts to ask the people in your life (friends, family, business associates) for their feedback on the company.

Implied Warranties

Another attempt to protect the car-buying consumer is something called implied warranties. These warranties are legislated by state governments and hold dealers responsible if the vehicles they sell do not stand up to certain criteria. Implied warranties are just what you'd expect: they are implied by the dealer and do not have to be written down or promised to the buyer. Be forewarned, however, that dealers in most states can use the words "as is" or "with all faults" on the Buyer's Guide to nullify an implied warranty. So watch the fine print and tell the dealer your terms before you buy.

Variations on Legislated Warranties

Under the warranty of merchantability, a product sold is expected to perform the duty it is purchased to perform. For example, if a dealer sells you a car, the car should do what one would expect a car should do—take the driver from point A to point B. A dealer is liable if you can prove the reason the car will not run existed when you bought the car.

The warranty of fitness is applicable when you are advised by a dealer to purchase a certain type of vehicle for a certain type of job. For example, if a dealer advises you to buy a vehicle for carrying heavy equipment on a daily basis when the vehicle does not have enough horsepower, that dealer may be liable under the warranty of fitness. It's always a good idea to check implied warranties if you have a problem that isn't covered under the dealer warranty.

Before-You-Buy Inspection

The before-you-buy inspection is a step you may be tempted to forego, but don't! Have any and all used cars inspected by a technician before you purchase no matter what warranty or certification comes with the vehicle. Ask for technician referrals from family and friends. And make sure the shop you pick displays the logo Automotive Service Excellence (ASE).

ASE logo.

Auto-Biography

The independent, nonprofit National Institute for Automotive Service Excellence (ASE) was established in 1972 to help consumers distinguish between competent and incompetent mechanics. ASE's mission is to improve the quality of vehicle repair and service through the testing and certification of repair and service professionals. Because the ASE recognizes that technicians must keep up with technological advances in auto repair, technicians retest every five years. At present there are about 400,000 professionals with current certifications working in every segment of the automotive industry. For more information, check out ASE's website at www.ase.com.

When you find an ASE-certified shop that will perform this inspection, make sure you know exactly what systems the technician will be checking and the cost. According to the FTC, you should not have to pay over $100 for this service. And as always, you need a paper trail. Get all of this information in writing before the technician begins the inspection. Request a written printout of what needs work and the estimated cost of repairs. If you don't understand some of the repair language, ask for clarification. The information you get from this inspection is invaluable when deciding whether to purchase a used vehicle. You can also use the information from the mechanical inspection (what it will cost to make needed repairs) to render a fair and informed price for the vehicle. Doing a little legwork and research before you buy a used car (or a new car, for that matter) is empowering.

Meet the Mechanics/Technicians at the Dealership

Nowadays, you may want to call your mechanic a technician. It seems to be the new buzzword with all the computer scanning going on in shops. Becoming acquainted with the technicians at your dealership is normally not an easy thing to do. The faces you will see are the service writers or shop manager, but probably not the person who will actually work on your vehicle. Why? Technicians work on cars and are not part of the frontline customer-service team. Still it is in your best interest to establish a relationship with a technician. And if you find a shop you like, it shouldn't be too difficult to inquire about and meet your technician or technicians. As repair work becomes more and more specialized, you may find that technicians are certified to work on certain car systems, not the entire vehicle, so you may have more than one technician. And as always, make sure the shop is ASE certified. This lets you know the technicians have been tested by the best in the automotive-repair industry.

CarLogic _____

When you walk into a dealership, focus on the surroundings: does everything seem to be running smoothly? Is the staff courteous and helpful without making you feel pressured? If you really want to check out the dealership, ask for a copy of its Customer Satisfaction Index (CSI) report. This report tells how other customers think the sales and service department measures up. Call the dealership to request this report if you'd like to peruse it before you go into a dealership.

Choosing a Technician Outside the Dealership

Choosing a good technician outside the dealership may be as easy as word of mouth and a displayed blue seal that recognizes the shop as ASE certified. It's a good idea to begin your search for a repair shop before you encounter a repair problem. Ask family and friends—especially those you know are particular about their vehicles and who own the same make and model car you do—to recommend a good repair shop.

Or you can ask the shop manager whether the shop has experience working on your make and model vehicle. Find out if the shop will be able to handle all your vehicle repairs. Along with an ASE certification, being AAA approved is another sign the shop is worthy of your inspection.

Here are some other things to look for when choosing a good repair shop:

◆ A neat, well-organized facility, with vehicles in the parking lot equal in value to your own and modern equipment in the service bays.

◆ A courteous staff, with a service consultant willing to answer all of your questions.

◆ Signs of professionalism in the customer-service area, such as civic, community, or customer-service awards.

◆ Policies regarding estimated repair costs, diagnostic fees, guarantees, acceptable methods of payment, and so on.

Meet the Body-Shop Personnel

When choosing a body shop, look for one that employs technicians certified by the ASE. ASE-certified professionals usually wear blue-and-white ASE insignia or a lapel pin and carry credentials listing their exact area of expertise. Consumers should look for facilities that display the ASE Blue Seal of Excellence logo. When a shop displays the ASE sign, you'll know the staff is qualified and computer literate.

As I mentioned, vehicles continue to evolve and the evolution doesn't stop with vehicle systems: bodies of cars are always being updated, too. Because of new designs, new techniques for repairing dents and reshaping fenders, and so on, body-shop technicians have to be specially trained as well. You may find your car dealership doesn't have an in-house body shop—some do, some don't. If your dealership doesn't have a body shop, ask who they recommend or ask your technician for the nearest ASE-certified shop. For more information on how dealership service departments are keeping up with the times regarding retaining skilled specialists, check out www.nada.org and click on Education and Training.

Keeping Your Technician Happy

You've found a repair shop you feel looks out for your best interest—keeping you and your family safe on the highways—and one that offers reasonable repair rates.

Here are a few things you can do to make sure the repair-shop personnel know you appreciate their efforts the next time you need to bring in your car:

- Remember this is a business and they schedule appointments, so unless you have an auto emergency, call early the day before and try to make an early-morning appointment for the next day. You'll know to tell them what needs to be done for routine maintenance. Use this book for reference. If you have a repair problem, describe the symptoms: odors, sounds, handling, and when the problem occurs. (Refer to Appendix A for a guide to troubleshooting vehicle symptoms.)

- Drive through a carwash the night before if your car is dirty, especially if there is mud on the bottom/undercarriage of the car. This will keep your technician from getting dirt in his eyes if he's working under the vehicle. A clean car also tells the technician you care about your vehicle.

- If the repair will require that the technician has trunk access, clean out any unnecessary items (for example, clothes you were supposed to drop off at Goodwill).

- If you think the technician did a good job, say so! Put it in writing so the shop manager can put the letter in the technician's file.

Keeping your car in great shape can become a headache if you let little jobs go until they become huge. Warranties are great to have, but you need to make sure you get exactly what *you* need. Ask your trusted technician what he thinks.

The Least You Need to Know

- Don't be pressured into buying extended warranties until you've done your homework.

- Used cars must come with a Buyer's Guide (if you buy from a dealer or independent), which tells you if the vehicle is still under manufacturer's warranty, if the vehicle comes with a warranty or if you can purchase a warranty, or if the vehicle comes "as is."

- Always have a used car inspected by an independent mechanic *before* you buy it.

- Pick the shop that will take care of your repair work with care.

- Remember to thank the technician who works to keep you safe on the highway.

Tools: What You'll Need

In This Chapter

◆ Putting together a basic auto toolbox

◆ A wrench for every occasion

◆ Basic screwdrivers, pliers, and hammers

◆ Gauges and other handy tools

◆ What you should carry in your car's trunk

Everyone has used a tool at some time or another, whether it was helping Santa put toys together or driving a nail. Experience probably taught you that the correct tool and a quality tool make any job much easier. Buying tools is like buying anything else, knowing what tools you need and why will take that "so many tools and never enough time to find the right ones" look off your face. We'll tell you exactly what you'll need so all you have to do is take the list when you shop or visit neighbor Tim's toolbox.

And don't worry about breaking the bank; you don't have to buy all the tools in one shopping spree. Face it: no one will ever have a complete toolset. What fun would it be to not have a new tool to salivate over? Can't see yourself making a to-die-for tool list? Give yourself some time under the hood and you might be surprised how interesting new tool innovations are. Here's a rule of thumb: buy what your budget will allow now and more as you can. If you don't have the tool you need for a project, borrow what you need until you have the basics. And don't forget to put your toolbox in your trunk or buy a separate toolbox to carry in your trunk for—heaven forbid—breakdowns. You probably won't need it, but it's best to be prepared.

Toolboxes: You've Gotta Have One (or Two)!

It takes a devout and focused clutter-holic to live in a messy work area and still be able to keep up with where every tool and gizmo is located. Most of us need some sort of tool-organization system. Another advantage of storing your tools in a toolbox is that they are kept away from the elements. A good rule of thumb is to always wipe your tools off after using them, and especially if they are dirty.

CarLogic

Ask someone you trust to point you in the direction of *the* store in your area to buy tools. Ultimately you will be looking for a store that sells quality tools and has a great sales staff that knows tools and is eager to help customers. And it never hurts to find a store that has great sales!

There are many great systems to choose from, from lightweight yet sturdy toolboxes with ample compartments for nuts, bolts, and screws to roomy fabric tool bags that are kind to your walls and doors. Check local stores for toolbox selections and decide what fits your needs best. Or if you're feeling handy, try making your own customized toolbox.

Here are some other options to consider:

- Wall organizers with lots of pockets for tools

- Trunk-compartment box for roadside emergencies

- Different sized metal boxes with or without storage trays

- Wheeled tool chests so that you can roll the chests wherever you need them in your work area

- Pickup-truck toolboxes in different styles and sizes to store your basic tools and other items—such as groceries—that you don't want to blow out of the bed of the truck

Buying a Toolbox

If you are just starting out buying tools and don't anticipate buying more than the basics we suggest in this book, one toolbox that does double duty for both home and trunk is sufficient. A good way to determine what size toolbox you need is to collect your tools either literally or in your mind and estimate the toolbox size. Buy a larger box than what will hold the tools you own. As you think about your tools, also think about how many compartments you'll need for nuts, bolts, and so on. If you have a large collection of tools, you might want to also buy a small toolbox to store your most used items, or pack a small toolbox to keep in the car trunk.

Speedbumps

Remember your back when you pack the toolbox. At some point you will have to pick up the toolbox and carry it, so try to balance the way you pack your tools to distribute the weight evenly.

Tool Checklist

Keep up with what you have and what you will need in your toolbox by using this handy list (we'll tell you more about many of these tools in the rest of the chapter):

- ❏ Standard screwdriver
- ❏ Phillips screwdriver
- ❏ Pozidriv screwdriver
- ❏ Torx screwdriver
- ❏ Ratchets: ¼", ½", ⅜"
- ❏ Combination wrenches: ¼" to ⅞" *SAE*; 8mm to 22mm metric
- ❏ Offset wrenches
- ❏ Ignition wrenches
- ❏ Allen (hex) wrenches

- ❏ Torque wrench
- ❏ Socket wrench set: ⅜" to ¾" SAE; 8mm to 19mm metric
- ❏ Extensions for socket wrenches: Flex-head 1" to 12"
- ❏ Ball-peen hammer
- ❏ Combination slip-joint pliers
- ❏ Wire and taper feeler gauges
- ❏ Flat feeler gauge
- ❏ Compression gauge

Drive Time

The most common wrenches are standard, also known as **SAE** (Society of Automotive Engineers), and metric measurement wrenches.

What Tools Cost

The initial investment of tools may seem an extravagance, but in the long run the money you spend now will save you time, money, and aggravation. Take a few minutes and peruse this list. See what you think your budget will stand now and plan what you will buy or borrow down the road. Prices vary, but this list gives you a basis to work from:

- Jumper cables ($8–$30)
- Jack (from $17)
- Lug wrench (from $10)
- Pliers ($5–$20)
- Funnels ($1.50)
- Combination wrenches (from $9), or combination wrench set (less than $10 for a basic 11-piece set, and more for better sets)
- Offset wrenches (from $5, but usually sold in sets)
- Ignition-wrench set (from $15)
- Allen (hex) wrenches (from $3)
- Socket wrench set (from $30 for a quality set)
- Torque wrench (from $60)
- Continuity tester (from $19)
- Hand degreaser ($1.50–$3)
- Rags (around $35 for 50 shop rags, or free if you use your own clean rags)
- Oil filter wrench ($7–$13)
- Rubber gloves ($4–$8)
- Work gloves ($4)
- Spark-plug wrench ($2)
- Rubber mallet ($4–$16)
- Ball-peen hammer ($6–$8)
- Tire pressure gauge ($4–$35)
- Utility knife ($3)

- ◆ Screwdrivers ($3)

- ◆ Socket set ($9–$15)

- ◆ Stiff nonwire brush ($10)

The Basic Wrench: A Toolbox Staple

Let's start with the fundamental tool for your auto toolbox, the wrench. There are many sizes and variations of the basic shape, but for the auto maintenance and repair we discuss in this book you'll only need a handful or so. Remember, always compare prices and find out when major chains have sales, but you always want to buy quality tools. (Hopefully quality tools that are on sale!)

Check your owner's manual to see what type or types of wrenches you will need to work on your vehicle. This is what you need to do whether you own an American- or foreign-made car. The most common wrenches are standard, also known as SAE (Society of Automotive Engineers), and metric measurement wrenches. Many vehicles have uses for a mix of standard and metric. If you own an American-made vehicle, it's a good possibility you'll need standard and metric wrenches. So the rule of thumb: read your owner's manual and then go shopping. If you are uncertain what to buy when you get to the store, carry your owner's manual in with you and ask the salesperson.

Open-End, Box-End, Combination, and Adjustable Wrenches

When shopping for wrenches, you'll come across several different kinds:

- ◆ Open-end wrenches are self-explanatory: they have openings at each end. Because the ends are open, they slip into tight places easily. Open-end wrenches are not for the final tightening of nuts or bolts.

Open-end wrench.

- ◆ Box-end wrenches fit completely around the nut or bolt and are used for final tightening.

Box-end wrench.

◆ Combination wrenches are a must-have for a basic toolbox. They give you an open end and a closed end so there's no need to buy both open-end and box-end wrenches unless you just want to. You can purchase combination wrenches in sets with various sizes.

Combination wrench.

◆ Adjustable wrenches adjust to fit different size nuts and bolts, but you'll find the combination wrench a sturdier tool.

Adjustable wrench.

Offset Wrenches and Ignition Wrenches

When working on your auto, there will be times when a tool will have to have a bend in it in order to get into tight areas, especially around the engine. Offset wrenches are great for just this type problem. Having one or two of these in your toolbox will keep your knuckles in good shape and save on your first-aid expenditures. Another set of wrenches you'll want to add to your toolbox is a set of combination wrenches to work on your ignition. These ignition wrenches come in small sizes.

Offset wrench.

Ignition wrenches.

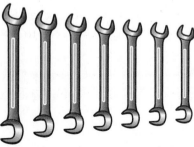

Allen (Hex) Wrenches

Your vehicle will have some screws that require different types of wrenches. You've probably heard about them. They are called Allen or hex wrenches. Hex, of course, is short for hexagon, or six sided. Allen wrenches aren't expensive and we suggest you buy a set. This tool is used to drive Allen screws and bolts, which have a hexagonal socket in the head.

Allen (hex) wrench.

Socket Wrenches

If you are going to work on your vehicle, you are going to have to buy a set of socket wrenches. Well, you don't *have* to, but then again, you don't have to wear a warm coat on a cold day, either. A quality set of socket wrenches will make your auto-repair work more comfortable.

Socket wrenches are bought in sets. For basic repair and routine maintenance you can get by with a set for under $30. You can get straight SAE sets, straight metric sets, or a combination of standard and metric. Check your owner's manual or ask a salesperson at the auto-supply store for the type or types of sockets you will need. A socket has either 6 points or 12 points inside. The 6-pointed sockets are for bolts with rounded corners and 12 points are best used in tight places. A 6-pointed socket wrench probably will suit most of your needs.

Your set of socket wrenches should contain the following basic parts:

- ◆ Sockets, the cylindrical part of a wrench, come in the basic size of ⅜" drive. (The drive is the square hole in the back of the socket that adheres to the driver, which turns the socket; you turn the driver as you would a screwdriver.) A good standard for metric sizes is 8mm to 19mm.

- ◆ You will also want to invest in a spark-plug socket. Spark plugs come in different sizes, so take your owner's manual with you to make sure you get the correct size.

- ◆ Socket sets usually come with one or two ratchet handles. Some come with more and of course you can always add more as time goes on.

◆ Flex-head handles are useful for working around engines. Being able to hold the handle at various angles is ideal for working in tight spaces.

◆ Socket extenders enable you to reach nuts and bolts deep inside the engine.

The parts of a socket wrench.

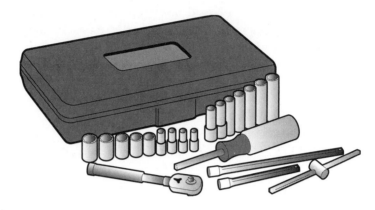

 CarLogic _____

The best way to tell a quality socket wrench set is to look at its teeth. We're not teasing. You'll find most ratchet handles have 20 to 30 teeth, but the best ones have up to 60 teeth. The more teeth, the better it can fit into tight places.

Torque Wrenches

You will be happy to know that a torque wrench will aid you when you are just learning. Why? Because torque wrenches tighten to the precise degree needed. However, torque wrenches are optional. Good ones are expensive. Your best bet is to borrow one and see how much it helps with the repairs and maintenance you are going to do before buying. You may be able to do just as well working with a good socket set.

Torque wrench.

Wrench Safety Tips

Here are some general tips for using wrenches safely:

◆ Select the correct jaw size. This will help keep the tool from slipping and injuring you.

◆ Wear safety glasses anytime you are working under the hood.

♦ Wear gloves to protect your hands and knuckles.

♦ Make sure your stance is steady so that you don't fall into the car should the wrench slip.

♦ Use a wrench with a straight handle rather than an offset handle if possible. You have more control with a straight handle.

♦ Make sure the open end of the wrench (jaw) fits snugly over the nut or bolt before you try to loosen the bolt.

♦ Turn an adjustable wrench against the inflexible jaw.

♦ When using a *ratchet wrench*, you want the ratchet wheel to fit the *pawl* so there is no slippage. To achieve this, you begin by putting ratchet to bolt by employing a bit of pressure to the ratchet.

♦ Use smooth, steady movements when using a wrench.

Drive Time _____

A **ratchet wrench** has a toothed wheel so that the teeth can hold a device made to employ the teeth. This device is called a **pawl**.

Using Combination Wrenches: Easy as One, Two, Three

The combination wrench is the one wrench we suggest for your basic toolbox. It has a boxed end and an open end. The open end is jawlike. The jaw may be flush with the handle or at angles, with the most common angle being 15°. You can use the box end for loosening or tightening bolts. Slide the jaws around the bolt and turn a couple of times. You'll find turning the open end is easier than working with the box end because you have to set the box on the nut or bolt each time with each rotation. The box end is safer in that you don't incur the possibility of slippage as much. The box end fits snugly over the nut or bolt. You'll use the box end with 12 points most often. It has a medium swing angle and is good for working in tight spaces.

Speedbumps _____

Never use a wrench that is too big or too small for the job. A wrench that is too big can slide off, leaving you with banged-up knuckles, or can damage the nut or wrench. One that is too small won't fit anyway no matter how many times you kick a car tire in exasperation trying to make it work.

Always remember when working with a combination wrench to have a wrench that fits the nut or bolt snugly. You will need to use a pulling motion on the wrench. Don't push the wrench unless you just want to use some of those neat superhero bandages on your knuckles or there is no other way. If that's the case, be careful and let the handle of the wrench rest in the palm of your hand—guide the wrench from there.

It will take practice to know if you have nuts and bolts tightened correctly, but keep trying and you'll be a pro in no time. If you find a screw or bolt that is almost rusted and hard to loosen, use a penetrating oil such as WD-40. The oil goes into or penetrates narrow spaces between the threads of parts so you can loosen the parts without a lot of elbow grease.

Screwdrivers

Well, we all know about screwdrivers, don't we? There's the kind with the straight head and then there's the one with the funky head. Now we'll name them. The most common type is called a standard or slot screwdriver. And the other kind is the Phillips screwdriver. And now the duh moment. You use Phillips screwdrivers with Phillips screws, and standard screwdrivers with standard screws. Yes, we all know to do that, but we don't always do what we're supposed to do, and that can damage the screw. Always use a screwdriver with a head that is the same type and size as the screw you're working with.

Two common types of screwdrivers with several types of screw heads.

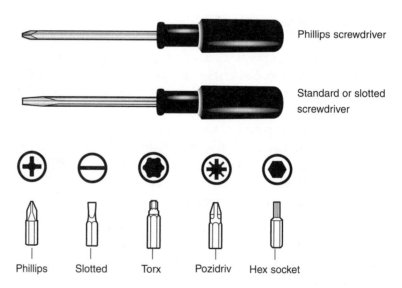

Phillips screwdriver

Standard or slotted screwdriver

Phillips   Slotted   Torx   Pozidriv   Hex socket

You will need a variety of sizes of screwdrivers. You can buy them in sets: standard-only sets, Phillips-only sets, and mixed sets. The length and shafts vary as well. This happens because screws can be in deep crevices.

You can get all the screwdrivers you need for relatively little money. Look for sales on plastic- or rubber-handled screwdrivers in sets of varying sizes.

Pliers

Needle-nosed or slip-joint pliers are great to have in your auto-repair toolbox. These hand tools are used for a variety of projects because of the way they work—taking the power of a hand grip and making it more powerful and precise.

Needle-nosed pliers (left) and combination slip-joint pliers (right).

Hammers and Mallets

A ball-peen hammer should also make it into your toolbox. Sometimes you might need to give a gentle tap on nuts or bolts to help loosen them. If you use a hammer, remember that when you're frustrated with some repair that is not going well, step away from the hammer. You'll find taking your frustrations out in that manner will create a bigger problem than you had to begin with. Also make sure your hammer is in good repair, which means it is fastened securely so that the metal part doesn't fly off and damage your car or injure you.

Another handy tool to keep in your toolbox is a rubber mallet. They are good for things like tapping your hubcap back on after changing a flat.

Speedbumps

Always use insulated pliers and other tools when working on your vehicle electrical system to avoid being shocked. And use the right tool for the job at hand—don't improvise!

Ball-peen hammer.

Gauges and Other Essentials

Yes, working on your vehicle can be done once you learn the basics and have the right tools, but there are gauges that will let you know whether you have put in enough fluids, added enough air to your tires, etc. We'll tell you what you'll need.

Drive Time

A **computerized ignition system** means the timing and firing of the spark plugs is controlled by an electronic control unit. **Gapping** is adjusting the space between the spark plug points.

Tune-ups aren't necessary as often for cars with *computerized ignition systems*, but things like spark plugs and wires have to be replaced periodically, so check your owner's manual for correct times. Things like how hard you drive your vehicle and the type of spark plug installed in your vehicle make a difference in how long you can go without a tune-up. If your vehicle is equipped with a computerized ignition system, you won't need the gauges we're about to discuss because that is taken care of by a computer that sends electrical currents to spark plugs. But if you have an older vehicle with a nonelectronic electrical system you'll want to pick up the following gauges for spark plug *gapping*.

The following gauges help you fine-tune your ignition:

♦ Wire feeler gauges are used for gapping spark plugs. Spark plugs need to be a precise distance apart so that the spark can spring over with the appropriate force. But unless you have an old car, this information will not apply.

Wire feeler gauge.

◆ Flat feeler gauges are thin strips or blades of a precise size that help you adapt the distances between auto parts—valves and ignition touch points.

Flat feeler gauge.

◆ Compression gauges are used in the spark plug hole of the cylinder head to measure cylinder compression pressure. You'll want this gauge especially if you have an older-model car, because it will expose defective piston rings and valves. Ask the salesperson for the best gauge for your needs.

Compression gauge.

Work Lights

Work lights are invaluable. You have to be able to see what you are doing in order to avoid damage to you or your vehicle. Tell the salesperson what you will be using the light for. He or she will most likely advise you to buy a well-insulated quality light with a long cord. Rule of thumb: buy a light that has at least a 25-foot retractable cord and a cage around the bulb. Be sure to hang the light on something that is not electrical.

Work light.

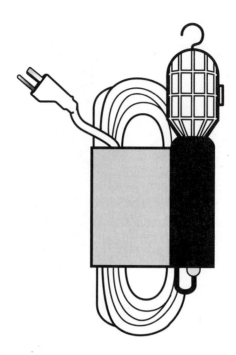

Jacks and Jack Stands

You must have a jack in your car at all times for changing tires. New cars come with a jack, but it's a good idea to check it out and see how it works before you need it. For older cars, or if you bought a secondhand car, take a look at what you have and then decide whether you need to buy a new jack. There are different types of jacks, but a hydraulic jack (pictured in Chapter 1) is your best choice. There are also scissor types of jacks (pictured in Chapter 1) if that's what you prefer, but check your owner's manual and go shopping to see what is the safest and easiest jack for your vehicle. Don't ever shy away from asking sales personnel at the auto shop. They will be happy to help you find what you need. And if you find that isn't the case, find a better auto shop to deal with.

You will also need to invest in a pair of jack (support) stands that you can position underneath the vehicle to keep your vehicle from falling on you, as discussed in Chapter 1.

CarLogic

Check your owner's manual to make sure you know which type jack you will need for your particular vehicle. It's not a one-size-fits-all situation. And once you have the jack you need for your car, lube the jack each time you change your oil.

Jack (support) stands.

Creepers

You've seen mechanics roll around on their backs under cars. Those boards with wheels they're lying on are called creepers. You can, of course, buy one or you can make one yourself. You might want to see how much time you'll be devoting to auto repair and maintenance before you invest in a creeper. They make maneuvering under your vehicle much easier. But always remember to make sure your car will not fall on you before you slide even a thumb underneath it.

Creeper.

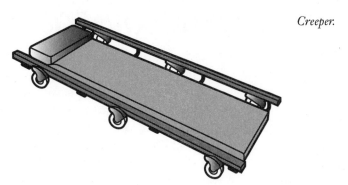

Fire Extinguishers

A working fire extinguisher is a must for your auto repair and maintenance buying list. You will want an ABC dry chemical fire extinguisher handy in your work area at all times. (An ABC fire extinguisher covers "A" paper, lumber, etc; "B" flammable liquids such as gasoline; and "C" electrical fires.) You will also want to carry a fire extinguisher in your car. Keep it within easy reach while doing maintenance or repair work on your car.

Your fire extinguisher needs to be inspected every year to make sure everything is set to operate properly when needed. There are fire extinguisher companies that offer this service. In many cases, a fire extinguisher just needs to be examined or weighed (CO_2 extinguishers). Your fire department may offer this service, so check with them. You can also opt to buy a new fire extinguisher. A monthly check to make sure the gauge is pointed in the green section—which means "ready"—needs to be performed. The older fire extinguisher should be inspected internally (pressure tested), and then reassembled, recharged, and marked indicating the service date. A discharged fire extinguisher can be recharged if it has metal fittings instead of plastic fittings—check with your fire department or a fire extinguisher company.

Funnels

Plastic or metal funnels are inexpensive and can save time and aggravation. You will need one when pouring fluids, so pick up a few and remember to clean them after each use. Also make sure they are clean of dust, lint, grass, etc. when you need to use them. Some funnels even come with precision hoses that fit directly into fluid containers.

Other Things You Will Need to Carry in Your Car

When deciding what to carry in your trunk, think about the trip you are taking. If you are doing your routine to work and home and the commute isn't far, you'll just need your regular stocked toolbox. However, for road trips, you will want to anticipate weather conditions and what you might need if you are stranded in those situations. Here are several items you should tuck away in your trunk for daily commutes:

- Spare tire
- Flashlight with fresh batteries
- Quality jumper cables
- De-icing fluid (essential for daily commutes if you live in a cold climate)
- First-aid kit

- Working fire extinguisher

- Reflector triangles or flares

- Jack

- Gloves

- Blanket

- Jug of water for the radiator

- For snowy climates: tire chains or a bag of sand or cat litter (for traction on snow and ice); a snow shovel

While it's a good idea to have as many of these things as you can, a fully charged cell phone is still your best safety device in case of an emergency. Have your cell phone at your fingertips while driving. Don't get in your car without one!

The Least You Need to Know

- When buying your basic auto-repair tools, buy what your budget will allow and more as you can.

- One toolbox for home and car is sufficient, but if you have a lot of tools, consider having one for home and one in the trunk.

- Combination wrenches kill two birds with one stone.

- It's good to buy standard and Phillips screwdrivers in sets so you will have a variety of sizes.

- When visiting your auto-parts store, pick up some spare equipment like belts, nuts, bolts, and fuses for your shop toolbox.

- Keep your trunk toolbox equipped with essentials in case of breakdown, and pack your trunk for weather conditions as well when going on a road trip.

Establishing a Regular Maintenance Routine

In This Chapter

- ◆ The importance of establishing a regular maintenance routine
- ◆ Checking the oil, the air filter, and belts
- ◆ Checking, cleaning, and replacing the battery
- ◆ Checking the radiator, coolant, and hoses
- ◆ Checking fluids
- ◆ Other important checks you should make

The Car Care Council says four out of five cars driving on our roads need maintenance. Is your car one of them? Well, it could very well be your car does need some service work done. If not, congratulations! And keep up the good work. For the rest of us, let's make a list of routine maintenance jobs and check it twice. Just think how much money you will save by taking care of your car so you won't have major problems in later months. Not that you won't ever have to repair your vehicle, but keeping up with maintenance will keep your car running, driving, and looking good the greater percentage of the time. And that's good for your health and your wallet.

You will be surprised how little time it takes to establish a car maintenance routine. Make sure the car has not been driven for a couple of hours before you do routine maintenance. All you need to do is open the hood (we tell you how in Chapter 1). Make sure you have a clean rag with you. Remember, a clean rag hanging out of your back pocket is a necessity for any auto job. Old, clean T-shirts headed for the trash make good auto rags.

You will find regular maintenance routine checklists in Appendix B. Before you write on them, make a copy for each vehicle and for the number of years you intend to keep the vehicle(s). The checklists help you keep track of what services need to be performed and when. You will also want to note parts replaced and those dates.

We also provide a vehicle fact sheet in Appendix B so you can record all the facts about each vehicle in one handy place. Make a copy of the page for each vehicle. This page will make your trips to the auto-repair store more efficient. Why? Because when salespeople ask important questions about your car, you'll have answers a fingertip away, even if you don't drive the vehicle you're buying parts for.

Let's get to work. Once you learn what to do, you'll zip through the maintenance check in no time—20 minutes max!

Check the Oil

It's best to check your oil each time you fill up your gas tank. Also, if the oil is dirty and grimy or smells of gasoline, it probably needs to be changed. If the oil level is low, you will need to add oil, but you do not want to overfill. Here's how to check your oil:

1. Make sure your vehicle is on level ground.

2. Let your car sit for a few minutes after turning off the engine. This allows the oil to drain back into the oil pan.

3. With your vehicle's hood open, find the dipstick. Pull the dipstick out, wipe it clean with a rag, and reinsert it.

4. Pull the dipstick back out and hold it horizontally so that you can read the oil level. The oil should be between the markings High ("H") and Low ("L") on the dipstick. (You might instead see MIN and MAX, standing for minimum and maximum.)

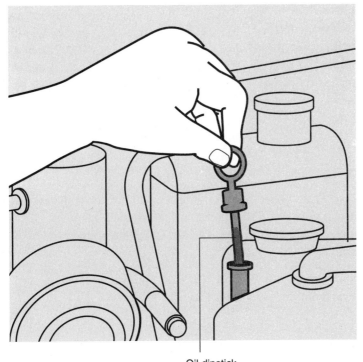

The engine oil dipstick can usually be found on the side of the engine on rear-wheel drive autos and on the front of the engine if you own a front-wheel drive vehicle. Check your owner's manual.

Oil dipstick

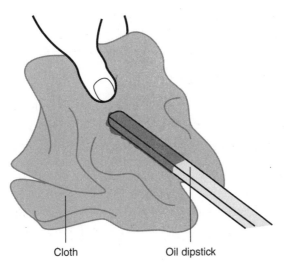

Preparing to wipe pulled-out dipstick.

Cloth   Oil dipstick

Check the oil level.

5. If the oil is below the L, you need to add the proper oil. Check your owner's manual for the correct viscosity. Take the top off the capped opening. This is usually located on top of the cylinder head cover. Carefully pour in the oil, being careful not to overfill.

6. Insert the dipstick and check the oil level again after adding oil. One quart should raise the level from the low to high level.

Speedbumps

Your oil will always read lower than it really is when the engine is hot. It's best to wait at least 15 minutes after you shut the car off to check the oil. But if you are doing this at the gas station that may not be possible. Still check your oil when you fill up, but unless your oil is very low, wait and check it again when you get home—after your car is cool—then add oil if needed. By adding oil to the full level on the dipstick when the engine is hot, you may overfill. This can damage your engine.

While you are under the hood, top off other fluids: coolant, transmission, brake, and power-steering to the levels indicated. (We'll tell you how later in the chapter.) Make sure you put the correct fluids in your car. Check your owner's manual for specifics. If you find your car low on any fluid you've just refilled a week ago, you'll need to investigate or ask your auto technician.

Check the Air Filter

Filters come in a variety of sizes. Check your owner's manual to see what type you need and write the type down in the vehicle fact sheet provided in Appendix B.

Here's how to check the air filter:

1. To locate the air filter, unscrew the wing nut on the lid of your air cleaner and undo any other devices that hold it down. You'll find the air filter inside. You may find your under-hood filter cover is held with plastic button fasteners. If that's the case, pry them up carefully with a standard screwdriver. Lift the filter out and check it for any holes or tears.

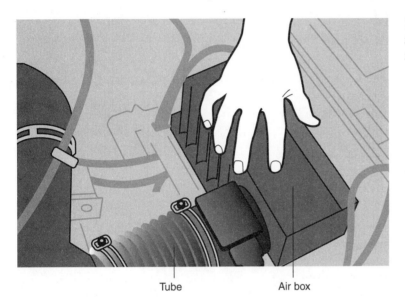

To locate the air filter, follow the tube from the engine to the air box.

Tube   Air box

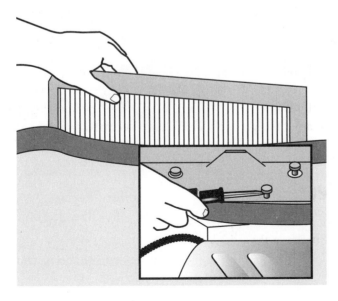

Unscrew wing nut or pry fasteners up gently. A steady hand and a standard screwdriver work well if your air box is secured with fasteners.

Air filter

Be careful when removing the dirty air filter so that you don't dislodge important wiring.

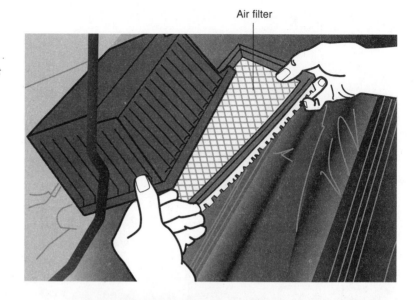

Tidy up with a quick air-box vacuum before sitting the new air filter in place, and then fasten the box securely. Your new filter should be good for 12,000–15,000 miles.

CarLogic

Most modern fuel-injected vehicles use flat-panel filters. They are available at your auto-parts store.

2. Put your work light in a position to tell if you can see a glow of light through the filter. No glow? Replace the filter. Replacing your air filter isn't difficult. Just follow the directions on the package.

3. If the filter is dirty or has holes or tears, replace the filter.

Check Belts

The next thing you'll want to do is look at the belts, at least every three months. Your vehicle may have multiple belts or one belt handling all devices. Check your owner's manual for the type of belt or belts your vehicle is equipped with. If you have multiple belts—belts that work the fan, the alternator, etc.—you will be checking slack. Should a belt have more than ½" of slack when pressed, you can try to adjust it if the belt isn't cracked and is in otherwise good shape. A belt that is cracked, frayed, shiny, or gives more than ½" and won't adjust should be replaced.

If you have a late-model car, the odds are good that you have a *serpentine belt.* If so, the previous information won't apply because such a belt drives several devices. The serpentine belt is more efficient than older multiple-belt systems. Why? Because the serpentine belt is a single wider belt instead of several narrower and thinner belts. The wider the belt, the more tension can be applied without stretching. And that's

Drive Time

A **serpentine belt** is a snakelike (it snakes around pulleys) single belt used to propel many under-the-hood mechanisms such as alternators, power-steering pumps, coolant pumps, and A/C compressors.

good for many reasons, but the major one is this: higher tension reduces slip and this requires less work from the engine, which increases gas mileage and engine power. The drawback of this single belt is that if the belt breaks, the vehicle loses all devices such as the fan, alternator, air-conditioner compressor, etc.

Serpentine belt.

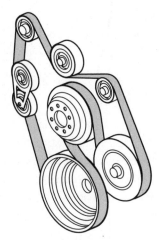

Check the serpentine belt for wear each time you are under the hood. The belt should not show signs of sagging and should sit directly in the middle of the pulleys, as shown in the illustration. Another good way to check for a loose serpentine belt is to listen for a squeaking noise. The serpentine belt and pulleys should be inspected every six months for evidence of wear such as excessive cracking (on serpentine belts, some cracking is normal), fraying, incorrect alignment, and incorrect tension.

Check the Battery

You're probably familiar with vehicle batteries. Usually at some point in life, you either hear about or experience a dead battery. Your vehicle's battery has more energy than a two-year-old. That may be hard to believe, but it's true. And all that energy is used to start your car's engine, run your CD player, turn on the lights, and so forth.

Cars and light trucks have 12-volt batteries. You will most likely find that your battery is maintenance-free, which means you won't have to add water. However, you can still purchase maintenance-required batteries. They are cheaper but you must monitor the electrolyte level, which means you have to add water. The fluid inside your battery is a mixture of acid and water. The location and type of your battery terminals vary. Some are on the side of the battery while others are on top. Keep them clean and corrosion-free.

The CCA or Cold Cranking Amp rating of a battery is the power the battery has to start on cold mornings (0°F). Check your owner's manual to see what CCA your vehicle requires.

Ask your trusted auto-parts dealer questions about batteries. You might want to check into the batteries that come with built-in charge indicators to tell you whether they need charging.

Now that you know the basics about your car's battery, be sure to check on it every three months or 3,000 miles.

On some maintenance-free sealed batteries, a built-in hydrometer, sometimes called a magic eye, is used for checking the fluid level and specific gravity readings. If the battery is equipped with an eye, use it for checking the condition of the battery by observing the color of the eye. A green eye indicates good condition and a dark eye indicates the need for service, but read the manufacturer's directions to do what is required for the specific battery you purchased.

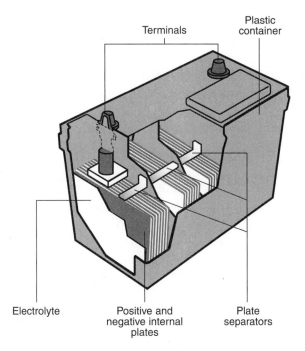

Terminals

Plastic container

Electrolyte

Positive and negative internal plates

Plate separators

The battery is usually located on either side of the engine near the car's frame. It's a rectangular box with two wires that you will see are connected to the battery terminals. The terminals are located either on the top or the side of the battery.

For batteries that require maintenance, read the manufacturer's directions, but you will probably be told to check the electrolyte level at least once a month, or more often in hot weather or during times when you drive a lot.

Speedbumps

Car batteries can be explosive if not handled properly. Cigarettes, matches, and any items that could cause a spark should be kept away from the battery. Wearing protective items such as a mask, gloves, and safety glasses are a good idea. Never try to jump-start a battery that has a crack in the plastic container—the battery could explode. Make sure the battery is replaced and be careful not to get any electrolyte on your skin.

Checking the Level

The electrolyte level can be checked in a couple of different ways. You may be lucky enough to have a battery with a translucent case that allows you to see the level in comparison to a line marked on the outside, or you may have a battery with caps that can be removed allowing you to look down into the cells. The electrolyte level should be half an inch above the plates and a quarter of an inch below the vent slots. If the level is low, add distilled water (not tap water) to bring the electrolyte solution to the proper level. Each of the six cells is self-contained and must be checked and filled individually. If the temperature is below freezing, distilled water should be added only while the car is in a warm garage or after allowing the car to warm up.

CarLogic

Although adding tap water to your battery once is not going to ruin it, always adding tap water can damage your battery and shorten its life. Why? The electrochemical reaction in your battery is reversible to allow the discharge and recharge cycles. Chlorine, calcium, magnesium, and other chemicals in tap water create side reactions that are not reversible, degrade the plates, and inhibit the production of electricity, all of which damage the battery. If you live in an area where the tap water is very hard, the damage can be worse. Play it safe and use distilled water only.

Checking the Gravity

Checking the *specific gravity* of each cell in your battery should be part of your regular maintenance routine. Once a year should be fine for newer batteries and more often for older ones. You will use a hydrometer to check the specific gravity directly on a maintenance-required battery. Purchase one for batteries at your auto-parts store. Don't confuse a hydrometer with a coolant tester, which looks similar. You may prefer the type with a float level as opposed to the type with multiple floating balls.

Drive Time

Specific gravity is the weight of a liquid. The weight of water is used as a reference point, 1.000. A specific gravity of 1.260 means that the solution weighs 1.260 times as much as water. Concentrated sulfuric acid has a specific gravity of 1.835. An electrolyte solution with a specific gravity of 1.260 has about 65 percent water and about 35 percent sulfuric acid.

Before checking the gravity of each cell, put on safety goggles and rubber gloves. Insert the nozzle into the electrolyte solution, use the squeeze bulb to draw some of the solution into the float chamber, and read the position of the float. Keep the nozzle in the cell opening during the entire procedure and squeeze the solution back into the cell after you get a good reading. Be very careful that you do not get the solution on anything. It will burn skin and eyes, remove paint, and destroy fabric. Get a reading for each of the six cells. If the readings vary by more than .050 for any two cells, the battery should be replaced. Maintenance-free batteries may have a built-in indicator on the top of the case that displays battery condition. This is usually a mini-hydrometer that reads only one cell. You can use a voltmeter to check your battery's state of charge, which indirectly tells you about the specific gravity. If you use a multi-tester, carefully read the instructions on how to test battery voltage. The voltmeter should read about 12.5 volts on a fully charged battery with all accessories off and engine off and about 13.5 to 14.5 with accessories off and the engine running.

On most batteries, if the indicator is a light color the battery can be assumed to be okay. If the indicator is a dark color, the specific gravity is low, and the battery should be charged or replaced. There should be specific notations on the battery as to what color the indictor should be depending on the battery's state of charge.

Maintenance-free battery   Voltmeter

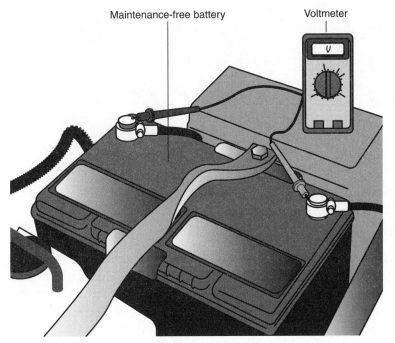

Checking state of charge with a voltmeter.

Maintenance-required battery   Hydrometer

Check the electrolyte level of each cell. If under the low level line, replace the battery or add distilled water.

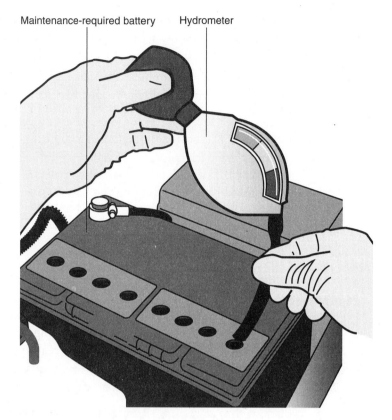

Cleaning Terminals and Cable Clamps

Before we get started, let's gather some tools. You will need proper-size wrenches to loosen the bolts on the clamps or terminals and the hold-down clamp. If you have top posts on your battery, an inexpensive clamp puller available at any auto-parts store is very handy and can prevent damaging the posts. Another handy tool is a post and terminal cleaner. This is a specially designed set of wire brushes, also inexpensive and readily available at auto stores. You will need some kind of cleaning solution to neutralize the corrosion. Water and enough baking soda to make a diluted paste works well. Some people swear by using a can of diet cola. (Use the diet kind to avoid the sticky residue from the sugar.) Last, but most important, is your safety protection. Always wear rubber gloves and safety goggles.

Make sure the car is turned off and the keys are out of the ignition switch, so that you can safely remove the battery cables. When disconnecting the battery cables, the negative is always the first one off and the last one on. Be careful not to accidentally touch the two terminals or posts with the wrench while removing the terminal ends or clamps. Major sparks will occur and you could actually weld the wrench across the terminals, causing a fire and at the least ruining the battery. Carefully loosen the clamp bolts if you have top posts, and use the puller to remove the clamp from the post. If you have side terminals, remove the bolts. Move the cables out of the way and loosen or remove the hold-down clamp so that you can lift the battery out of the car. Clean the battery tray of any dirt or debris. If you find some corrosion there, clean it with the baking-soda solution. If you find rust, use the wire brush to remove the loose scale and give it a coat of rust-inhibiting paint.

Now turn your attention to the cables. Clean the terminals with the wire brush until they're shiny. Use an old toothbrush and the baking-soda solution if there is a lot of corrosion present. Examine as much of the cable as you can for defects, especially nicked or missing insulation. A short between the positive cable and the frame can cause a fire. Check that the clamps or terminals are securely fastened at the end of the cable. If the cable or terminal is defective, replace the entire cable with one of the same gauge and type. Auto-parts stores stock most sizes. Now clean the posts on the battery with the wire brush. You want all contact points to be shiny and free of dirt or corrosion, which can inhibit starting and charging. Carefully clean the battery case, especially the top, since moisture and dirt can create a circuit between the terminals that will discharge the battery. If you use the baking-soda solution or any liquid cleaner, be careful that none enters the battery cells.

When everything is clean, return the battery to its tray, clamp it down, and reinstall the clamps or terminals. The post clamps should reinstall with a slight twist. Never use force to remove or install, since the posts are lead and will break off fairly easily. Coat the clamps with a thin coat of grease after installation to prevent corrosion. Doing this procedure once a year should prevent problems until your next battery replacement.

Battery-terminal brush and clamp cleaner.

Speedbumps _____

Car batteries are lead-acid batteries. Always wear rubber gloves and safety goggles when working with them. The posts and terminals are lead. Wash your hands immediately if you handle these with bare hands. The electrolyte solution is sulfuric acid. The white powdery residue often found around the terminals is also corrosive. The powder or solution can cause burns to bare skin and serious problems if it gets in your eyes. Flush with clean water and go to the emergency room if necessary.

Replace the Battery

The most obvious sign that it's time to replace the battery is when it goes dead, but like any other component in the vehicle, batteries have a finite service life and will need to be checked periodically. To avoid the situation where you turn the key and nothing happens, you'll want to have your battery checked by a professional as part of your periodic maintenance routine. This is usually done as part of an overall charging-system check, where the voltage output of the alternator or generator is measured to make sure it's operating properly.

Most charging systems operate at about 14.5 volts. The technician will use a voltmeter to check the charging system output and something called a carbon pile tester to check the battery condition. This equipment puts a load on the battery to make sure it is still operating within specifications, and it detects a weakening battery condition to indicate it's time for a new one. Keep in mind that a dead battery could indicate a problem elsewhere in the charging system, but if your battery is more than about five years old, it's probably time for a change.

When it's time to replace your battery, tell your trusted auto-supply person what you are looking to buy. You will need to know how long you'll keep your car so that you don't buy a battery with a longer warranty period than you will own the car. Where you live and drive your car will also determine the type and quality of battery you buy. In cold climates your car's engine is more difficult to start, requiring a battery with higher Cold Cranking Amps (CCA). Hot climates stress a battery even more through increased corrosion and evaporation of electrolyte. There are batteries designed for either or both of these extremes.

Other basic considerations when choosing a battery include …

- Your vehicle manufacturer's requirements.
- What you want to pay, if you want a maintenance-free battery.

♦ Where you will be driving your car (you'll need a stronger battery casing if you drive off-road much of the time).

If you buy a battery from a dedicated auto-supply store, you will get better service. Many times the store's technicians will install the battery for you free of charge and recycle the old battery appropriately. Most will even give you a discounted price for your new battery if you bring in the old one. And you'll feel better knowing you've disposed of a potential environmental hazard appropriately. If you choose to install the battery yourself, take the old battery to an auto-parts retailer that offers a battery-recycling program.

 CarLogic

Consider installing a more powerful battery if you install electrical and electronic accessories in your car, such as a bigger sound system.

Installing a new battery is a job most vehicle owners can handle themselves with just a few hand tools, but there are some important precautions to observe. First is to read this entire replacement procedure before you begin. Remove all metal objects, like jewelry, that can cause an inadvertent short circuit while you are working. You'll need the proper-sized wrenches to loosen the battery terminals, the proper sized socket wrench with about a 6- or 8-inch extension to loosen the battery hold-down clamp, and a wire brush or specific battery terminal cleaner brush. You'll also want to be wearing a pair of work gloves. You can buy mechanic's gloves in any parts store.

To replace the battery, open the hood and inspect the battery cables for corrosion or damage. There may be a rubber or plastic cover over the positive terminal. Remove any corrosion with a wire brush, being careful not to get any of this material on your skin or clothes. You can clean the terminals with a mixture of water and baking soda to neutralize the acid, if necessary. Once the terminals are clean, use your wrench to disconnect the negative (usually black) terminal first. This is done by simply loosening the terminal clamp bolt on top-terminal batteries, or the connecting bolt on side-terminal batteries. Whatever the fastener type, turn it counterclockwise to loosen and be careful not to strip the bolt head.

Speedbumps

Caution: When disconnecting or reconnecting the battery terminals, be very careful not to have your wrench contact any metal parts of the car. This will cause a short circuit and possible injury.

Once the negative terminal is free, carefully position it out of the way and repeat the process·for the positive battery terminal. Once both terminals are free and positioned out of the way, locate the battery hold-down and remove or loosen the retaining bolts. Some vehicles may have a framework or box holding the battery in the car, while others may have a simple clamping device that is located at the base of the battery. You may need to have a socket wrench with an extension for this job, since your hand wrench probably won't work in such tight quarters. Once the battery is free, carefully lift it out of the engine compartment and set it aside. Again, avoid contact with clothing or skin. Batteries are heavy, so be careful you don't drop it. Once the old battery is removed, inspect the battery tray and remove or clean any dirt or corrosion you find there. This is also the time to use a wire brush to clean the battery terminals on the replacement to ensure a good electrical connection when you install the new battery. You can buy a special battery terminal brush that makes this job easy, but steel wool or sandpaper will also work.

Once you have everything clean, install the new battery. It's always a good idea to compare the new battery with the old one before installation, checking for correct size and terminal locations. Getting the positive and negative terminals connected properly is critical, and you want to make sure your replacement battery is an exact match in size and terminal location and type as the old one. Carefully place the new battery in the tray and reinstall the hold-down clamp, then reconnect the positive and negative battery cables. Be careful not to overtighten the battery connections, or to touch any metal surfaces with the wrench while you're working. Tighten the connections until they are snug, but don't go more than about a quarter turn from that.

Again, properly dispose of the old battery if you didn't already exchange it for a new one at the parts store. Taking it back to the store that sold you the replacement battery is the usual process. Do not put it in the trash.

Check the Radiator and Coolant

About 20,000 BTUs of heat energy are produced from burning a gallon of gasoline. Your car's cooling system must efficiently dissipate most of this heat. The radiator and engine coolant are two essential components of the cooling system that require regular attention to keep them functioning properly. The engine coolant must have the correct proportions of antifreeze and water to provide boiling and freezing protection, and the correct amount of corrosion inhibitors to protect all of the cooling system components.

Antifreeze comes in a variety of types. There are standard types, based on ethylene glycol or propylene glycol, that last about two years before they need to be replaced. There are long-life versions, lasting up to five years or 150,000 miles. And there are greener versions that are less toxic to animals and the environment. To keep the cooling system in your car working efficiently, it is crucial to check the coolant level frequently and to check the strength and condition at least annually. Additionally, the coolant must be replaced before the corrosion inhibitors are completely depleted. Carefully read your owner's manual to see which type of antifreeze is required and how to add it safely when necessary. Some types are incompatible with others, and long-life types can be compromised by mixing with standard types.

Speedbumps

Antifreeze is extremely toxic to people and animals. Properly used and stored, antifreeze presents little danger. But when improperly disposed of or when there are leaks from your vehicle's cooling system, conventional antifreeze can be lethal, especially to toddlers who tend to put everything in their mouths or to pets who might lap at a spot of antifreeze on the driveway. Because of its sweet taste, coolant is attractive to wild animals such as squirrels as well as pets. If you spill some or have a sizable leak, dilute it thoroughly and wash it away with plenty of water.

You have read your owner's manual and are familiar with how to check the coolant level. There are basically three different scenarios. If you need to check the level in the radiator, you will remove the radiator cap and look into the neck to see the coolant level. Generally, the coolant should be above the cooling channels and about ¾" below the bottom of the neck. The next situation involves a pressurized expansion tank. You see markings on the side labeled as max and min or hot and cold. The last typical situation is a nonpressurized overflow tank. This should also have similar markings.

Here are some tips for keeping your radiator in mint condition:

♦ Check the coolant level regularly, whenever you check the oil level or you have the hood open. If you need to add coolant, add equal amounts of antifreeze and distilled water or premixed coolant.

♦ Use only distilled water when mixing with antifreeze. The chemicals in hard water or softened water interfere with the corrosion inhibitors.

♦ Check the cooling system hoses for swelling, cracks, and other signs of deterioration on a regular basis. Look for leaks where hoses are clamped and tighten if necessary, being careful not to overtighten. Inspect the radiator for damage or leaks and remove any debris that may have accumulated.

◆ Never add cold coolant to a hot engine!

If your car has a coolant-recovery system that incorporates a pressurized expansion tank, follow the same procedure in removing the cap as you would for the radiator cap, especially when the system is hot and pressurized.

Never attempt to unscrew the radiator cap while the engine is still hot.

A coolant reservoir attaches to your radiator.

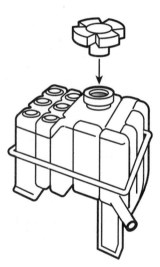

Speedbumps

Never remove a radiator cap from a hot engine. You can get burned by radiator steam. You will need to wait until the engine cools down. Test for a cool engine by touching the upper radiator hose. If it's cool to warm, you're okay. If it's hot, wait and try again in about 15 minutes.

Here are some suggestions for checking engine coolant strength and condition:

1. Your engine coolant should be a 50/50 mixture of distilled water and antifreeze. Any proportions above 65% antifreeze inhibit the coolant's ability to carry heat, and proportions below 50% reduce freeze protection and minimize the amount of anticorrosion additives. You can check the proportion by using a hydrometer specific to your antifreeze type. Different types have different specific gravities, so be sure you have the correct one. Test strips, which indicate strength by color changes after being dipped in the coolant, are also available at auto-parts stores.

2. Replace your coolant at the recommended intervals to maintain the anticorrosion protection for all the cooling system, even if it looks clean and fresh.

3. When antifreeze is first produced, it is colorless. An increasing number of dyes are now added to allow you to distinguish it from pure water. Reds and oranges tend to be used for long life, yellow and green for standard, and pink and blue-green for more environmentally friendly versions. However, the color is not always indicative of the type. If your coolant doesn't look fresh, looks colorless or rusty, or has debris floating in it, it's time for a flush and new coolant. Instructions for when and how to do so are in Chapter 9.

4. If you notice an oily film on your coolant, you should have the cooling system tested for internal leaks where either engine oil or transmission fluid is contaminating the coolant. This requires specialized equipment that pressurizes your cooling system.

Check the Hoses

The hoses in your car's engine compartment are subjected to harsh conditions of extreme hot and cold along with salt, moisture, and road debris. The rubber that these hoses are made of has a limited useful life span. The upper and lower radiator hoses are also constantly subjected to significant changes in pressure. Check all your hoses regularly for cracks, swelling, and leaks. If you notice any defects or signs of deterioration, have them replaced as soon as possible, because they continue to deteriorate rapidly and could cause significant damage when they fail or leave you stranded.

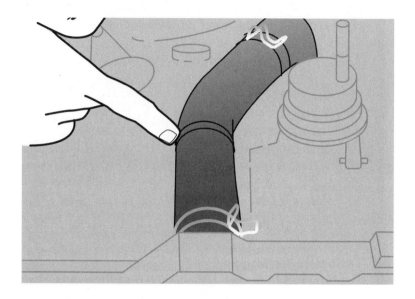

Check radiator hoses: two hoses run from the radiator, an upper hose and a lower hose.

Check the Automatic Transmission Fluid

The automatic transmission fluid (ATF) performs three functions in your car's transmission. It acts as a lubricant, as a coolant, and as a hydraulic coupling to transfer mechanical energy. You will want to periodically check the level, change the fluid at the recommended intervals, watch for leaks, and be kind to your transmission while driving.

Most cars with automatic transmissions today have dipsticks with which you check the ATF level. Read your owner's manual for the proper procedure and for the correct fluid to add if your level is low. The manual should show you the location of the transmission dipstick and differentiate it from the oil dipstick. Some newer cars have eliminated the dipstick in favor of a level sensor or refill/overflow holes. Follow the procedure in the owner's manual, which may recommend taking the car to the dealer for a level check.

Heat degrades the fluid over time, so changing the fluid at recommended intervals helps protect the most complicated mechanism in your car. Recommended intervals range from 30,000 miles to 100,000 miles to never. Fluid change almost always involves a filter change or strainer cleaning. While the job is a little messy and not too complicated, it is best left to a service facility equipped with a transmission flusher. At best, when you change the fluid you only change about 60 percent of it. With the proper equipment, an automotive technician can change almost 100 percent.

Watch for leaks where you park your car. If you find some spots on the driveway, try to determine where they might be coming from. ATF is usually a reddish-brown color. If you can trace it to the vicinity of the transmission, have it checked out. It may be just a leaky seal or gasket or a cover plate that needs tightening. Transmission repairs are not always expensive, but repairing damage from lack of fluid almost always is.

To check your automatic transmission fluid, follow these steps:

1. After driving the car, so that the engine is warm and transmission fluid is pumping throughout the transmission, put the gearshift in park. Set the emergency brake and leave the car running. Follow all the safety precautions for working around a running engine.

2. Remove the automatic transmission dipstick, and wipe it clean with a clean, lint-free rag. Reinsert it until it bottoms out and remove it.

3. Notice the level of the fluid on the dipstick. It should be between the full and fill marks. If not, use a funnel to add fluid down the dipstick tube. Pour only small amounts at a time, being careful not to overfill. The difference between the full and fill marks is often only about a pint of fluid.

CarLogic

Because there are so many different types of transmission fluids on the market, you need to be sure that you get the right kind. Check your owner's manual.

4. Transmission fluid typically has a reddish color. If it looks or smells burnt or if you can feel grit or particles as you rub some between your fingers, the fluid should be changed.

Check the Brake Fluid

Like any other fluid in your car, brake fluid needs to checked for quantity and quality. This is especially important for brakes, since compromising the ability to stop your car can have disastrous results. Brake fluid naturally absorbs and dissipates water. This is actually desirable, since you do not want water collecting in a puddle or "slug" in the system. When the water content of the brake fluid reaches a certain level, it lowers the boiling point of the fluid to unacceptable levels. Changing the brake fluid every two years prevents the boiling point from being lowered too much and prevents the accumulated water from damaging brake components.

Read your owner's manual for directions on how to check the level and what type of fluid to add should your level be low. If you have antilock brakes (ABS), you may have to follow a special procedure before checking the fluid. This typically involves pumping the brakes with the car off to return fluid from the accumulator back to the reservoir so that the level can be properly checked.

To check your brake fluid, follow these steps:

1. Most newer cars have translucent plastic reservoirs with markings of high and low or max and min on the side. Look at the level of the fluid and see where it falls in relation to these marks. You want the fluid to be close to the max or high mark. If you have a car on which the reservoir is an integral part of the master cylinder, you will have to move the retaining clip off the removable top with a flat blade screwdriver. Pull the top off; it may be a little snug due to the rubber seal. The fluid inside the reservoir should be about half an inch below the top.

2. If you need to add brake fluid, carefully clean around the reservoir to prevent any dirt from falling into the fluid. Take the cap or top off the reservoir and add enough of the recommended type fluid to bring the level close to the full mark.

3. Brake fluid in your reservoir should be reasonably clear. If it has become very dark, you are probably overdue for a fluid replacement. Color is not always a good indicator of condition, so follow the two-year replacement recommendation.

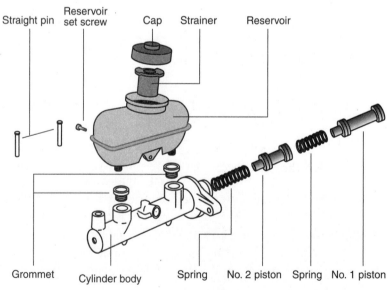

Exploded view of a typical brake master cylinder showing the interior components. Note the location of the fluid reservoir on top. That's where you check the fluid level. Brake fluid should be changed every two years.

Keep the following cautions in mind:

◆ Because it is an alcohol compound, brake fluid is a good paint remover. If you spill any on your car's finish or on any other painted surface, wipe it up immediately and rinse the surface with water. Properly dispose of the rag containing the spilled fluid.

◆ Minimize the time the reservoir is open and the brake fluid is exposed to the air.

◆ Be very careful not to introduce any contaminants into the brake fluid. Getting grease or oil in your fluid can ruin your hydraulic brake system.

◆ Brake fluid is a type of alcohol that attracts water. Always keep bottles of brake fluid tightly sealed to prevent the fluid from absorbing water vapor from the air. The water that can then be introduced into the brake system will corrode the brake components. Any leftover fluid should be recycled at a hazardous waste center. Inquire at your auto-parts store about how to recycle old fluid.

◆ If a brake fluid reservoir is empty—which hopefully will not happen in a well-maintained vehicle—you must bleed the system after the cause of the leakage is resolved.

◆ Brake fluid deteriorates with use. Have your mechanic replace the fluid if it looks dark in color. The fluid should be changed every two years to protect the hydraulic components from corrosion.

Check the Power-Steering Fluid

To check the power-steering fluid, locate the power-steering pump in your car (see the following illustration). If you can't find it, your owner's manual should tell you where it is. Then follow these steps:

1. Unscrew the cap and see whether the fluid reaches the fill mark on the dipstick (or whether it's near the top of the bottle).

2. If the level is low, check your owner's manual or dealership to see what kind of fluid your power-steering pump requires.

Power-steering pump.

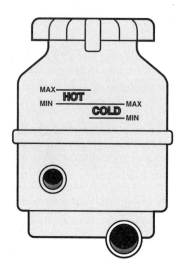

Check the Windshield-Washer Fluid

You will find your windshield-washer reservoir under the hood. It's normally a plastic bottle that connects to the windshield-wiper mechanism. Make sure the windshield-washer reservoir is full of fluid. You can find windshield-washer fluid at your auto-supply store or any gas station. As you top off the windshield-washer fluid, go ahead and pour some solvent on a rag and clean the wiper blades as well. Solvent won't squirt out if it's frozen, so be sure to buy solvent with antifreeze added during the cold winter months. If you live in a cold climate with dirty snow, it'll be especially important to keep your windshield clear.

CarLogic

Make sure you read the directions on the windshield-washer solution you buy. Also, while shopping ask your trusted salesperson about premixed solutions that contain antifreeze—especially if you live in very cold climes. Follow the directions the manufacturer suggests (which usually means do not dilute—you could be losing your cold-weather protection by making the antifreeze less potent).

Other Important Checks

Here are a few more important checks to ensure your vehicle is in good shape:

◆ Check windshield-wiper blades and replace if they show signs of cracks and wear. A good rule of thumb is to change the blades every six months or 6,000 miles.

◆ Check your tires at least monthly for proper inflation and condition (but it's best to check tires with each gas fill-up). Proper vehicle tire pressure isn't a universal number; consult your owner's manual to find out the recommended tire pressure for your car. Be sure to check tires when they are cold. (Not to worry, you will become well acquainted with the way a healthy tire looks in Chapter 7.)

◆ You probably know what damaged wires look like. Well, checking under your hood isn't a lot different than checking extension cords. If the wires are peeking through the insulation, if they feel inflexible, or if they have corrosion on them, it's time to change them. This is probably a job for your technician.

The Least You Need to Know

◆ Once you know what to check, a regular maintenance routine takes only about 20 minutes out of your week.

◆ Check your oil and all fluids when you fill up your gas tank.

◆ Buying batteries from auto-supply stores and then regularly checking and cleaning your battery are good car-care practices.

◆ Be very careful when working around antifreeze. It is extremely toxic to people and animals, so dilute and thoroughly wash away all spills. Dispose of used antifreeze properly.

◆ Check your car's belts, hoses, and windshield wipers for cracks and wear monthly, and check your tires for proper inflation and condition.

Part 2

Identifying and Troubleshooting Your Car's Systems

In this part, you are about to meet some pretty neat systems that make your car crank in the mornings, give you a comfortable ride, turn on your favorite music, allow you to stop for ice cream, go around curves, keep you cool in the summer and warm during the winter, and yes, eat all that expensive gasoline.

Not only will we introduce you to the steering and suspension systems, electrical system, fuel system, drive-train system, brake system, cooling system, and engine system; we'll also tell you how to troubleshoot problems occurring in those systems. We'll even tell you how to repair some problems and when you need to take the car to a technician. And as always, we'll remind you of two important words: safety first. While knowledge pertaining to how your vehicle works is *always* good to know for three basic reasons—safety, financial, and emotional—hands-on work requires time, study, basic tools, and having a spotter (it's never a bad idea to let someone know when you are working on your car). We're ready to make the introductions now! So turn the page.

Meet Your Car's Private Parts

In This Chapter

- ◆ The engine's four-stroke process starts with a turn of a key
- ◆ The steering and suspension system makes your ride smooth
- ◆ Your engine cools off and heats up with this system
- ◆ Keep car parts oiled with the lubrication system
- ◆ Get wired so that you can listen to all your favorite tunes, and more
- ◆ Brakes and drive train are there to make you stop and go

You put the key in the ignition and your car purrs. Do you ever wonder how that happens? If you don't, you aren't alone. Usually the wondering begins when the car malfunctions and doesn't purr. But you might be able to keep your car from stranding you a good percentage of the time by knowing basic facts about each system. Hands-on learning puts you in the driver's seat to knowing how your car runs.

It's not necessary for you to understand the engineering behind each of these systems, but you should have a basic comprehension of how they all work together to provide you with safe, reliable, comfortable transportation. Put simply, the engine and transmission provide the power, while the steering and suspension provide the control. The cooling system keeps the engine at proper operating temperature and provides heat for passengers. The brake system gives you the ability to bring it all to a safe stop.

There, now you can stop looking at your car like it's an alien spacecraft and your technician an alien leader with his or her own language. In fact, you'll soon find that many of your auto fears will be distant memories as you become proactive in learning about the systems that make up your car. So let's embark on a tour of your car's basic systems. (Chapters 6 through 19 will go into much more detail on each of the systems we touch on here.)

Ignition System: The Way It All Starts

Although modern vehicles have all sorts of computers and sensors that work together to make the engine start and run efficiently, let's look at how your vehicle starts in the simplest of terms. We'll begin with the most basic components, which are the ignition switch, neutral safety switch, starter, and battery. Think of your starter as a small electric motor with a small gear located at one end. This small gear engages a second, larger gear on the engine when you turn your key in the ignition to the start position. A safety switch prevents the car from starting if the transmission isn't in either Park or Neutral. As your engine is rotated by the starter, the pistons start moving up and down in the cylinders and drawing in the fuel and air mixture. The ignition system starts the combustion process by firing the spark plugs, which starts the engine turning over faster than the starter motor. Once the engine starts, the gear connected to the starter disengages from the engine gear.

Auto-Biography

The engine system has many subsystems, such as the fuel system, cooling system, ignition system, camshafts, turbochargers, and gears. However, the ignition system is where all the work begins. A turn of the ignition key starts the engine's four-stroke process.

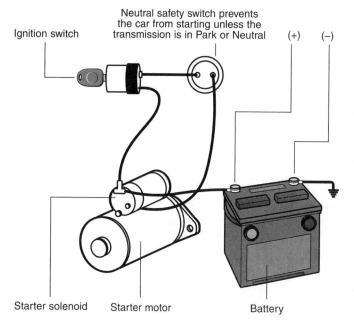

Ignition switch

Neutral safety switch prevents
the car from starting unless the
transmission is in Park or Neutral

(+)   (−)

*Starting your car involves
these basic components, but
this is a very simplified drawing. Modern vehicles also
have a host of computers and
sensors that have to work
together.*

Starter solenoid   Starter motor   Battery

Your car's ignition system has two important functions. First, it changes low voltage–
high amperage current into high voltage–low amperage current, and second, it distrib-
utes that current to each of the cylinders. Changing the current is done by the ignition
coil, and distributing the current is done by the distributor. In older cars, this was it.
The distributor had a replaceable cap and rotor that sent current to a spark plug in
each cylinder through a spark-plug wire. Ignition systems have evolved significantly
over the past few decades. Electronic control modules (ECM) were added to improve
efficiency, and the single coil was replaced by systems of individual or shared coils.
The distributor of old has been eliminated and replaced by a distributorless system
that has fewer replaceable parts and may not need attention or servicing for as long
as 100,000 miles. If you like your cars with low miles, you may never have to worry
about a tune-up again.

The initial source of energy to start your car comes from the battery. It provides the
power to ignite the spark plugs when you first start the engine. That voltage travels
through the ignition coil, which acts as a mini-transformer that boosts the voltage to
the high level required to create the ignition spark in the plugs.

Ignition system with a dis-tributor.

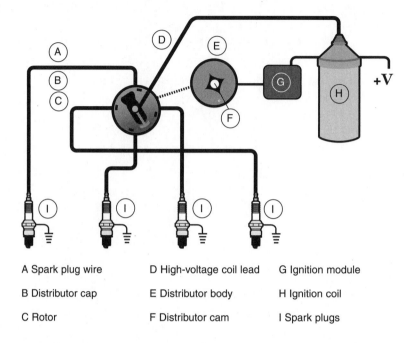

A Spark plug wire   D High-voltage coil lead   G Ignition module

B Distributor cap   E Distributor body   H Ignition coil

C Rotor   F Distributor cam   I Spark plugs

To provide the spark plugs with enough voltage to ignite the fuel and air mixture, the voltage from the battery or alternator has to be increased to tens of thousands of volts at a small fraction of an amp from the normal 12 volts of current. The coil, acting as a transformer, makes this conversion. The primary or low-voltage side of the coil brings in the 12 volts from the battery or alternator and converts it to very high voltage on the secondary or high-voltage side. This high voltage is then sent to the distributor or directly to the spark plugs, depending on the ignition system your car has.

As I said earlier, your car may have an ignition system entirely controlled by a computer. In this case, a crank angle sensor (CAS) and an ignition control unit replace the electronic control module and the distributor. Using the same principles as a distributor, the CAS reads marks on a ring or plate that correspond to the positions of the pistons in each cylinder. It sends a signal to the control unit, which then, in addition to other inputs, causes the coil to produce the spark at exactly the right instant.

The efficiency of the CAS and ignition-control unit has made the distributor obsolete. This new system is reliable and is designed in such a way that your car will keep running, although with some loss of engine performance, should any of the coils go bad.

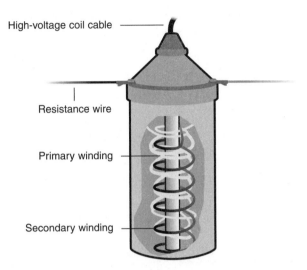

High-voltage coil cable

Resistance wire

Primary winding

Secondary winding

Your vehicle's coil rings work like a transformer to produce the exact high voltage needed to create the spark at the spark plugs.

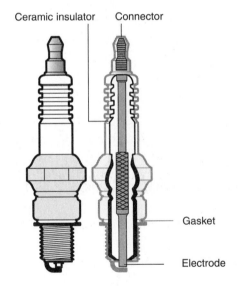

Ceramic insulator   Connector

Gasket

Electrode

The typical spark plug inside and out.

Speedbumps

The ignition-control unit stores information on the ignition settings. Should your ignition system malfunction, it is designed to go into "failsafe" mode and retrieve the stored data that will keep your car running. Be aware that in this mode, your car may have its speed or RPMs limited to protect the engine, so you'll notice a drop in power. The malfunction indicator light (MIL) on the dashboard will also alert you should there be any problem with this system. Modern computer-controlled cars will store "trouble codes" to let the diagnostic technician know which circuit the problem occurs in and help to determine the exact cause. If the MIL light comes on, it usually means the computer has detected a problem and recorded a trouble code in its memory. These codes are retrieved by the use of special test equipment.

Steering and Suspension System

Now that you have your car started, take the wheel! Your vehicle steering and suspension system has two basic jobs: to keep the car's wheels in contact with the road through all sorts of bumps and curves and to provide an easily controlled, comfortable ride. To keep your vehicle pointed where you want it to go, you will use one of two common steering devices—either the rack-and-pinion or the recirculating-ball system. These days, the rack-and-pinion is the more widely used, particularly on anything from the import manufacturers.

Your car is also equipped with springs and shock absorbers. These parts work hand in hand to make your ride comfortable and keep the wheels in contact with the road under all conditions. The springs absorb the vibrations and the shock absorbers disperse bouncing. How tightly the spring is wound determines how a car takes bumps. Large cars usually have springs that aren't as tightly wound so the dispersion of bounce is greater than in smaller cars. Smaller cars, however, make up for the less smooth ride in handling. So it's a tradeoff.

The basic suspension system in your car consists of shock absorbers, control arms, the frame, and steering linkage. These components keep your ride comfortable and reduce vibrations.

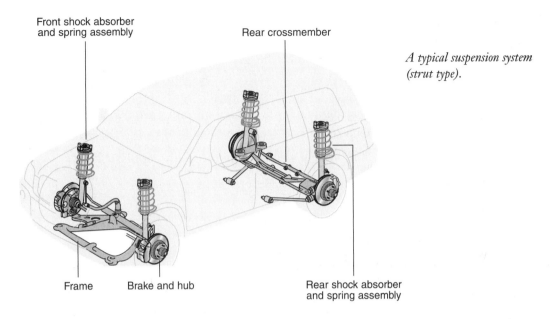

Front shock absorber
and spring assembly

Rear crossmember

*A typical suspension system
(strut type).*

Frame   Brake and hub

Rear shock absorber
and spring assembly

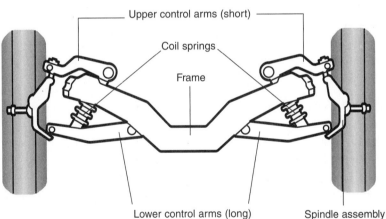

Upper control arms (short)

Coil springs

Frame

*Independent short and long
arm (SLA) suspension typical
of rear-wheel drive vehicles.*

Lower control arms (long)   Spindle assembly

Cooling System

Your engine's cooling system has two important jobs: to dissipate heat and to make a cold engine warm quickly. How? Well, the system removes excess heat from the engine by passing coolant (a 50/50 mixture of water and antifreeze) through a heat exchanger called the radiator to keep the engine operating at a temperature it can tolerate. Your engine runs best at a set temperature, which is pretty hot, and this is maintained by using a thermostat in the coolant-flow system. The temperatures generated by the combustion in the cylinders would quickly melt the engine if the cooling system weren't there. However, when the engine is cold, mechanical parts wear out faster, and the engine doesn't run efficiently. So the cooling system also allows the vehicle to warm up fairly quickly by closing the thermostat and keeping the coolant from circulating until the engine reaches normal operating temperature. Tell your engine to stay at its comfort level by keeping this system happy.

The many parts of the cooling system are shown in the following illustration.

Your vehicle's cooling system knows just the right temperature to keep the engine happy.

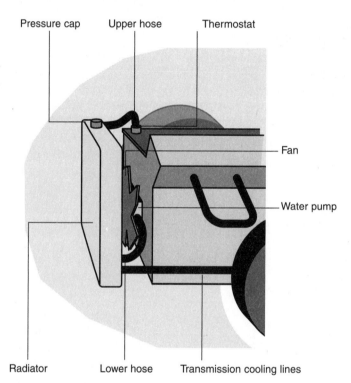

Lubrication System

Do you want to know why your vehicle needs to have the correct amount of clean oil? The oil pump sends oil circulating through your engine to make sure moving parts like pistons and connecting rods can move easily and don't generate more heat. The oil pump moves oil around. The oil filter keeps oil clean. Oil also works on keeping other moving parts from rubbing against each other. The lubricating properties of oil keep the engine from overheating due to friction and keep all the parts running smoothly. Oil keeps your whole engine running smoothly through three functions:

◆ It provides a thin cushion between two metal surfaces, eliminating friction.

◆ It helps dissipate heat.

◆ It carries dirt and other contaminants away from the moving parts to be deposited in the filter.

Electrical System

The electrical system is complicated, and electrical problems are some of the most difficult to diagnose and repair. Consider all the parts of your car that run on electricity: alternator, horn, ignition coil, lights, radio, antenna, speakers, sunroof, windows, starter, voltage regulator, and much more.

Think of the electrical system in your car as four interconnected subsystems:

◆ Devices

◆ Transfer

◆ Protection

◆ Storage and production

The electrical *devices* include accessories such as clocks, radios, sunroof motors, door locks, and power window motors; safety devices such as lights, turn signals, and horns; and essential components such as starter motors, cooling fans, engine sensors, and the ignition system. The electricity in your car is *transferred* to the devices through a network of wires and junctions. These devices are *protected* by fuses that are located in a central location (the fuse box) or by fuses that are in line with the wiring that provides electricity to the device. The electricity needed to start your car or to power your car's accessories when the car isn't running is *stored* in the battery. When the engine is running, it turns an alternator that *produces* current to keep the battery fully charged and to provide electricity to power all electrical components in your car, from the lighted vanity mirror to the spark plug.

Fuel System

The fuel system provides a precise mixture of fuel and air to the car engine. Virtually all vehicles built after 1981 use an electronic fuel-injection system that eliminates the need for a carburetor. These are computer-controlled fuel-delivery systems that deliver maximum performance and fuel economy with minimum engine emissions.

Engine System

The engine is the heart of the automobile. It converts fuel and air into the energy that powers your vehicle. You love to hear it purr. But how does the engine make your daily drive happen? It all comes together through the careful interaction of many internal and external engine parts.

Here are some basic engine terms you'll find useful to know:

- Cylinders—The tubes in which the pistons travel up and down. They may be bored directly into an iron engine block or made of steel sleeves inserted into the bores in an aluminum block. Cars come with different numbers of cylinders (4, 6, 8, 10, or 12) set in different configurations (in-line or V designs are the most typical).

- Cylinder block—The main structural engine component housing the cylinder bores and providing mounting attachments for the crankshaft and other engine components. The cylinder block is usually cast as one piece of metal in a foundry, and then machined as necessary.

- Cylinder head—The major engine component that completes the top half of the engine. It contains the combustion chamber and usually provides the location for attaching intake and exhaust manifolds, along with spark plugs and fuel injectors. It also typically houses the valves and may provide attachments for a camshaft in overhead-cam (OHC) engine designs.

All modern cars have a four-stroke, one-cycle engine that can be either gasoline or diesel design. The intake stroke, compression stroke, power stroke, and exhaust stroke comprise one engine cycle. When the fourth stroke is completed, the cycle begins again.

The process begins when the piston begins its descent to the bottom of the cylinder bore (intake). Pistons move up and down as the crankshaft rotates very much like your legs do when pedaling a bicycle. When the piston moves down, it creates suction within the cylinder, which draws in the air and fuel mixture through the open intake valve. The engine valves are opened and closed by the rotating camshaft in time with the process. The fuel-injection system is designed to deliver the correct amount of fuel and air during this intake stroke.

 CarLogic

This chapter gives you general information about how any car works. Refer to your car's owner's manual for specifics. You can also purchase manuals for your model car should you want to go a step further. These manuals know the design of most any car—say a 2005 Ford Mustang or a 1960 Chevrolet Impala—and give vehicle-specific information on how to do routine maintenance and repairs.

Once the piston reaches the bottom of its travel in the cylinder, the intake valve closes, sealing the cylinder and the piston begins to move up and compress the fuel/air mixture in the cylinder (compression). When the piston reaches the top of it's travel in the cylinder (Top Dead Center or TDC), the ignition system fires the spark plug, igniting the fuel/air mixture in a controlled explosion (ignition) that forces the piston back down. This is called the power stroke and is what makes the horsepower in an engine.

When the piston again reaches the bottom of its travel in the cylinder, the exhaust valve opens, allowing the rising piston to push out the burned gasses (exhaust). When the piston again reaches the top of the cylinder, the exhaust valve closes, the intake valve opens, and the piston begins the cycle all over again to draw in a fresh fuel/air charge to the cylinder.

In multi-cylinder engines, these cycles are timed to deliver smooth, continuous power by firing the cylinders in a specific sequence called the firing order. This mechanical ballet happens thousands of times a minute through the carefully timed interaction of the many internal and external engine components, all synchronized by the use of various shafts, gears, belts, chains, and electronic control signals generated by the computers controlling the engine.

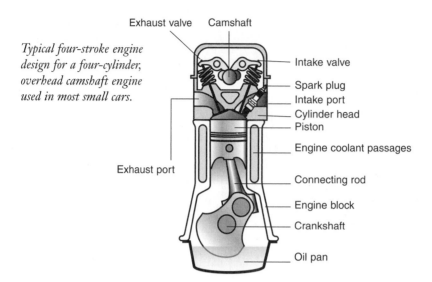

Typical four-stroke engine design for a four-cylinder, overhead camshaft engine used in most small cars.

Exhaust valve   Camshaft

Intake valve

Spark plug

Intake port

Cylinder head

Piston

Engine coolant passages

Exhaust port

Connecting rod

Engine block

Crankshaft

Oil pan

Drive Train System

Cars have either manual or automatic transmissions that are part of the drive train system. Your drive train has two duties: to send *power* from the engine to the drive wheels and to vary the amount of *torque*. Transmissions do this by using different gear ratios that are designed to maximize the engine power at various road speeds. We call this shifting gears. Automatic transmissions do this by the use of hydraulic fluid without direct input from the driver. Manual transmissions require the driver to move a shift lever at the appropriate road speed (mph) and engine rpm to change gears manually.

Transmissions are bolted to the rear of the engine and attach to the crankshaft to transfer engine power either through a torque converter filled with hydraulic fluid in automatic transmissions or through a foot pedal–operated manual clutch plate in manual transmissions. Depending on the vehicle design, rear-wheel-drive cars have a driveshaft connecting the transmission to a differential gear, which in turn transfers the power to the rear wheels. Front-wheel-drive designs usually have the transmission and differential in the same housing at the rear of the engine and use constant velocity (CV) joints to connect directly to the front wheel axles. Rear-wheel-drive models have the engine and transmission mounted in-line, front-to-back. Front-wheel-drive models mount the engine sideways under the hood, so the transmission/differential assembly is usually on one side or the other.

Drive Time _____

Power is the rate or speed at which work is performed. **Torque** is turning or twisting force.

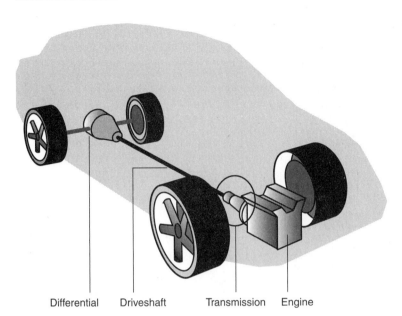

Typical rear-wheel-drive (RWD) transmission layout.

Differential   Driveshaft   Transmission   Engine

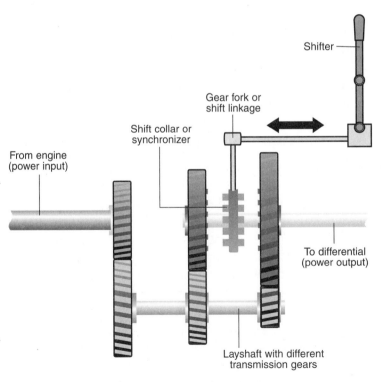

Manual transmissions require the driver to move a shift lever in order to change gears as the vehicle accelerates.

Shifter

Gear fork or shift linkage

Shift collar or synchronizer

From engine (power input)

To differential (power output)

Layshaft with different transmission gears

Brake System

The brakes are one of the most important safety devices on your car. They control the deceleration of your vehicle in an efficient manner. Most cars today come equipped with power or power assist brakes. You don't realize how much weight you are stopping in its tracks with the little pressure that you apply when braking. (And aren't we happy to hear *that!*) The most important system in your car needs your undivided attention and we will learn all about it in Chapter 18. Many modern vehicles are now equipped with antilock brake systems (ABS), which use computers and hydraulic controls to help keep the vehicle from skidding out of control during a stop in slippery conditions.

Here are the basic brake system components for a vehicle using a front disc and rear drum brake design. This layout is typical of most cars.

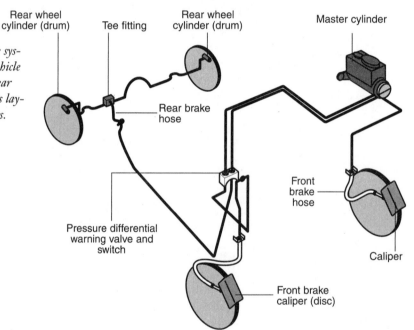

A/C and Heat System

When you move the lever on your car's climate-control panel to heat, you open a valve that diverts some of the engine's antifreeze solution to a heater core. The blower fan then moves cooler air through the core, heating it before it enters the passenger compartment. When you turn on the air-conditioning, the blower fan forces warmer air through the evaporator core, cooling it before it enters the passenger compartment.

The heater core acts like a radiator when the heat from hot engine coolant is dissipated. The A/C evaporator core acts as a radiator in reverse transferring the heat from the air to the refrigerant in the air-conditioning system, thereby delivering cool air to the passenger compartment.

The Least You Need to Know

- When you turn the key in the ignition you begin the four-stroke engine process.
- The suspension system smoothes out bounces and bumps and allows you to steer and control the vehicle.
- Because your engine gets very hot, your vehicle needs the cooling system to keep it at a specific operating temperature.
- Lubrication is critical for your engine to run.
- The electrical system plays a significant part in many aspects of your drive time—from ignition to turns to lights.
- Your brakes and drive train are there to make you stop and go.

Chapter 6

Steering and Suspension Systems

In This Chapter

◆ A closer look at the steering and suspension systems

◆ The parts that make guiding your vehicle almost effortless

◆ How shock absorbers work to smooth your ride

◆ Independent and dependent suspensions

When you're trying to merge onto a busy interstate, it's great for your vehicle to respond upon request. So there are times when horsepower rules! But you expect more from your vehicle than a great 0 to 60 acceleration. You expect your car to handle and ride smoothly.

Basically, the suspension in your vehicle is a system of shock absorbers and other supports that connect your vehicle to its wheels. Suspension systems keep your car's wheels on the ground where they can provide traction, while keeping you and your passengers comfortable and mostly isolated from routine road obstacles like speed bumps, potholes, and those strange grooves that make your car vibrate. These are lofty goals. However, car designers continue to make vehicles more and more passenger-friendly.

Let's take a tour of your car's steering and suspension systems, name basic parts, and give different designs of these systems. (In Chapter 7, we'll tell you how to perform routine maintenance and troubleshoot various problems on your steering and suspension system.)

The Steering and Suspension Systems at a Glance

- Ball joints
- Joints
- Springs
- Idler arms
- Bushings

- Tie-rod ends
- Steering linkage
- Steering damper
- Spring types: coil, leaf, torsion bars, air

- Shock absorbers
- Struts
- Tires

An Overview of Your Car's Steering and Suspension Systems

Sliding behind a steering wheel and steering your vehicle is a great feeling. Your vehicle responds to your hands' every command. We've all seen children walk around with various round objects pretending they were steering a car. They know it's a vital part of driving. And yes, you wouldn't get very far without your steering wheel, but your car's *steering system* is a little more involved than a steering wheel. The two most common types of steering systems are …

- **Rack-and-pinion steering,** in which the steering column is attached to a small gear (the pinion), which engages a toothed bar (the rack). Each end of the rack is attached to one of the front wheels. When the steering wheel is turned, the pinion gear moves the rack, which turns the front wheels.

- **Recirculating-ball steering,** in which the steering column is attached to a worm gear that engages a mechanism using ball bearings in a recirculating track. When the steering wheel is turned, the mechanism moves an arm that is attached to the steering linkage, which then moves the front wheels.

The seat you ride in is much better to your backside because of, yes, the materials it's made out of, but also because of your suspension system. Most of our roads today are fairly smooth, but even twenty-first century roads are blessed with plenty of bumps, dips, and potholes. It's these imperfections that apply uneven surfaces to car wheels. Engineers work diligently to make your car's suspension, with its various components, provide all of the solutions needed to absorb shocks while giving you a comfortable ride.

Drive Time

The **steering system** is a device that allows you to guide and direct your vehicle.

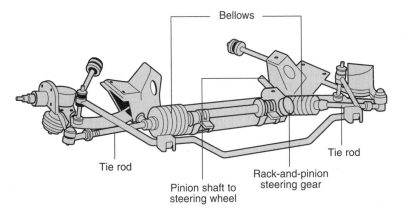

Bellows

Tie rod

Tie rod

Pinion shaft to steering wheel

Rack-and-pinion steering gear

Typical manual rack-and-pinion steering compenents.

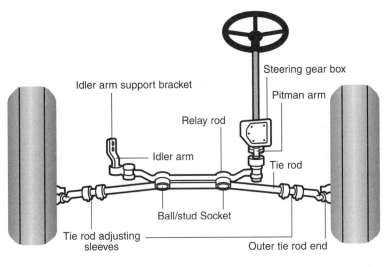

Typical steering system components on a recirculating-ball type design.

Idler arm support bracket

Steering gear box

Pitman arm

Relay rod

Idler arm

Tie rod

Ball/stud Socket

Tie rod adjusting sleeves

Outer tie rod end

◆ The suspension system is designed to properly distribute the weight of your car to each of the tires. It is also responsible for keeping your tires in contact with the road when you hit bumps or potholes and when you turn.

◆ The anti-sway bar is incorporated into your car's suspension system to minimize your car's tendency to roll when you go around a corner. They can be found on the front or the rear or both and are designed to keep all four wheels in contact with the road.

◆ Your vehicle's springs and shock absorbers form an essential, carefully balanced part of the suspension system. The springs suspend the weight of your car, so that there is movement at each wheel when you hit a bump or a dip in the road. The shocks eliminate the resulting bounce and keep the tires in contact with the road.

Parts of the Steering System

Whether you are turning on a smooth roadway or bouncing around a curve on a dirt road, the front wheels on your car need to move easily in whatever direction you are steering while they are moving up and down. The ball joints are one of the important components that allow this to happen. It functions like a ball-and-socket joint, similar to your hip joint, which allows a wide range of motion.

The steering knuckle is a heavy metal casting that provides means for attaching one or both ball joints, the steering linkage, and, very importantly, a front wheel. The ball-joint attachment provides the pivoting axis for the wheel, and the steering linkage attaches to an arm on the knuckle, providing a radius to turn the wheel. The front wheel is attached to a spindle, really just a short axle, by way of a couple of wheel bearings and an axle nut.

Your car will most likely have one of two common types of suspension at the front wheels. If your car has a MacPherson-strut suspension, the suspension system at each of your front wheels will only have a lower ball joint. The other type of suspension uses two control arms and is known by one of three names—double A arm, double wishbone, or short long arm (SLA). If your car has this type, it will have upper and lower ball joints at each front wheel.

◆ The steering linkage is an intermediate part of the steering system that is typically either a simple link that connects the steering rack to the front wheels or a series of interconnected links that connects the steering or pitman arm to the front wheels. In either case, the linkage helps translate the rotational motion of the steering wheel to the left-and-right motion that allows the wheels to move in the correct direction.

- ◆ The steering damper is a hydraulic mechanism found in some cars to minimize sudden changes in the steering system that can occur when hitting a bump. It can help maintain steering control under extreme conditions.

With all the ups and downs, lefts and rights, and loading and unloading of your car, the moving parts of your car's suspension and steering would wear out quickly without proper lubrication. Carefully read your owner's manual to see where and how often these parts need attention. Many newer cars have parts with sealed lifetime lubrication. The joints and fittings are packed with a high-quality grease and sealed to prevent leakage and contamination from water and dirt. You will not need to worry about lubrication, but watch for stiffness or looseness that may indicate a part needs to be replaced.

If your car's suspension and steering components need lubrication at regular intervals, do it yourself or have it done at the recommended intervals. The ball joints, tie rod ends, and other components depend on grease to provide a cushion that eliminates friction and keeps the joints free of dirt and water. Keeping these components greased will keep them operating smoothly and provide you with a car that's safe and comfortable to drive.

 CarLogic _____

Springs usually last the lifetime of your car, so you don't need to worry about servicing or replacing them.

Parts of the Suspension System

The following are parts of your vehicle's suspension system:

- ◆ Coil springs can be found on the front or rear of many cars. They usually require less overall room than other types of springs, providing some design advantages. They function like a torsion bar that has been wound around an axis.

- ◆ Leaf springs are attached to the frame with a hanger assembly and a moveable shackle. They may be a traditional steel multilayer type or they may be a single-layer constant-rate composite spring. They are typically used to attach the rear axles of larger cars and trucks.

◆ Torsion bars use the resistance to twisting of a steel bar to provide a means of minimizing the up-and-down movement of a wheel. One end of the bar is attached to the car's frame and the other end is attached to a control arm that is attached to an axle or knuckle. When the wheel hits a bump or pothole, the torsion bar twists and then returns to its original position.

◆ Air springs are typically a rubber container of air located between your car's frame and axle. The elastic properties of the rubber and the compressive properties of the air absorb axle movements and wheel vibrations. Some applications allow for adjustment of the stiffness of the ride or for adjustment for carrying heavier loads by increasing and decreasing the volume and pressure of the air in the container.

CarLogic

Test your auto IQ. Did you know these "springy" facts?

◆ The weight of your car that is supported by the springs is considered sprung mass, while the weight of the wheels and axles that support the springs is known as unsprung mass.

◆ The size of the spring, the number of coils, and the torsional resistance of the metal all contribute to how your car responds to the up, down, left, and right movements of the car as it goes down the road.

◆ To create a smoother, more comfortable ride, larger cars tend to have a softer ride. The longer wheelbase and a "looser" suspension contribute to this type of ride that results in a little more rolling movement when cornering.

◆ Smaller cars, especially sports cars, tend to have a tighter, less forgiving suspension. The shorter wheelbase and the stiffer springs create the sensation that the car grips the road better and maneuvers through corners with greater agility.

As children, we all became aware of the concept of a springing action from bouncing on beds or trampolines, but finding the correct balance for an automobile is a little more complicated. Springs absorb energy, but they have to have a place to put that energy. So car engineers have to find a way to control the incessant bouncing without transferring it to your seat.

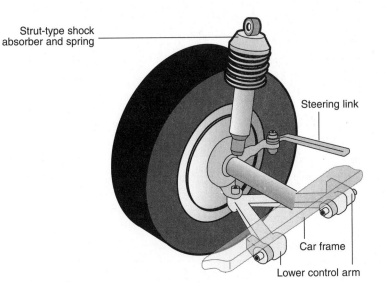

Strut-type shock absorber and spring

Steering link

Car frame

Lower control arm

Front suspension.

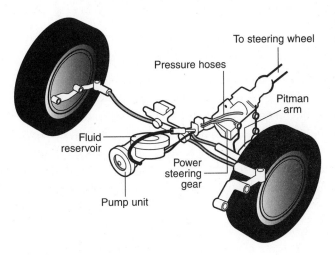

To steering wheel

Pressure hoses

Pitman arm

Fluid reservoir

Power steering gear

Pump unit

Conventional integral power steering components.

Linkage power steering components.

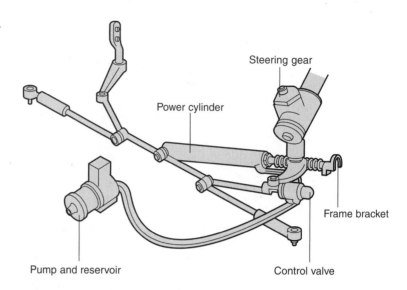

Absorbing Bumps in the Road and Rounding Curves

As we've discussed, a suspension composed of only springs would make for an extremely bouncy ride and, on particularly bumpy roads, an uncontrollable car.

Enter the shock absorber. Your car's shock absorbers control the incessant bouncing. They also control unwanted spring motion through a process known as dampening. Shock absorbers limit the range of up-and-down movement of the wheel along with reducing the frequency and magnitude of the bounces. How? These bounces are the stored and released energy of the springs. Since springs alone can only store and release energy, we need shock absorbers to dissipate and absorb that energy. Shocks do this by turning the kinetic energy being released by the springs into heat energy that is dissipated through the hydraulic fluid or gas in whichever type of shock is in your car.

To understand how this works, let's look inside a shock absorber to see its structure and function.

Most automotive shock absorbers today are of the hydraulic type. They are mounted to your car's frame at the top end and either directly to the axle or to a lower A arm at the bottom end. They provide the controlling link between the sprung weight (the top end) and the unsprung weight (the bottom end). The shock absorber is constructed of two tubes, one telescoping into the other with a piston connected to a rod that is attached to the frame of the car. The inner tube is the pressure tube, while the outer tube is the reserve tube, which stores and supplies hydraulic fluid for the pressure tube.

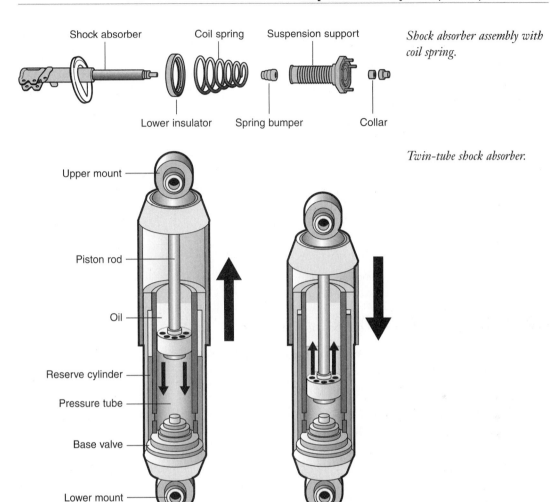

Shock absorber   Coil spring   Suspension support

Shock absorber assembly with coil spring.

Lower insulator   Spring bumper   Collar

Twin-tube shock absorber.

Upper mount

Piston rod

Oil

Reserve cylinder

Pressure tube

Base valve

Lower mount

Extension
cycle

Compression
cycle

When one of the wheels of your car dips into a pothole or hits a speed bump, the springs absorb the resultant shock to the suspension by coiling and uncoiling. To prevent the springs from shaking you and your car excessively, their motion is dampened by the shock absorbers. Now for the spring to coil and uncoil, it must extend and compress the ends of this shock absorber. However, the ends offer so much resistance to this motion that the coiling and uncoiling of the spring quickly fades. The resistance is created when the piston, which is connected to the top end, must force hydraulic fluid through valves in the pressure tube in order to move.

Whenever the shock is at either limit of its range of travel, it often keeps the rest of the suspension system from overextending. When you raise your car on a jack or lift by the frame, you will notice that the wheels drop. The shock absorber is typically fully extended in this situation, limiting any more extension of the rest of the suspension.

Fully extended shock absorber.

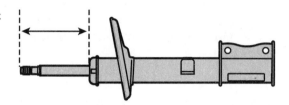

As your shocks wear out, they provide less and less resistance to the movement of the springs and can seriously affect the handling of your car. When struts wear out, in addition to the problems caused by worn shocks, they can affect the steering. The struts eliminate the need for an upper A or control arm and for an upper ball joint. The top end of the piston rod provides those functions.

When you drive around a curve, your car remains fairly level with the road surface. The laws of physics suggest that unless the curve is significantly banked, the inner wheels with respect to the curve should be rising off the road. Those clever automotive engineers have incorporated an anti-sway or stabilizer bar into your car's suspension to prevent that from happening and to keep all four tires in contact with the road. This bar typically spans the width of your car just inside the wheel wells. It is connected to the frame and to each axle or corresponding control arm. When one wheel moves up or down, the bar will transfer that same movement to the other wheel, keeping the car level and preventing body rolling when you go around a curve.

Speedbumps

The shocks and struts on your car contribute much to its handling ability, especially during emergency maneuvers or hard braking. Replace them at the intervals recommended in your owner's manual or when they fail the bounce test. If you push down hard on one corner of your car, it should rise back up and settle to where it was without multiple bounces. Other indications that your shocks or struts may need inspection are when you notice excessive body roll while cornering, uneven tire wear, and excessive dipping while braking hard.

Independent and Dependent Suspensions

You are driving around a curve and one of your wheels hits a pothole. Ideally, you want just that wheel to respond to the shock to the suspension system. If that does happen, you have an independent suspension system. If the shock is translated through the entire axle, then you have a dependent system (also called a solid axle). That's not necessarily a bad thing. Trucks, less expensive cars, and older cars tend to have dependent suspension systems. Independent systems can provide a more secure ride as each bump is isolated at only one wheel at a time.

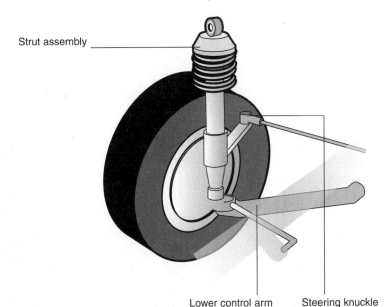

Strut assembly

Lower control arm   Steering knuckle

The MacPherson strut provides a steering pivot as well as a suspension mounting for the wheel.

Double-wishbone suspension.

A fully independent suspension grants a smooth ride.

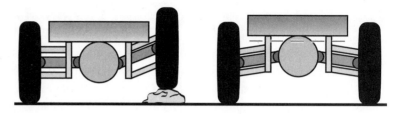

Encountering an object   Response

The Least You Need to Know

◆ Rack-and-pinion steering is a common type of steering in vehicles—but trucks, SUVs, and larger cars tend to mostly use the pitman arm assembly (which is used mostly on rear-wheel-drive vehicles).

◆ Shock absorbers absorb energy and make for a smoother ride.

◆ Your vehicle's springs absorb vibrations, but then need somewhere to put that energy.

◆ The steering linkage can connect the steering wheel to the front wheels.

◆ The MacPherson strut incorporates steering, spring, and shock into one unit—all three functions are equally important.

◆ Check your owner's manual for the type of suspension your vehicle is equipped with.

Chapter 7

Steering and Suspension Systems: Troubleshooting and Maintenance

In This Chapter

- ◆ All about your tires
- ◆ Rotating your tires
- ◆ How a tire is constructed
- ◆ Balancing the wheels
- ◆ Getting your tires aligned

What to buy? There are so many tire choices! Well, let's chat about that. Buying tires is no different than buying anything else. You must take a few minutes to find out what size tires your vehicle needs as well as what the manufacturer of your vehicle suggests. It's best to have basic knowledge of what you need before you shop. You need to know basic information like how tires work to support your vehicle, why it is so important to keep the correct air pressure in your tires, the construction of tires, what the numbers on the sidewall mean, and how to spot and diagnose tire problems.

In Chapter 6, we told you about the parts of the steering and suspension systems. Now we'll tell you how to troubleshoot your steering system. All you want to do is check for "play" in your steering wheel. That means if you can turn your steering wheel even a little without your tires moving, you need to have your technician look at your steering wheel and check to see if your tires need to be aligned.

Tires 101

Although an eye-catching set of wheels gives a great visual, tires that are in good condition are a must. There isn't so much to do to tires really. Checking them each time you fill up your gas tank is a good idea. You will also need to check the tire air pressure, rotate the tires (or have your technician rotate them), and replace them before they become unsafe.

Checking the tire pressure isn't difficult. You will need to know the proper air pressure for your tires. You can find that out by looking in your owner's manual. Refer to Chapter 1 for the steps involved in checking your tire pressure and adding air if necessary.

Radial tires have been the industry and safety standard for the past 20 years. Combined with steel belts, these tires provide excellent traction and control during their normal treadwear life span. When you look at your tires, all you see is the black rubber. Inside that rubber coating you will find plies (layers of textile cords) made of polyester or nylon and belts made of steel. These materials are carefully designed and engineered to provide your tires with the strength and stability that today's driving requires.

Radial tires are standard on most new cars. They rate high on the following criteria: cornering, rolling, and stopping.

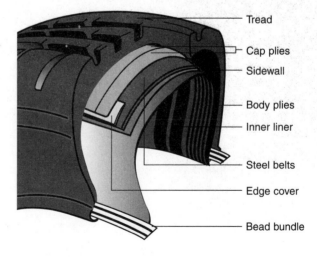

- Tread
- Cap plies
- Sidewall
- Body plies
- Inner liner
- Steel belts
- Edge cover
- Bead bundle

Let's go outside and check the condition of the tires on your vehicle.

CarLogic

It's time to buy new tires when the tread has about 1/16" of thickness remaining. If possible, buy a complete set of tires; replacing just one tire may cause balance problems. When buying new tires, listen to the salespeople, but realize it is not possible to know how long a tire will last. Things like braking habits (hard-braking skids will wear out tires faster), road conditions, keeping the correct air pressure in your tires, and having them rotated at the proper times all determine the life of a tire.

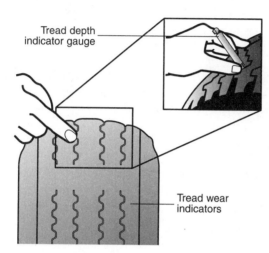

Tread depth indicator gauge

Tread wear indicators

Tire wear indicators have been standard on tires made since 1968. These bars show up as 1/2"-wide smooth bands across the tire. When tire wear indicators become visible, replace the tire. You can also check wear with a gauge or penny. If you can see the top of Lincoln's head on two adjacent grooves, the tire has less than 1/16" tread left and should be replaced.

Tire Rotation

Find out what your manufacturer recommends for the pattern of rotation for your vehicle. There are several ways to rotate tires according to the type tire you own. Radials are rotated in a cross-rotation pattern or modified X pattern. Cross rotating will even out wear and prolong tire life.

Tire rotation.

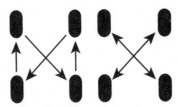

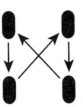

1) *Rearward cross pattern* and
2) *X pattern:* Use the rearward
cross or X pattern for rear-wheel-
drive and four-wheel-drive vehicles.

3) *Forward cross pattern:* Use the
forward cross pattern or X pattern
for front-wheel-drive vehicles.

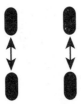

4) *Front-to-rear pattern:* Use
the front-to-rear pattern on
vehicles that have the same size
directional wheels.

5) *Side-to-side pattern:* Use the side-
to-side pattern on vehicles that have
differently sized nondirectional wheels
and tires on the front and rear axle.

The Making of a Tire

Much time and effort goes into the research and development of tires. They are carefully engineered to meet the more demanding requirements of increased vehicle weight, higher speeds, calls for more efficiency to reduce fuel use, and increased performance.

Tires are made from natural and synthetic rubber along with additives like sulfur and carbon black. Polyester and nylon are used to produce the cords, plies, and belts. Steel wire is also used to produce belts and form the bead for some tires.

Several machines take these materials and produce the six individual components that will later be assembled and molded into a tire. The tread rubber and sidewalls are extruded and cut into carefully measured lengths. The plies are produced by mills that coat nylon and polyester fabric with rubber. Fine-gauge steel wire is woven into belts. An impermeable layer of rubber forms the liner and finally, steel wire is wound into a circle to form the bead. These six components are assembled into an uncured tire, which is then placed in a mold to be cured under pressure and heat. The finished tire is then carefully inspected before being shipped off as a new car tire or replacement.

These six components provide important functions. The bead anchors the sidewall, provides a seal along the rim, and resists the deformation required to mount the tire on the rim. The plies provide strength. The sidewalls provide lateral stability and protect the plies. The belts provide puncture resistance and keep the tread flat on the road. The tread provides traction and resistance to wear. The liner provides a leak-proof coating inside the tire, eliminating the need for an inner tube.

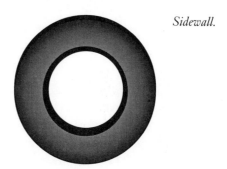

Sidewall.

What Do All the Letters and Numbers Mean?

You can learn how to buy a new set of tires by learning how to decipher the numbers and letters on the set that has gone its last mile. Let's say your tire has the following letters and numbers embedded in the rubber: P18560R1482H. Here's what that means:

- The **P** designates that the tire is a passenger vehicle; other designations are **LT** for light truck and **T** for temporary or spare tires.

- The **185** is the width of the tire in millimeters (mm), measured from sidewall to sidewall. Since this measure is affected by the width of the rim, the measurement is for the tire when it is its intended rim size. This number tells you the height of the tire, from the bead to the top of the tread. This is described as a percentage of the tire width.

- The **60** represents the aspect ratio, which means the ratio of sidewall height to width.

- The **R** tells you the tire is a radial-ply construction. If there is a B you'll know the tire is a bias-ply construction (bias-ply tires are obsolete for all but antique vehicles).

- The **14** refers to your vehicle's wheel diameter in inches.

- The **82** is the tire's load index, which gives you an idea of how much weight it will support.

- The **H** is the tire's speed rating. The H rating indicates the tire can run at speeds up to 130 mph. Other letters you might see are S (113 mph), V (149 mph) and Z (149+ mph).

Tire Grades

You've only just started your fascinating inquiry into the exciting world of tire characteristics and ratings, all of which can be found in concentric circles around the sidewall. The federal government requires tire manufacturers to grade their tires on treadwear rate, traction performance, and temperature resistance. The Uniform Tire Quality Grading System (UTQGS) provides standard guidelines for comparing tires:

- The *treadwear grade* indicates relative tire wear. The higher the number, the longer the tire should last. A grade of 200, for example, indicates a tire that should last twice as long as one with a grade of 100.

- The *traction grade* indicates the tire's ability to stop on wet pavement. The higher the grade, the shorter the distance required. You will see grades of AA, A, B, and C. To come up with these traction grades, car tires are tested on a straight stop, not during a curve. Those with the best rating are AA, while those with a C rating are poor but still legal to use on your vehicle.

- *Temperature grades* indicate a tire's resistance to heat. The higher the grade—A (speeds over 115 mph), B (speeds 100 to 115 mph), or C (speeds 85 to 100 mph)—the more resistant to heat, which can accelerate deterioration, cause blowouts, or cause tread separation.

There is still much more, such as the Department of Transportation (DOT) ID number, the number of plies and materials used in the tire, the maximum load rating (not to be confused with the load index number), and the maximum permissible inflation pressure.

Another marking on the sidewall that is used to indicate an all-season tire are the letters MS, which stand for mud and snow. An all-season tire is the best all-around choice for the family chariot, particularly if you live in a seasonal climate that involves extremes from hot to cold and rain and snow. Most new vehicles built as family cars, including SUVs and minivans, typically come new with MS-rated all-season tires.

If your driving tastes tend toward sport sedans or performance cars, there are tires built to run much faster than the national speed limits, but if you must have the best, look for a Z rating. These performance tires come in many styles and designs, from low-profile sidewall construction to unidirectional tread designs for maximum grip and performance at high speeds. There are also high-performance rain tires with specific tread designs to channel water away from the tire at road speeds. As you might expect, the higher the performance and capabilities of the tire, the greater the cost. The best advice if you're not sure what tire to buy is to talk it over with your local tire shop. You should discuss the type of driving you typically do and the kind of loads and road conditions you typically encounter. There's a different tire depending on whether you're hauling the kids to soccer practice in the minivan or SUV or pushing the limits on a twisty back-country road in the Corvette. Take the time to find out how much tire you really need to buy.

Tire Wear

Uneven tire wear shortens the life of your tires, costs you money, and is hazardous. Here are some causes of uneven tire wear:

- If your car was used when you bought it, there could be frame damage.

- If there is excessive wear at the center of the tire, you've overinflated it.

- Excessive wear at both edges signals underinflation.

- Scallops indicate your tires have not been rotated as needed or your suspension needs servicing.

- Bald spots indicate a bad tire or a wheel that needs balancing.

- Excessive wear at one edge indicates too much camber angle between wheel and pavement. (We'll tell you more about camber in a moment.)

Improperly and properly inflated tires.

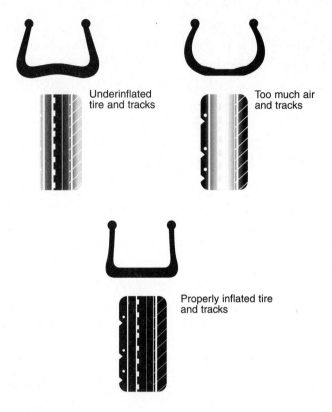

Underinflated tire and tracks

Too much air and tracks

Properly inflated tire and tracks

Balancing Your Wheels

If you have an unbalanced wheel, not only will it wear out before its time, but it will also interfere with a smooth ride. Balancing your vehicle's wheels is a job that is best done by your technician. Your technician will also rotate your tires, so this is a place where you can have two jobs done at once.

There are two types of balancing:

♦ A wheel that is *statically balanced* has an equal distribution of weight around its circumference and will come to rest in any position after being spun. If a wheel is not statically balanced, it will always come to rest with the heavy part down. When spun at higher speeds, it will tend to "hop" or shake up and down. Static balance can be checked and corrected using a bubble balancer.

♦ *Dynamic balancing* is usually done by a computerized spin balancer. It ensures that there is an equal distribution of weight on both sides of the wheel and indicates where additional weight must be added, if necessary, to achieve this balance. Wheels lacking dynamic balance will shake in a sideways, back-and-forth motion.

Having Your Tires Aligned

Aligning the tires is a job best left to your auto technician. Using a very precise alignment machine aided by a computer, he or she will check and adjust the caster, camber, and toe angles, returning them to the specifications recommended by your car's manufacturer. Most modern vehicles require all four wheels to be aligned, not just the front, and the latest alignment equipment is designed to do this very accurately. It's all about the angles, and here's what those names mean:

♦ The *caster angle* indicates he backward or forward slope of the steering axis determined by the upper and lower ball joints or by the MacPherson strut. Caster angle is expressed in degrees. Caster is considered positive if the top of this axis tilts toward the rear of the car, and negative if it tilts forward.

♦ The *camber angle* indicates how far a wheel tilts away from the vertical when viewed from the front. Camber angle is expressed in degrees, and is considered positive when the tops of the wheels tilt away from the center of the car and negative when they tilt toward the center.

♦ The *toe angle* indicates the exact direction each wheel is pointed when compared to the center line of the vehicle. Toe angle is expressed either in fractions of an inch or in degrees. Positive toe or toe-in has the wheels turning into each other. Negative toe or toe-out has the wheels turning away from each other.

> **Speedbumps**
>
> All three angles significantly influence handling and tire wear. Any deviations from the manufacturer's specifications can become exponentially exaggerated as speed increases because your tires are not working as they were designed to work.

Excessive caster angle makes steering heavier and less responsive.

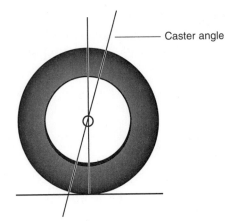

Caster angle

Camber angle alters how a car handles. For example, negative camber (bottom of wheel is further out than the top) improves cornering grip.

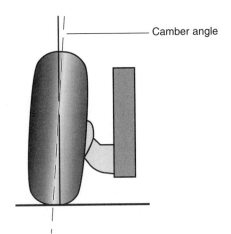

Camber angle

Toe settings impact tire wear, straight-line stability, and corner entry handling.

Toe-in   Toe-out

The Least You Need to Know

◆ Inspect your tires each time you fill up—looking for abnormal wear, bubbles on the sidewalls, cuts, or embedded nails.

◆ To extend the life of your radial tires, rotate in a cross-rotation pattern or modified X pattern.

◆ Learning what the numbers and letters on your sidewall mean will help you with your next tire purchase.

◆ Talk over your typical driving conditions and type of vehicle with your tire dealer to determine which type of tires are best for your car, van, or SUV.

◆ Balance your wheels in order to keep your car driving smoothly.

◆ Aligning and balancing the wheels and rotating the tires are jobs usually best left to trained auto technicians.

Chapter 8

Cooling System

In This Chapter

- How your car's cooling system regulates engine temperature
- A tour of the cooling system
- How the water pump works
- The radiator and radiator cap
- The job of the thermostat
- The cooling fan and heater core

In all likelihood your car has a gasoline engine. There are other kinds of engines, such as diesels (which are becoming more commonplace), but most cars today run on gasoline. Engineers work to make the most of any expenditure of energy, but about the best they can do right now is turn over the dissipated heat (the heat that's driven away from the engine) to your vehicle's cooling system. (Over half—around 70 percent—of the energy produced by gasoline is turned into heat.) It would be nice if some of the wasted chemical energy could be turned into mechanical power. Maybe one day that will be the case. But for now, let's talk about the important job your car's cooling system takes on. (In Chapter 9, we'll tell you how to perform routine maintenance and troubleshoot various problems in your cooling system.)

> **The Cooling System at a Glance**
>
> ◆ Radiator/pressure cap ◆ Fan
>
> ◆ Thermostat ◆ Hoses
>
> ◆ Water pump ◆ Coolant reservoir

An Overview of Your Car's Cooling System

If you looked inside your running engine, you'd see all that high-priced gasoline constantly burning. (Painful thought—and don't try it for safety reasons!) A lot of the heat from this combustion goes out the exhaust system, but some of it soaks into the engine and heats it up.

Internal-combustion engines operate most efficiently at higher temperatures. Once the engine is warmed up, the engine cooling system keeps the operating temperature at around 200°F (93°C). Several factors contribute to this efficient operation. Oil at higher temperatures flows more easily, allowing the moving parts in your engine, including the oil pump, to rotate more easily with less resistance and wear. The cylinder head that contains the combustion chamber keeps the temperature hot enough to completely vaporize the fuel, ensuring better combustion and reduction in harmful emissions.

This constant temperature is maintained by engine coolant that protects the cooling system components from corrosion, prevents boiling over, and doesn't freeze. The coolant is circulated by the water pump, so that it can carry excess heat away from the engine. The coolant releases its heat in the radiator before returning to the engine to start the process over again. A thermostat regulates the flow of coolant, and a pressure cap controls pressure and releases excess pressure.

Parts of the Cooling System

Engines in most cars today are liquid cooled. In the past, there were a few manufacturers producing air-cooled engines. However, liquid-cooled engines have a few advantages. The engine temperature is easier to control, making it easier to produce more efficient and less polluting engines. The liquid coolant provides a more efficient and effective way to warm the passenger compartment on cool days. Automatic-transmission fluid heat exchangers can be conveniently located in the radiator tanks.

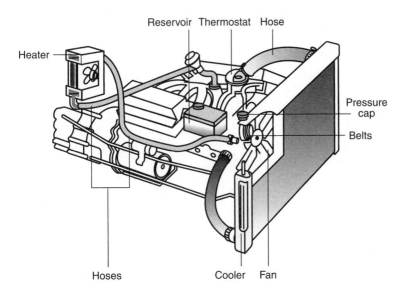

Reservoir Thermostat Hose

Heater

Pressure cap

Belts

Hoses   Cooler Fan

Most cars are equipped with a liquid-cooled cooling system.

Water Pump

Most water pumps are driven by a belt that wraps around the crankshaft pulley. A few are driven directly by gears from the crankshaft. However it is driven, the pump is always circulating coolant when the engine is running. With the thermostat open, coolant from the radiator is pumped through the engine block and cylinder heads to the radiator and back to the block and heads.

 Auto-Biography

Older-model vehicles that were air cooled produced up to 50 percent more pollution than modern liquid-cooled engines.

The engine block is designed with many passages and cavities around the cylinders, and the cylinder head has passages to allow for maximum dissipation of heat into the coolant.

The water pump has a crucial role in keeping the engine temperature in a range where it will operate efficiently and where it won't self-destruct or seize. The temperatures inside the combustion chamber can reach 4,500°F. The exhaust valves are especially vulnerable since the hot exhaust gases must pass over them. The passages in the cylinder head are designed to allow coolant to flow efficiently, keeping the valves from warping.

Coolant is circulated through the engine by the water pump.

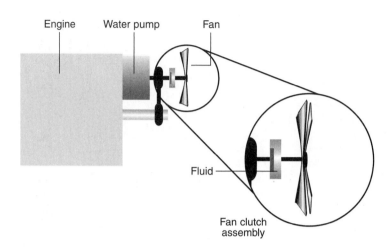

Engine   Water pump   Fan

Fluid

Fan clutch assembly

Radiator

Radiators are simple heat exchangers. That is, your car radiator transfers heat from the hot coolant to the air that is being blown through the radiator. There are basically two designs of heat exchangers:

- *Cross-flow* radiators have two tanks, one mounted on each side of the radiator core with a system of horizontal parallel tubes connecting them. Coolant flows in the top of one side tank and is drawn out from the bottom of the other side tank.

- *Down-flow* radiators have the tanks on the top and bottom with a vertical system of parallel tubes connecting them. Coolant flows into the top tank and is drawn out of the bottom tank. While the coolant is flowing through the tubes, heat is being dissipated to a multitude of fins surrounding the tubes. The heat is then transferred to the air being blown through the fins by the fan.

The tanks can be plastic or metal, usually aluminum or copper, and the tubes and fins are aluminum, copper, or an alloy of either or both. The size of the radiator and the design of the tubes and fins have been carefully matched to the engine in your car to provide efficient cooling.

If your car has an automatic transmission, you will see two metal lines attached to one of the radiator tanks. These are the inlet and outlet lines for the transmission cooler. There is a heat exchanger inside the tank that initially helps bring the automatic transmission fluid up to operating temperature and then helps keep it from overheating.

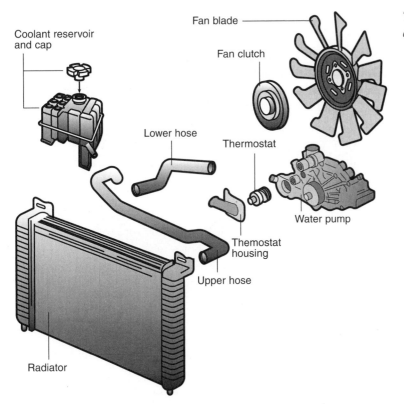

Fan blade

The radiator is a heat exchanger.

Coolant reservoir and cap

Fan clutch

Lower hose

Thermostat

Themostat housing

Upper hose

Water pump

Radiator

Pressure Cap

If you have a closed system with fluid circulating through it, and you apply heat to it, the pressure in the system will increase. This can be beneficial in that the boiling point of the fluid is raised under pressure. This allows the fluid to remain a fluid at higher temperatures and continue to transfer heat. However, too much pressure would be difficult to contain, so a relief valve is necessary. This is the job of your radiator or pressure cap. Most cars have caps set to relieve pressure when the fluid pressure reaches from 7 to 15 pounds per square inch.

Newer cars now have expansion tanks or coolant overflow tanks to catch the coolant that is being released under pressure by the cap. When the radiator cools down, it creates a vacuum, drawing coolant back in from the expansion or overflow tank.

Thermostat

The coolant flow in most cars is controlled by a thermostat. A few cars have coolant flow controlled by the Power Control Module (PCM). The thermostat allows your engine to warm up quickly, and then maintain a constant operating temperature. It does this by opening and closing a valve. When cold the valve is shut, so coolant circulates only through the engine until it reaches a temperature of about 180°F, when the valve begins to open. By the time the temperature has reached about 200°F, the valve is fully open and coolant is flowing to the radiator and back through the engine.

Thermostats are available in slightly different heat ranges to compensate for different operating conditions and for changes to the cooling system.

If you have the chance to examine an automotive thermostat, be sure to appreciate the simplicity of this amazing device. Then put it in a pot of water on your stove and watch as the water approaches boiling temperature. You should see the valve open and then close as the water cools. The valve is connected to a rod that enters a small metal cylinder. That cylinder is filled with a petroleum wax that has a specific melting point. When the wax melts, it expands, pushing the rod, opening the valve.

Fan

Earlier in this chapter, we talked about needing to cool the coolant in the radiator. A fan is needed to pull air through those fins to get rid of the heat. Older cars had a mechanical fan mounted to the water pump that turned whenever the engine turned. Newer cars are outfitted with fans that have a silicon clutch, so that when you are moving down the expressway and plenty of air is passing through the radiator, the fan can spin with the airflow, rather than creating resistance and drag. With transverse mounted engines, this type of setup was no longer possible, so electric fans were mounted right behind the radiator. These have the added benefit of being easily controllable. A temperature-sensitive switch turns the fan on when needed.

Heating

One of the benefits of a liquid cooling system for an engine is being able to easily provide heat for the passenger compartment. The heater core is another heat exchanger that operates like a small radiator. It is located under your dash. A fan blows air through it that is warmed by the coolant from your engine. It typically draws coolant from the cylinder head and returns it to the water pump, so that you don't have to wait for the thermostat to open to get some heat.

The Least You Need to Know

- The primary job of your car's cooling system is to keep the engine from over-heating; it also regulates engine temperature to keep it running smoothly.

- Cars today are liquid cooled (usually water mixed with antifreeze) instead of air cooled.

- Your vehicle's water pump starts circulating coolant as soon as the engine starts running.

- Radiators are heat exchangers.

- Newer cars now have expansion tanks or coolant overflow tanks to catch the coolant released under pressure by the cap.

Cooling System: Troubleshooting and Maintenance

In This Chapter

- ◆ Why a car overheats
- ◆ Checking your coolant level and adding coolant
- ◆ Flushing the radiator
- ◆ Replacing the thermostat
- ◆ Help for squeaky belts and leaky hoses
- ◆ Keep your cool with A/C know-how

In Chapter 8, we told you about the parts of the cooling system. Now we'll tell you how to troubleshoot and fix those parts. We'll also tell you when it's time to call a technician. The cooling system works to keep your engine from overheating, and that is a very important job. If your vehicle overheats, it can mean the death of your engine.

So what are the signs your car is about to have a hot flash? Your first indication will either be your temperature gauge going into the red zone or a check engine/temperature light that just appears. It's a good idea to go ahead and check on your vehicle as soon as one of these signs comes to your attention to avoid being stranded on the roadside. Another plus to having this checked out is the next sequence of events unfortunately may mean a big repair bill. If cooling system repairs are not done correctly, you risk ruining your engine as well as the environment if antifreeze is not disposed of properly. We recommend that you keep this system properly maintained and when you have a problem, let your technician make the needed repairs. However, if you buy a vehicle-specific manual (see Appendix C) and feel comfortable making the repairs yourself, be sure to study the directions in the manual before you begin the repair.

Why Is My Car Blowing Its Top?

There are many reasons your car may overheat. Are you in rush-hour traffic? Or is it sizzling hot outside? Then your car may be overheating simply because of the circumstances. If you do find yourself in this predicament, turn off the air conditioner, open your windows, and turn your heater on wide open. This will help draw some heat from your engine and unfortunately into your car. You do not want your vehicle to overheat, so if a service station isn't in sight and the other measures didn't work, you need to pull over and shut off the engine immediately.

Here are some other reasons your car may get hot:

◆ Leak in your cooling system

◆ Thermostat problem

◆ Fan belt is loose

◆ Water pump problem

◆ Low oil level

◆ Bad hose

◆ Dirty radiator plugged with debris

◆ Timing needs adjusting

◆ Needs coolant

Checking and Adding Coolant

Regularly checking fluids is a good plan for your wallet and for your safety. Let's begin by learning how to take off the radiator cap. But before we do, a few words of warning are in order. *Never* try to remove a radiator cap when the engine is hot. You will want to wait at least 20 to 25 minutes so that your engine can cool off. This is even if you had to pull over by the side of the road. It may be inconvenient, but you do not want to be sprayed with hot coolant. So if you are stranded, pop the hood and get back into your car. Make sure it's pulled a safe distance off the road, though, before you sit in it. Observe safety rules (pull back long flowing hair, take off dangling jewelry, etc.) when working under the hood. Take your cell phone out to dial a relative and maybe your auto club or technician to let them know what is going on. Chat a while before you try to take off the radiator cap again.

Speedbumps

To avoid possible injury, always wait at least 20 to 25 minutes before removing a radiator cap to allow your engine to cool off.

After the engine has cooled, remove the radiator cap by following these steps:

1. Some cars have safety caps that after being popped allow pressure to escape. If you have a safety cap, very carefully pop it now. Step back while the steam escapes and then go back and twist the cap in a counterclockwise motion. If you don't have a safety cap, you'll want to pull out one of those old tee-shirt rags from your toolbox and place it over the cap before you turn. This will keep your hands from getting burned.

2. After turning the cap, if things have not settled down—that is, if there is a lot of hissing and steam or coolant escaping—righty-tighty the cap back on. You'll need to wait for the engine to cool more.

3. When it's safe to take the top off, twist in a counterclockwise motion and open the cap away from your body.

The radiator cap is pressurized.

Drive Time

The **coolant recovery tank** is an overflow reservoir in the engine compartment.

Now check your vehicle's coolant. You will be checking how much fluid you have and the quality of that fluid. Most vehicles built since the 1970s have a *coolant recovery tank.*

If you have an older car or one without either an expansion tank or a coolant recovery tank, you must check the coolant level at the radiator. When the engine is cool, remove the radiator cap and look into the neck; you should see coolant about ¾" below the top of the tank or the bottom of the neck. The coolant should easily cover the ends of the tubes. If the level is low, you will need to add some coolant. It's important to match whatever coolant is being used in order to preserve its protection qualities. The color of anti-freeze is no longer an adequate guide as to how long a coolant will last. You should use standard antifreeze, if that's what is in your system. Or use long life if that's what's in there. Long-life antifreeze means the corrosive inhibitor of the antifreeze lasts longer—up to 5 years or 100,000 miles. Always follow the guidelines in your owner's manual. You can purchase premixed coolant or you can purchase antifreeze that must be mixed with equal parts of distilled water. Add the coolant to the radiator to bring the level up to where it should be.

If your car has an expansion tank, checking the coolant is a little easier. The tank should be made of a translucent plastic through which you can see the coolant level. There should be markings on the side that indicate hot and cold level. See where the coolant level lies in relation to these marks. If the engine is cool, you can add coolant by removing the pressure cap and bringing the level up to the cold mark. If the engine is hot, you will have to wait for it to cool down before removing the pressure cap to add coolant. If you have a coolant recovery tank, you simply flip the cap to open it since it is not pressurized. If your engine is hot, you should wait for it to cool down, since cold coolant and hot metal do not always agree with one another. If you find either the expansion tank or the coolant recovery tank completely empty, there is a good chance the coolant level is low in the radiator, too. If you have a cap on the radiator, remove it when the engine is cool and top off the radiator before filling the expansion tank or the coolant recovery tank.

If you own an older car, follow the same safety measures, but add water or coolant directly to the radiator. You can buy and install a coolant recovery reservoir. Just ask your trusted auto-parts salesperson. You can also buy a pressurized cap for your radiator should you need one.

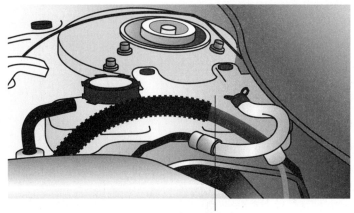

The coolant reservoir generally has "high" and "low" markings for an easy way of checking the coolant level. However, if you need to remove the cap, always wait until the engine cools.

Coolant reservoir

Flushing Your Vehicle's System

Flushing the radiator helps keep the cooling system clean of rust and settling debris. The maintenance schedule in your owner's manual will tell you when you should have your cooling system flushed and refilled. The most common service interval recommendations are every 24 to 36 months or 24,000 to 36,000 miles, but many later-model vehicles now have coolant that is designed to last 100,000 miles. Find out for sure what your particular vehicle warrants from your technician and write this information in your maintenance log or vehicle fact sheet (see Appendix B).

There are a few different techniques for flushing your cooling system. Your auto-parts store will stock several flushing products and some aftermarket devices, like tee fittings for the heater lines, to make the job a little easier. You'll want to keep a couple of things in mind when deciding whether you want to do this. Are your radiator and engine fitted with drain cocks? Some cars are and some have only one or none, and require you to remove the lower radiator hose to drain the system, which can be a bit messy. More importantly, be aware that you will need to properly contain and recycle several gallons of flushing solution and old coolant. Don't just let it run down the storm drain. Your auto-parts store or your community recycling center should be able to provide you with a recycling location. So think carefully about whether you would like to leave this potentially messy job to the service technicians who have the proper flushing equipment and onsite storage for these toxic fluids.

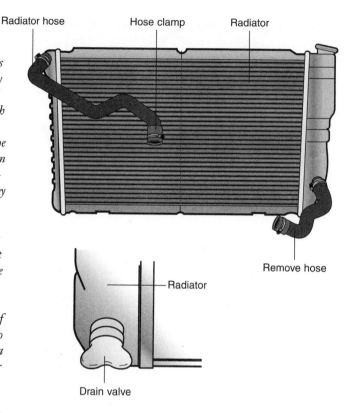

Most radiators have larger upper and lower water hoses and on modern vehicles they are often specifically molded to fit. All are secured at both ends by hose clamps, which may be of either a screw-type or spring-type design. Loosen the screw type with a screwdriver and the spring type by squeezing the tabs together with a large pair of pliers. It's best to replace both hoses at the same time. Also, most radiators have a drain valve at the lower corner (generally the right lower corner as you are facing the front of the car) which can be used to carefully drain coolant into a container for proper reuse or disposal. Coolant is toxic. Be careful not to let children or animals drink it accidentally.

Radiator hose   Hose clamp   Radiator

Remove hose

Radiator

Drain valve

Given the environmental concerns alone, flushing a cooling system is a service that is best left to the professionals. If you decide to go ahead with this procedure on your own, carefully read and follow the directions. Check your owner's manual for any special directions when flushing and for recommendations for replacement coolant. A vehicle-specific repair manual should have a detailed step-by-step procedure.

Speedbumps

Remember, antifreeze or coolant has a sweet smell and taste, but it is toxic and can be fatal if even a small amount is ingested. Keep it away from kids, pets, and storm drains. Wear protective clothing so you don't get any on your skin. Thoroughly rinse off any spilled coolant immediately. You should always put the top back on an open container of coolant and keep it out of the reach of children or pets. Also, it is important to dispose of this chemical properly (check with local authorities) or you run the risk of harming people, animals, and the environment—and there are fines levied for disposing of coolant illegally.

The antifreeze tester is an inexpensive tool (you can get it at a discount or auto-parts store) that lets you know if your vehicle has enough antifreeze. Normally you need a mixture of 50 percent water and 50 percent antifreeze, but check your owner's manual for your particular vehicle.

Coolant/antifreeze tester.

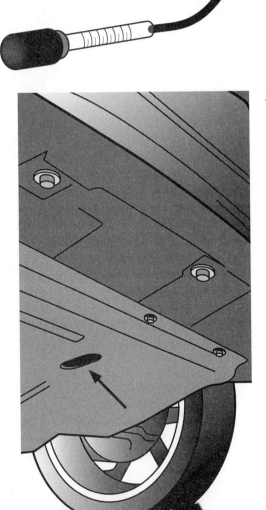

Radiator drain-plug location.

Checking and Replacing a Thermostat

Here are a few things to check before deciding to replace your thermostat: coolant level (as described in previous section), drive-belt tension (refer to Chapter 4), and temperature gauge operation (by putting a thermostat on the radiator). An engine that seems to be taking longer to warm up, or is running cooler than normal per your temperature gauge, may indicate the thermostat is stuck open. If that is the case, you will need a new thermostat. The only way to really check the thermostat operation is to remove it, place it in a pan of water, heat the water slowly, and observe the operation of the spring and valve as the water reaches about 200°F. The thermostat valve should open gradually. If you take the thermostat out of a cold engine and it's already open, you can pretty much assume you need a new one. Given the relatively low cost of the part, if you're going to go to all the trouble of removing it in the first place, why not just replace it?

Most thermostats are located under a metal housing (usually called a "goose neck") at the upper radiator hose connection to the engine, but some import models may have them elsewhere. In all cases they are relatively easy to reach and replace, since they are designed to be serviced periodically. Any good vehicle-specific service manual sold at a parts store should show you this location on your particular vehicle.

Your vehicle's thermostat is located between the engine and the radiator.

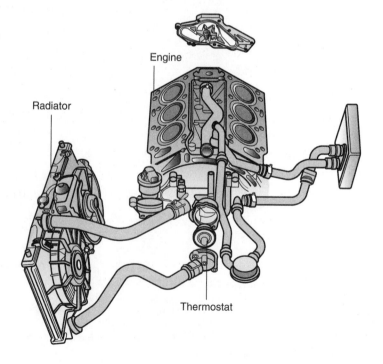

Engine

Radiator

Thermostat

If you find you need a new thermostat, it's a good idea to go ahead and flush and clean your cooling system at the same time (or have your technician do it). Why? Because you will have to drain a certain amount of coolant when you replace the thermostat, so if it's almost time for this maintenance (coolant change), you might as well go ahead and have it done when you change the thermostat. Radiator hoses and the radiator pressure cap should also be checked for wear and rust.

Removal and replacement of the thermostat typically involves the following (check a vehicle-specific repair manual to see if there are any departures from the following procedure):

1. Park your car on level ground. (When working under the hood and with toxic chemicals, remember all safety rules—wear safety goggles and gloves.)

2. Drain the cooling system. Unscrew the thermostat housing and connecting water hose. (Remember the previous information on flushing and cleaning; also, if you are flushing and cleaning the radiator and cooling system, you should tackle this before the thermostat.)

3. If you are only replacing the thermostat, drain just enough of the coolant to a level slightly below that of the thermostat housing. If your coolant is less than a year old, drain it into a clean container and reuse it when the thermostat is reinstalled. If you see draining the coolant as problematic or are uncomfortable working around this toxic fluid, leave this repair for your technician.

4. Note the location and placement of your thermostat so you can set the new thermostat back in place.

5. Check for corrosion or old glue from thermostat housing and remove. Carefully clean the thermostat housing and all mating surfaces of any old gasket material to avoid leaks.

6. Put the new thermostat in place, put on new gasket, and replace housing. Some vehicles will require that any air be bled out of the cooling system once it's refilled. Again, check a vehicle-specific service manual for this procedure.

7. Everything is back in place now, so you can check your work by running the engine for a while and check for leaks.

8. Go for a drive and make sure the temperature gauge stays at full operating temperature (check your owner's manual).

9. Check for coolant leaks again, and your job is done!

Usually if you do routine maintenance, you can prevent overheating by checking the level of liquid in the system and maintaining it properly. If the cooling system is not maintained properly you run the risk of overheating, which can mean heavy repair bills that won't guarantee the car won't overheat again. The best advice is to keep the cooling system in good repair. Keep an eye on the coolant level and have your technician keep an eye on the entire system, doing maintenance as needed.

Checking for Leaks and Troubleshooting Your Water Pump

The cooling systems in today's cars often involve more hoses than just the two radiator hoses and the heater hoses. Engine coolant is sent to different locations in the engine compartment by way of other hoses. Some of these will have permanent fittings, others may have removable clamps, and others may have some type of quick connect. Any of these connections have the potential for leaking. If a permanent fitting is leaking, you may have to replace the entire hose assembly. You may be able to retrofit it with a traditional hose and clamp. Check with your auto-parts store to see what kind of repair kits are available. A fitting with a removable clamp may just need to be retightened. Check that the hose is still in good shape. Quick-connect fittings may just need to be removed and reinstalled.

Hoses are not the only parts of the cooling system to develop leaks. The water pump may wear out and begin leaking through a weep hole designed into the case. When the shaft or bearing wears out enough to allow the impeller to contact the case, it shears a part of the gasket covering the weep hole, allowing coolant to escape. This is your warning that the water pump will soon fail. Radiators will develop leaks from external damage or from external or internal corrosion. Engine blocks and cylinder heads can also develop leaks, often caused by coolant freezing.

Checking the Hoses for Leaks and Cracks

A car used to have four hoses: upper and lower radiator hoses, and in and out hoses for the heater. You could buy a length of hose off a spool and with two adjustable clamps you had your replacement. This is no longer the case in many cars. Hoses have special fittings. They may be molded to fit into tight and convoluted routes. They may have tee's and wye's—types of hose fittings—with different sizes at each end. They still perform the same function of carrying fluid, but they can be very expensive to replace. Check the hoses for leaks around fittings. Also check to see if the hoses are cracked or have indentations that may become cracks in the near future and replace if necessary.

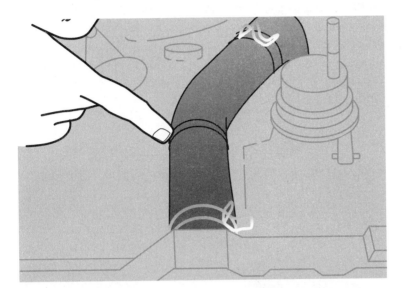

Find the hose/hoses.

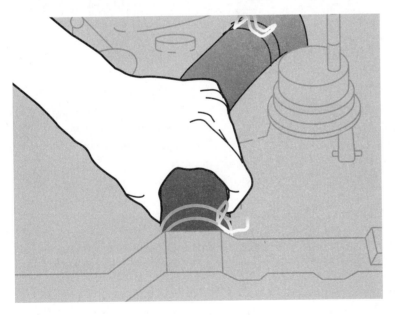

Check hose.

Replacing Belts

You can check your belts in a couple of ways. One way is simply to listen. With the hood open and the car in Park, have someone step on the gas pedal while you listen for a squeaking noise, which can indicate you have a loose belt. Another way is to visually inspect the belts after the engine is cool. You are looking for belt edges that are cracked or frayed or that have tears, rubber that is beginning to split, or material that is shiny. All belts should be replaced around 60,000 miles (but check your owner's manual for recommendations for your vehicle).

Belt wear and causes.

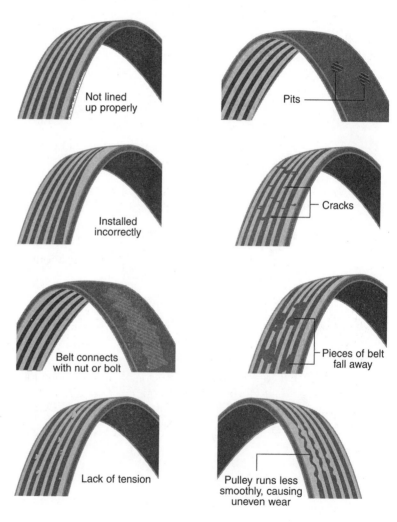

Keeping the Air Conditioner Operating at Peak Efficiency

The air-conditioning system in your car consists of a condenser mounted in front of the radiator, an evaporator located under the dash; a compressor driven by the engine; an accumulator located in the engine compartment; and a network of hoses, switches, and sensors. Today's air-conditioning systems are extremely reliable and require just a little attention. Low refrigerant levels are the most common problem that can be easily remedied by your A/C specialist.

All repairs to the system should be done only by qualified technicians, because of the complexity of the system and the special equipment needed to service it.

Doing the following maintenance procedure on a regular basis will ensure that your air-conditioning system continues to operate at maximum efficiency.

- Check the tension of the compressor drive belt and adjust if necessary.

- Check the condition of the hoses. Have any questionable hoses replaced by a qualified technician.

- Check the cooling fins of the condenser for debris. Remove if necessary using a soft brush, being careful not to damage the fins.

- Maintain the correct refrigerant charge.

- Operate the system at least once a month for about 10 minutes to keep the seals from hardening and failing.

CarLogic

Air-conditioner stinkies? This is usually caused by mold spores nesting in the moist environment of the evaporator case. You can have a technician get rid of this problem with a spore-killing disinfectant. Running just the fan will dry out the system and help keep the stinkies out of your car's A/C.

The Least You Need to Know

◆ Your maintenance routine will alert you to problems with your cooling system.

◆ Check your coolant by looking at the coolant reservoir.

◆ Listen for squeaky belts, but observe safety precautions.

◆ Check belts and hoses for leaks and wear every 60,000 miles or as recommended in your owner's manual.

◆ A/C systems are more reliable these days but can still fail.

◆ Most cooling system repairs are best left to a skilled technician.

Chapter 10

Electrical System

In This Chapter

- What kind of ignition system does your car have?
- How distributorless and distributor systems work
- The starting system: the battery and starter
- The charging system: the alternator and voltage regulator

Romantics know it takes that special spark to ignite a relationship. The same concept works for starting your car. There has to be an electrical spark. (Learning about electricity can be fun, huh?)

Your vehicle's ignition system fires your spark plugs. To do so, the battery sends current to the ignition coil. This hot spark goes on to the spark plugs either through a distributor, if you have an older vehicle, or directly to the spark plugs, if you have a newer one. In this chapter, we'll look at the components of your car's electrical system, and see how this spark makes the heart of your vehicle, the engine, come alive. (In Chapter 11, we'll tell you how to perform routine maintenance and troubleshoot various problems in your electrical system.)

The Electrical System at a Glance

- Spark plugs
- Coil
- Distributor
- Battery

- Starter
- Ignition system (subsystem of electrical system)
- Alternator
- Voltage regulator

The Ignition System

The ignition system not only has to provide the spark for combustion to occur, but just as importantly it must also provide that spark at just the right time and be capable of adjusting that time a little ahead or a little behind to compensate for different operating conditions, such as accelerating and changing gears.

If your car was built before the mid-1970s, it probably has a mechanical distributor and points. These worked fine, did their job, and you could replace those parts as they became worn. Starting in the mid-1970s, however, many cars were built with electronic ignition systems, which eliminated mechanical breaker points and added an electronic control module (ECM) to advance and retard the timing of the spark. Efficiency improved, there were fewer mechanical parts to need replacement, and tune-ups were spaced farther apart.

The ignition system has continued to evolve, so much so that the distributor has been eliminated and replaced by an ignition system. This system is controlled by a computer that picks up signals from sensors about engine conditions and determines the most efficient timing for sending the spark to the spark plugs. These new systems have even fewer replaceable parts and can go as long as 100,000 miles between recommended servicing.

 CarLogic

Check your owner's manual to see when and what kind of service is recommended for your ignition system. You may also find some of that information on a label in the engine compartment.

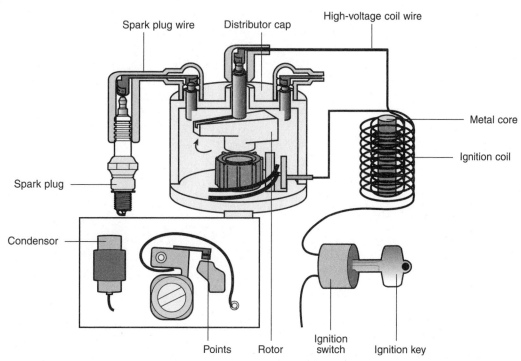

The basic ignition system on pre-1970s vehicles consists of the rotor, distributor cap, high-voltage coil wire, ignition coil, metal core, ignition key, ignition switch, points, distributor, spark plug, spark plug wire, and condenser. This nonelectronic ignition system has been replaced with solid-state components.

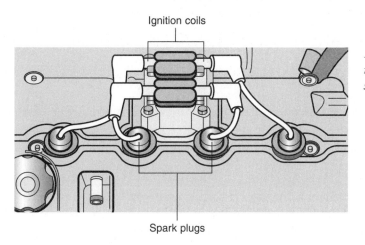

Distributorless electronic ignition systems use a coil for each spark plug.

The electronic ignition coil packs fire the spark plugs under computer control.

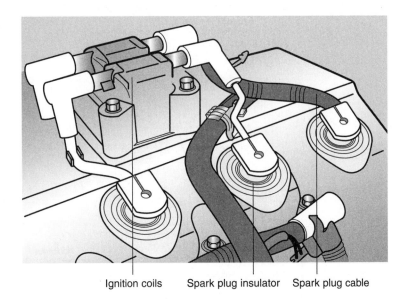

Ignition coils   Spark plug insulator   Spark plug cable

Whether it is the primary coil in older systems or one of the individual coils assigned to each cylinder in newer systems, the ignition coil acts as a transformer to boost the voltage to the level needed to create a spark. The primary or low-voltage side of the coil brings in 12 volts from the battery and converts it to very high voltage on the secondary or high-voltage side to send to the distributor or directly to the spark plugs.

The business end of the spark plug has two electrodes that lie in the combustion chamber when the spark plug is installed. An arc across the electrodes is produced by the high voltage supplied by the coil. This spark is precisely timed to ignite the fuel and air mixture. The resulting expansion of combustion gases forces the piston down and provides the power to move your car. That voltage goes to the coil, which is a mini-transformer. It boosts the voltage to the level required by the demanding spark plugs.

The coils are split into two sides: primary and secondary. The primary or 12-volt side has a large-diameter wire wrapped around it that creates a magnetic field. The secondary side has yards of smaller-diameter wire wrapped around it. The high voltage that your spark plugs need is created by electromagnetic induction.

A spark is needed to ignite the fuel and air mixture. It logically occurs at the spark plug, but to produce the spark the voltage has to be increased to tens of thousands of volts at a small fraction of an amp from the 12 volts of current at the battery. The coil, acting as a transformer, makes this conversion. The primary or low-voltage side of the coil brings in the 12 volts from the battery and converts it to very high voltage on the secondary or high-voltage side to send to the distributor or directly to the spark plugs.

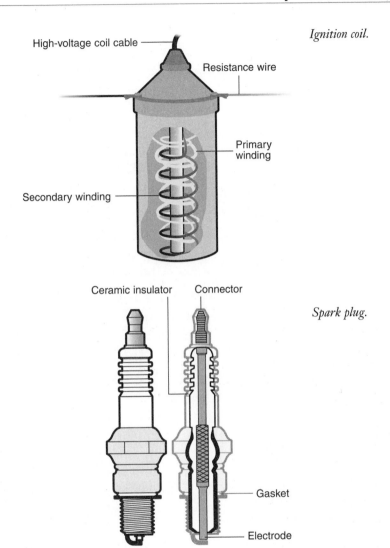

High-voltage coil cable

Resistance wire

Primary winding

Secondary winding

Ignition coil.

Ceramic insulator

Connector

Gasket

Electrode

Spark plug.

The Distributor

So far we've boosted the voltage to create the spark and we've located the spark at the spark plug. Now we need a trigger or switch to control when the spark should occur. The distributor has long been the standard device for doing this. It has a mechanically driven rotor, making one revolution for every two revolutions of the engine. Each spark plug is connected to the distributor by a spark plug wire terminating in the distributor cap. Inside the cap is a terminal corresponding to each spark plug, which completes an electrical circuit when the rotor passes by that terminal. At that instant, current is released from the coil by the breaker points and a spark is created at the spark plug electrodes.

Distributor cap.

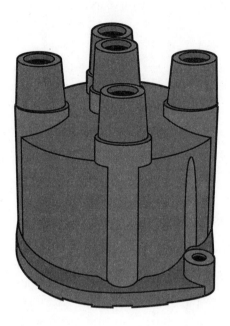

If your car was built within the last 10 years, it probably has an ignition system entirely controlled by a computer. In this case, a crank angle sensor (CAS) and an ignition control unit replace the electronic control module and the distributor. Using the same principles as a distributor, the CAS reads marks on a ring or plate that correspond to the positions of the pistons in each cylinder. It sends a signal to the control unit, which then, in addition to other inputs, causes the coil to produce the spark at exactly the right instant.

The Starting System

As you turn the key in your car's ignition switch, you pass the On position, which energizes the coil or coils in preparation for creating the spark. Reaching the Start position means you've completed the circuit to energize the starter motor. This is accomplished by the starter solenoid. The solenoid is essentially a large electromagnet that performs two important tasks. When the solenoid is energized, it pulls a plunger that completes a circuit allowing current from the battery to reach the starter motor. In most cars it also moves the starter pinion gear to engage the ring gear on the fly-wheel or flexplate.

In addition to the battery, starter motor, solenoid, and ignition switch, the starting system may include a starter relay, which reduces the amount of current that the ignition switch circuit must carry.

The last component of the starting system is the neutral safety switch, which prevents your car from being started while in gear. If you have a manual transmission, you probably have a clutch switch that prevents your car from being started unless the clutch pedal is depressed. Most of these components either work or they don't and need to be replaced. There is usually no repair that can be done; the contacts simply wear out. You should periodically check to make sure the connections are tight and not corroded.

The Battery

The primary function of the battery in your car is to provide a surge of current for the starter motor to get your engine going. After that, the alternator recharges it for the next time you need to start your car. The electricity produced by your battery results from an electrochemical reaction caused by lead and lead dioxide plates immersed in a strong sulfuric acid electrolyte. This reaction is reversible allowing the battery to discharge and recharge over and over again. Most batteries today are sealed and considered maintenance-free. Previously, water had to be added to the battery cells to replace water in the electrolyte lost by evaporation.

The battery in your car produces 12 volts at about 500 amps when fully charged. The amperage will vary depending upon the size of your engine and the quantity and demand of the electrical components in your car. A car battery has two ratings:

◆ The Cold Cranking Amps (CCA) rating is the number of amps that the battery can produce at 0°F for 30 seconds. The CCA gives you a way to compare a battery's ability to start an engine in cold weather.

◆ The Reserve Capacity (RC) rating is the number of minutes during which the battery can produce 25 amps while keeping its voltage above 10.5 volts. The RC tells you how long the battery can provide current to keep your car running should the alternator fail.

CarLogic _____

Some batteries have built-in charge indicators to tell you whether they need charging. A green dot in the window means the battery is at least 75 percent charged, no dot means it needs recharging, and a clear or yellow window means you need a new battery because the water level inside is low. Don't try to jump-start or charge such a battery. You might be able to salvage the battery if you can pry the sealed caps open and add water, but usually the battery must be replaced.

Batteries aren't all that attractive, just a box with a little color. Red is the positive terminal. The negative terminal is usually black. The clamps on the cables that you use to jump-start a dead battery are usually colored red and black so that you can tell which one goes where.

Most cars are negative ground. This means the wire from the negative terminal is attached to the frame of the vehicle to ground it, and the wire from the positive terminal leads to the starter ignition.

Car battery.

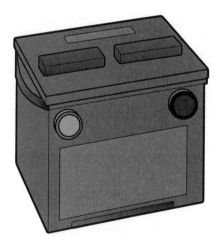

The Starter

The starter consists of an electric starter motor and a starter solenoid. When you turn the ignition key, the starter motor spins the engine a few revolutions so that the combustion process can start. It takes a powerful motor to spin a cold engine.

The starter motor in your car is a small, powerful electric motor that converts the electrical energy from the battery to mechanical energy to turn the engine over. It has a small pinion gear at one end that engages the ring gear on the flywheel or flexplate when the solenoid is energized. The spinning of the starter motor is now transferred to the engine. The pistons begin the intake stroke, drawing in the fuel and air mixture, and the ignition system begins the combustion process, which starts the engine turning over faster than the starter motor. As you move the key back to the On position, the solenoid is no longer energized, the starter motor is no longer energized, and a spring returns the pinion gear to its disengaged position.

The Charging System

Once your car is started and running, the alternator takes over as the source of electricity. The battery now assumes another role in the charging system. Along with the alternator and battery, your car's charging system includes a drive belt for the alternator, a voltage regulator, a bunch of wiring, and a gauge or warning light.

The Alternator

Your car's alternator supplies electricity to power all of the essential components like cooling fans, sensors, and the ignition system, the safety components like lights and wipers, and all of the accessories such as the radio and climate-control fan. It also supplies current to recharge the battery in preparation for the next startup. It produces alternating current by a rotating magnet with a magnetic field. This alternating current (AC) is rectified into direct current (DC) by diodes inside the alternator.

CarLogic

Your car probably has an indicator light on the dash panel to alert you to a problem in the charging system. You may also have a voltmeter or an ammeter. While the engine is running and no accessories are in use, the voltmeter should indicate a charging voltage of about 13.5 volts. An ammeter should have the needle centered between the plus (+) and the minus (–). Small fluctuations are normal. Read your owner's manual for more information about this gauge.

The Voltage Regulator

The voltage regulator in your car is probably inside the alternator. It does what its name implies. When you are driving at high speeds with minimal accessory use, the regulator lowers the alternator output voltage. If your engine is idling and you are using many accessories, the regulator increases the voltage output. When voltage regulators fail, the whole alternator is usually replaced.

Diagnosing charging problems can sometimes be challenging. It usually involves eliminating components or conditions one at a time. A common cause is a loose alternator belt. Wiring connections need to be checked to be sure they are tight and corrosion-free. Batteries can be sneaky suspects. Most auto-parts stores can check them out for you. Many can also check out your alternator or voltage regulator, too. Battery and alternator testing requires some fairly sophisticated equipment.

The Least You Need to Know

- The ignition system provides the spark for engine combustion to occur.
- Newer-model cars have ignition systems entirely controlled by a computer.
- The starting system includes the battery and starter.
- The charging system includes the alternator and voltage regulator.
- The battery in your car provides a surge of current for the starter motor to get your engine going.
- Your car's alternator supplies electricity to power all of the essential components.

Electrical System: Troubleshooting and Maintenance

In This Chapter

◆ Troubleshooting problems with the battery

◆ How to jump-start your battery

◆ Keeping your alternator juiced

◆ Troubleshooting the starter

◆ How to install new spark plugs

◆ Fixing lights, gauges, and fuses

In Chapter 10, we told you about the parts of the electrical system. Now we'll tell you how to troubleshoot and fix those parts. Today's auto electrical systems are intricate, and in many cases have to be repaired by a technician. These repairs can be painful to your wallet. We know that's not the best news; however, we will go through each part of the system and make every effort to keep all parts serviced and happy. We'll also spill all the beans we have to help you troubleshoot problems.

Remember that this system will require some study time before you attempt a repair. You will need to study a schematic or diagram of your particular vehicle's electrical system. Check your owner's manual. For more thorough information on your model of car, check out a vehicle-specific manual such as Chilton or Haynes (see Appendix C to find out how to order vehicle-specific manuals).

Troubleshooting Your Battery

When your battery begins to show signs of not doing its job, this is what you should do: look at the battery. Yes, it is that easy. Why? Knowing the health of the battery is the best way to know whether to suspect other system components, and can prevent the unnecessary installation of a starter or alternator. And even if you do install a new starter or alternator and later find out the problem was the battery, you'll still have to buy a new battery to get going again.

If you've performed routine maintenance, your battery should be in good shape with no corrosion or cracks in the case. If not, refer to Chapter 4 on how to clean your battery and get rid of the corrosion.

Check the "eye" if you have a battery with this technology. The color of the eye reveals what condition your battery is in. For instance, if you have an Atlas Delco battery and the eye is green, that's good, but if it's clear or light yellow, that indicates the battery is dead. If you don't have a battery with an eye, check the condition of your battery with a DVOM (digital volt ohmmeter).

DVOM (digital volt ohmmeter).

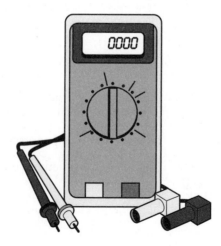

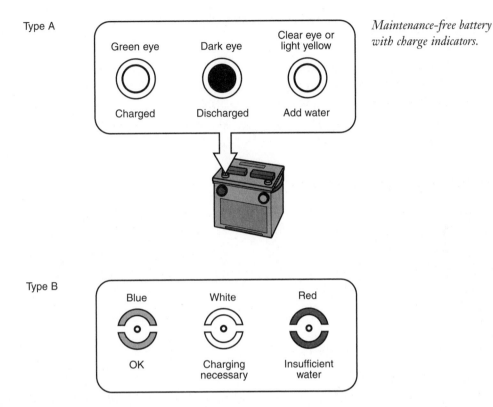

Maintenance-free battery with charge indicators.

Jump-Starting a Battery

Jump-starting your car's battery is not hard, but you do need to follow the directions to the letter. Bear in mind the makeup of your battery. It *does* make a difference if you put the wrong cable on the wrong post—a dangerous difference. Most cars can be jump-started, but you will need to check your owner's manual or ask a technician about your particular car before you try to jump-start your vehicle. (Some vehicles cannot be jump-started; you must install a fresh battery.) And if you have a battery with an "eye" that is showing clear or light yellow, there is no reason to try and jump-start your car. In this case, you will need another battery. However, if your battery shows it can still be charged, go for it if the case is in good shape with no cracks.

Here are some cautions to keep in mind when you jump-start your vehicle's battery:

♦ Carefully read your owner's manual to see whether you run the risk of damaging some of the delicate electronics.

♦ Reach out to connect the cable clamps and keep your face turned away from the battery.

◆ Some technicians suggest you turn on the lights and put the fan on high if your car is the donor car. These actions act as a buffer to protect the rest of the system in the event of a voltage surge or drop.

◆ Wait a few minutes before trying to start the dead car to allow the dead battery to regain some charge; otherwise, not enough current gets to the starter. You can ruin electronic brains in your car from careless jump-starts—or worse, small explosions can occur above a battery if you aren't careful.

Speedbumps

Be careful when charging or jump-starting batteries. Batteries are flammable, explosive, and caustic. Always keep the battery clean to allow proper ventilation. Never try to jump-start a cracked, swollen, or frozen battery. A cracked battery is dangerous and should be replaced. A common cause of battery-case cracks is the electrolyte freezing and swelling. This usually only happens when the battery has lost its charge and the concentration of sulfuric acid is very low. The battery can explode or at the very least spew acid.

Learning how to jump-start your vehicle's battery is like learning how to change a tire. It is best to know how to do it *before* you are in the position of having to do the job. Follow the guidelines in your owner's manual to avoid injury and damaging vehicle components.

Follow these steps to jump-start a battery:

1. Remember your safety rules. Before working under the hood, remove all jewelry, make sure your clothing isn't flowing or loose, and pull back any long hair. When a battery is discharged and you begin to put a charge into it, the electrochemical reaction involves hydrogen gas, which is very explosive. Extinguish cigarettes, wear gloves and safety glasses, and don't hover under the hood any longer than necessary when doing this procedure.

2. Pull your booster (jumper) cables out. The best jumper cables have 4- or 6-gauge copper wire (the smaller the gauge number the thicker the wire); 8-gauge cables may be used in warmer climates. Your cables should be at least 12 feet long—or long enough so you can get a jump-start from a car behind you, if need be. They should fit neatly in a carrying case. When buying, remember, you want copper

clamps (sometimes referred to as alligator clips) that will work with top, front, and side battery terminals. The booster cable clamps should be color-coded and clearly labeled.

3. Park the donor car near your car. Make sure they do not touch. It is possible for a metal-to-metal contact to cause a ground and take current needed to boost your vehicle's dead battery.

4. Turn off the ignition in both cars, and make sure any accessories such as the radio or air conditioner are also turned off. Put both cars in Park or Neutral and set the parking brakes.

5. Connect a clamp of the red (positive) booster cable to the positive terminal (marked + or POS) of the weak battery. Attach the cable's other red clamp to the + or POS terminal of the donor car. Don't allow the booster cable clamps to touch the car body, each other, or the other battery terminal. Keep metal tools from touching the + or POS terminal.

6. Connect the clamp of the black (negative) booster cable to the negative terminal (marked – or NEG) of the donor car's battery. Connect the other clamp to a clean metal part on the engine in the car with the weak battery. Get the clamp as far from the battery as possible.

7. Start the engine of the donor car. Rev the engine just a bit. Then try to start the other car. If it doesn't start, turn off the ignition of both engines and make sure the booster cable clamps are attached securely. Try again. If the engine starts, wait to make sure it doesn't stall, and then disconnect the booster cables in this order: negative cable from the ground connection, then from the – (NEG) terminal of the donor car; positive cable from the + (POS) terminal of the donor car, and then from the + (POS) terminal of the other car. Always connect the black cable last and disconnect it first!

Speedbumps

Never attach the negative booster cable to the – (NEG) terminal of the weak battery. If you do, sparks may fly when the metal clamp touches the terminal. This could ignite hydrogen gas given off by the battery. Many people have been killed or injured by battery explosions.

*Put positive (+) cable to posi-
tive (+) post of dead battery.*

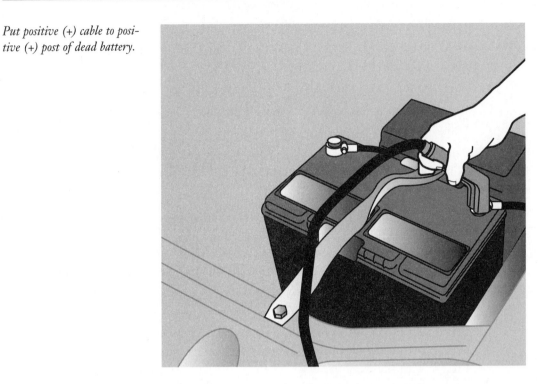

*Connect other end of positive
(+) cable to positive (+) post of
good battery.*

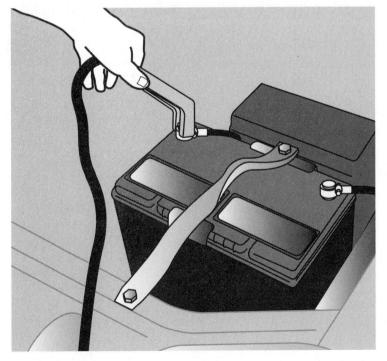

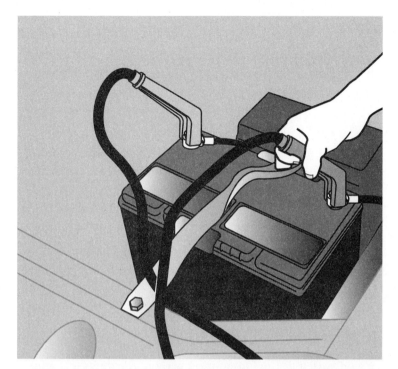

Connect one end of negative (–) cable to negative (–) post of good battery.

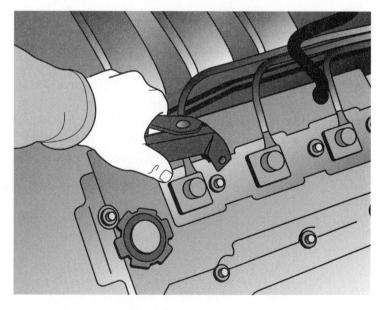

Connect the other end of the negative (–) cable to a solid metal part under the hood of the dead battery car.

When to Replace a Battery

You don't want to replace a battery before you know for sure that's the root of your problem. Another possible scenario is a weak alternator. Remember, most batteries have an approximate service life of at least three to five years. However, climate will play a factor in the life of a battery. Remember that extremes in temperature can shorten a battery's life.

Although the most obvious sign that the battery needs replacement is when it stops holding a charge and goes dead, the best way to determine the health of your battery is with a system check by a professional. Most repair shops will have a battery load tester that can determine the condition and verify that it's time for a replacement. A full charging system check is recommended whenever you find a dead battery.

When the time comes to replace the battery, the replacement should be the same size as your old battery, have a comparable CCA (Cold Cranking Amps) rating, and have compatible connections.

Checking Your Alternator Warning Light

When you turn your ignition switch to the On position without starting the engine, the alternator warning light should come on. If it doesn't, first check the fuse that protects that circuit. It may be a dedicated fuse or it may be a fuse that protects all of the dash warning lights and gauges. Check your owner's manual for its location. If the fuse is okay, go to the alternator and locate the terminal marked #1, I, L, or D+. It may be an individual connection or it may be part of a connection with multiple wires. Disconnect it from the alternator and ground it by touching it to a bare metal part of the engine. If the light comes on, the circuit is okay but the alternator is defective. If the light still does not come on, check the wiring for a break or missing insulation. Also, check the bulb at this point. A repair manual with labeled diagrams of the alternator connections and detailed wiring diagrams can make the job a bit easier.

Any other alternator problems are best left to the service technicians who have the proper equipment to make accurate diagnoses.

Starter

As we told you in Chapter 10, the starter is a motor that turns the engine crankshaft through the flywheel, starting the combustion process. Your vehicle's starter gets its power from the battery. After you check to make sure the battery and cables are clean (no corrosion) and the battery isn't dead, check the starter and solenoid connections for corrosion, wear, and tear. You may not always be able to tell what the problem is by taking the steps we've given. So if you try to start your car and all you get is a click and the engine doesn't turn over (and if it's not your battery), the motor in your starter may have gone bad. This repair requires you to purchase a vehicle-specific book (see Appendix C)—or leave it to a technician.

CarLogic

Major accessories should be turned off when you start your vehicle. This will keep your starter healthy longer. Some vehicles automatically keep your air conditioner and alternator (both power drains) off until your engine is up and running, but turning off accessories after you put your vehicle in Park is a good idea. Another way to keep your starter healthy is to keep starter connections clean. If your starter motor malfunctions and needs to be replaced, go ahead and replace the starter and the solenoid.

How to Change Spark Plugs

For most cars, spark plugs need to be changed every two years or 30,000 miles. Doing this will keep your engine purring and hopefully improve gas mileage. The 30,000 mile/two-year recommendation is not vehicle-wide, however. Read your owner's manual for instructions for your particular vehicle, because some vehicles can go as long as 100,000 miles before spark plugs are changed.

Here's what you will need to change your vehicle's spark plugs:

◆ ⅜" drive spark-plug socket, extension, ratchet, and torque wrench

◆ New set of spark plugs

◆ Spark-plug gapping gauge

◆ Clean rag or brush

Raise your hood and take a look around for a decal that gives the correct spark-plug gap for your vehicle. Then check to see the brand name of the plugs in your car. It's a good idea to replace them with the same kind. Follow these steps to replace the spark plugs:

1. Make sure the car has been off for a while and the engine is cold. Only remove spark plugs from a cold engine. Removing spark plugs from a hot cylinder head increases the risk of damaging the threads in the cylinder head. The easiest way

to find the spark plugs is to follow the ignition wires to the engine. On in-line engines, the plugs are located on the top of the engine between the camshafts and may be covered with a plastic shield that has to be removed. On V6 or V8 engines, the plugs are on the side of the engine above the exhaust manifold. If you have a front-wheel-drive car, with a V6 or V8 engine, half of the plugs will be right in front of you and the other half behind the sideways-mounted engine. If in doubt, get a vehicle-specific service manual for the location of the spark plugs and instructions on removing any covers.

Locate the spark plugs.

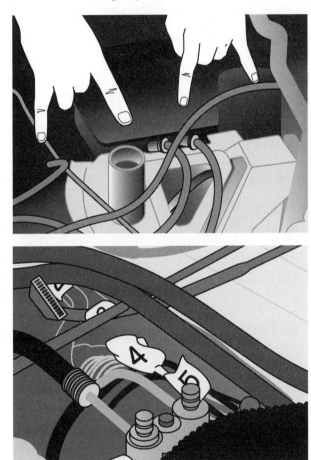

Disconnect the positive cable of the battery and label the spark plug wires, or remove just one at a time, so you put them back in the proper firing order. Newer vehicles with distributorless ignition systems eliminate the plug wires altogether and have the coils connected directly to the spark plugs at the cylinders, but if you have to remove the entire wire set, make sure you get a model-specific service manual, which will have diagrams and explain the proper firing order for replacing the wires correctly. Firing orders are not the same for every engine. If you do this incorrectly, the engine either won't start at all or will run very poorly. Your safest bet is to work on the plugs one at a time and eliminate the problem.

2. Remove the spark-plug wire from the spark plug only by pulling on the boot covering the top of the spark plug. Never pull on the wire itself. If you do, you will pull the wire out of the boot. If the boot resists coming off, gently twist it back and forth while pulling. If you are having real difficulty or if the plugs are in an awkward place, you may want to purchase some special pliers designed for removing these boots.

 CarLogic _____

Replace the plugs one at a time, so that you don't mix up the wires. If you do pull all the wires off at once, make sure they are labeled so that you can rein- stall them in their proper location.

3. Before you actually remove the plug, clean the area around it so that dirt does not fall into the cylinder. An air compressor is handy for blowing out the debris.

4. Place your spark-plug socket securely on the plug and turn the socket wrench counterclockwise to loosen it. Once it's loose, continue turning it until you can remove it from the head. Spark-plug sockets are specifically designed for this purpose. They have the correct depth to securely grab the plug for removal or installation and they have a rubber insert that holds the plug, making it easy to remove and install plugs in awkward or less accessible locations.

5. Once your old plug is out, examine it carefully. The condition of the plug can tell you a lot about the condition of your engine. Most repair manuals will have full-color pictures of plugs indicating different problems. You want to see a brown to grayish-tan color and slight electrode wear. If the electrodes are black with a sooty residue or covered with oil, it might be time to check with your professional technician. Likewise if the electrode is damaged or burned away completely.

6. Make sure that the spark plug gaps on your new plugs are set correctly for your engine. You will find the correct specifications on a label in the engine compart- ment or in the owner's manual. Use a feeler gauge or a spark-plug gapping tool to check the gap. The gauge should just fit in the gap between the electrodes. Adjust the gap if necessary by bending the outer electrode gently using a small screwdriver or a pair of needle-nosed pliers. Some gap measuring tools, like the circular type shown in the illustration, will automatically set the gap when you move the gauge under the electrode to the proper measurement.

Slide the gauge under the electrode and set the gap. You find the gap specifications in your owner's manual.

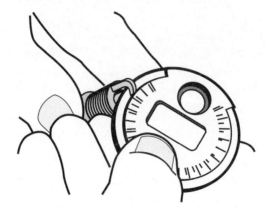

7. Make sure the cylinder head threads are clean and straight. Apply a thread compound to the plug threads if recommended by your owner's manual. The compound is often available in single-use packets where you buy spark plugs.

8. Carefully screw in the new plug by hand using the socket and an extension if necessary. Be careful not to cross-thread it, and continue screwing it in until it finally seats itself against the head.

Tighten with a torque wrench.

9. You must now read the owner's manual to find the correct tightening technique. Depending on whether you have plugs with metal gaskets or not, or if you have aluminum heads, there will be a specific procedure that needs to be followed to make sure the plugs are secure and the head threads are not damaged.

10. Reattach the spark-plug wire to the new spark plug. Push it on it until you feel and hear a click.

Other Problems

Checking on problematic lights is not difficult. Your main goal is to make sure there is no corrosion. If you are having problems with lights and other electrical devices in your car, the cause and solution can usually be found in one of three places:

◆ Check the bulb for cracks or a broken filament, or check the device for obvious damage. Bulbs are usually inexpensive to replace, so that's a first step.

◆ Check the connections. Make sure they are tight and free of corrosion. Clean them and tighten them if necessary.

◆ Check the wiring that supplies the light or device. Look for breaks and missing insulation. That should solve most problems.

If your electrical device is expensive to replace and still doesn't function, it's probably time for a technician with more sophisticated equipment to have a look.

Replacing a Halogen Light

If one of your halogen lights is not working, find the connection behind the headlight assembly and wiggle it. If the light starts working, you only need to tighten that connection. If it doesn't, you will need to remove the bulb socket and replace the bulb.

The bulb socket has a lock ring that usually unlocks with a quarter turn. Pull the socket back and remove it from the headlight assembly. Remove the old bulb from the socket and replace with a new bulb. Return the socket to the headlight assembly and lock it in place with a quarter turn. There are a few variations on sockets and bulbs. Your owner's manual should provide details for replacing your headlights.

Speedbumps

Put on gloves before working with bulbs. Never touch the bulbs with your bare hands; the oil from your skin will shorten bulb life.

Determine what type of headlight you have. This will tell you if you should replace the entire headlight or just the halogen bulb.

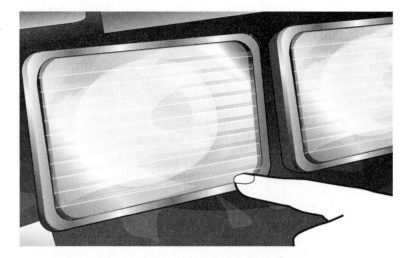

For bulb replacement, open the hood and look for a black knob on the back of the headlight. Unscrew; the bulb is attached to the black knob.

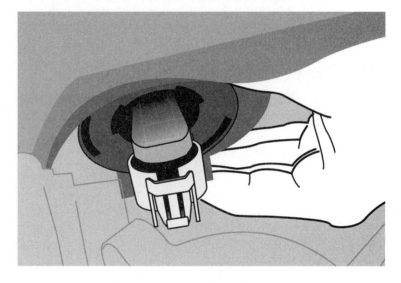

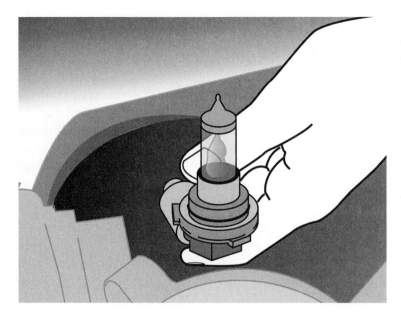

Without touching the glass on a halogen bulb, screw the bulb into place.

Aiming Your Headlights

You can buy an aiming device at your auto-parts store. You adjust your headlights by turning the vertical adjustment screw, located at the top (can be on the side or bottom) of the headlight with a Phillips screwdriver. When it's time to travel and you are pulling a heavy load behind your car, you will want to adjust your headlight beam as extra-heavy baggage in your rear makes your lights point upward.

Nervous Gauges

If you notice one or more of your gauges behaving erratically, the usual suspect is a loose ground wire. Gauges may have individual grounds or may share a common ground. With a wiring diagram from a repair manual, you may be able to find this wire and its connections. If you can't, you can have a service technician check the wire and its connections.

Speedometer won't be still? What a pain! Does it also make a noise? Some older vehicles use speedometer cables, which terminate in various places, normally some place in the transmission. Get a vehicle-specific manual or have your technician check out this problem.

Fuses

Newer cars have an incredible amount of wiring that powers devices, sends signals, and indicates problems. Those devices and those circuits are protected by fuses. Most of the fuses are found in the fuse panel. Some cars have more than one panel, and all cars will have some fuses inline with the wiring. Whenever some electrical device stops working, the first place to check is the fuse protecting that circuit. Look at your fuse panel and familiarize yourself with the circuits that are being protected there. The cover of the fuse panel may have a directory, or your owner's manual should have it. Sometimes a temporary surge blew the fuse and all you need to do is replace the fuse. If the second fuse also blows, you need to find the cause of the problem. Do not attempt to use a higher-rated fuse in the circuit. You risk starting an electrical fire that can eventually ignite the fuel.

There are a variety of types of fuses; however, all fuses have a thin filament that melts when a circuit has a short. Look carefully at a spare fuse and you will see where the filament thins out. Some cars use more than one type. The fuse panel in your car may include some spares and even a puller. If not, go to your auto-parts store and buy a variety pack for your car. They are not expensive, and having a spare might save you some serious inconvenience one day.

The Least You Need to Know

- Electrical repairs can be costly, so keep your system well maintained.
- Jump-starting your vehicle's battery is not difficult, but there are safety rules you must follow to protect yourself and your battery.
- The alternator warning light should come on when you turn your ignition switch, but if it doesn't, first check for fuse malfunction.
- Read your owner's manual to see how often your spark plugs should be changed.
- If you are having trouble with a vehicle light, first check for bulb damage.
- Keep extra fuses in your car just in case you need to replace one.

12

Fuel System

In This Chapter

♦ How fuel is delivered from the gas tank to the engine

♦ How fuel injector systems work

♦ A look at some of the sensors in your car and what they do

♦ Throttle body fuel injection versus multiport fuel injection

In this chapter, we'll discuss a system that requires a chemical we have to buy whether we can afford it or not: gasoline. It's a catch-22; if we don't buy it we can't get to work, but the high price of gas is starting to make us think hard about working from home. But no matter how much we might wish our engines could work their magic with just air instead of the air/fuel mixture needed to start and run them, we all end up at the gas pump to "fill 'er up."

But let's look at the bright side. The old saying of when we end up with a lemon (that is, high gas prices), it's best to find a way to make lemonade is very true when it comes to the fuel system. We still need to buy the main ingredient, gasoline, but we can also remember to keep tires properly inflated; change the oil, oil filter, and air filter regularly; and tune up the engine on time. All of these things affect your gas mileage. And it never hurts to know the parts of each system and how vehicle systems work, so we'll begin with a look at the fuel system found in today's cars. (In Chapter 13, we'll tell you how to perform routine maintenance and troubleshoot various problems in your fuel system.)

The Modern Fuel System

If you are familiar with TV's *That '70s Show* or lived prior to and through the 1970s, you know "pollution" was a buzzword and gas was said to be in short supply. During the middle of the twentieth century, we were faced with a hard fact: natural resources sometimes do become sullied and depleted. Automobile emissions came under scrutiny. During the 1970s, most U.S. automobiles changed the way fuel was metered. Metering is measuring the amount of fuel and how it is transferred to the engine. Before that time carburetors were used, but it was found that a small amount of gasoline was not being used and this fuel was sent out through the exhaust pipe into the atmosphere. From the 1980s on, automobiles in the United States have rolled off assembly lines with electronic fuel injectors (EFIs). EFIs are able to meter air to gasoline with no unburned fuel left over. Before we discuss EFIs in more detail, let's take a look at the parts of the modern fuel system.

Typical modern fuel injection system.

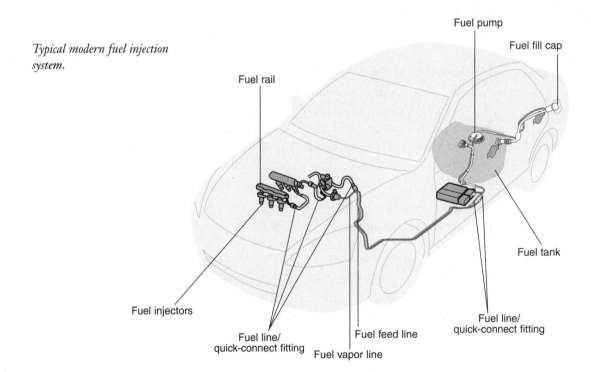

Fuel pump

Fuel fill cap

Fuel rail

Fuel injectors

Fuel line/ quick-connect fitting

Fuel vapor line

Fuel feed line

Fuel line/ quick-connect fitting

Fuel tank

The Fuel System at a Glance

- Fuel injectors
- Fuel tank
- Fuel filter
- Fuel pump
- Fuel-pressure regulator
- ECU (engine control unit)
- Fuel lines

Fuel Tank

The fuel tank is as familiar to most car owners as the gas pedal. You probably already know how to find and open the door to the fuel tank. If not, check your owner's manual (and see Chapter 1 for the basics on pumping gas). Most fuel tanks are made of steel, although plastic is also used if the manufacturer wants a lighter tank. The gas tank doesn't come in a particular form. Tanks are usually made to slide snugly into the spot allotted for the gas tank of a particular model vehicle by car designers.

 CarLogic

You can do a little homework and find a vehicle that gets better gas mileage by going to www.fueleconomy.gov.

Placement of the fuel tank is an important fact to know. Why? Fuel tanks should never be located in places on the car known to be crush zones. The correct placement of a gas tank is inside the frame rail. Because the gas tank is where gasoline is stored before it goes to the engine and because gasoline is extremely volatile, any defect in design or placement of the gas tank puts you at great risk of a fire or explosion in the event of an accident. Make sure you know where a gas tank is located before you purchase a vehicle. Some car makers have incurred lawsuits because of placing pickup fuel tanks in the crush zone or the outside of the vehicle's frame. This design flaw allegedly resulted in ruptured gas tanks, so automakers made a design change.

Internal Organs: Fuel Tank Anatomy

Have you ever wondered how your dashboard fuel gauge knows how much gas is in the tank? There is a float that is called a sending unit. This float is normally made of foam with a metal rod attached called a variable resistor. The variable resistor keeps track of the current running through the fuel tank. When the tank is full, there is a lot of current flowing so the indicator on your dashboard measures the electrical current and shows Full. When the gas in the tank is depleted, the current drops to all the increments of Full.

Most of us rely heavily on the gas gauge and know how much farther our vehicles will go when the gauge tells us it's time to stop and fill up. If you put off buying gas when the gauge is reading near empty, one day you *will* find yourself stranded by the side of the road feeling really put out with yourself.

Let's say it is five minutes past the time you were supposed to leave home. You jump in the car and take off, only to look down at the fuel gauge and remember what you forgot to do yesterday. Should you go the extra miles out of your way to the gas station when you are already late? How much gas is *really* in the tank when it registers "E"? You are already stressed so it's not a good time to find out, and you're already late. Here's how to find out how much fuel is in your vehicle when the gas gauge registers empty. First, get out your owner's manual and find out how much fuel your vehicle's gas tank will hold. Jot down that number for future reference in the vehicle fact sheet we provide in Appendix B. When you notice your tank is empty, fill your tank. On the gas pump, note the number of gallons it took to fill your tank. Now you have your equation. Subtract the number of gallons it took to fill the tank from the gallons the tank is said to hold (per your owner's manual). This figure tells you how much gas is left in the tank when the gauge registers empty.

CarLogic _____

A good rule of thumb is to never park your car at home without enough gas to get you to the nearest hospital emergency room should you need to drive there quickly.

Fuel Lines and Fuel Pumps

Fuel pumps do just what you'd think: they pump gas through fuel lines to the engine. Fuel lines are made of steel or copper. Most fuel lines are copper-plated to keep them free of rust. Fuel lines are placed where they encounter the least amount of friction and heat. Friction and vibration can cause damage over time. Heat sources like mufflers may cause vapors to occur that will decrease engine efficiency, so fuel lines are routed around sources of extreme heat.

Fuel lines attach to the fuel pump. Mechanical fuel pumps were the norm in pre-1970s cars. These pumps were attached to the engine and pumped to the motion of the engine. The fuel was metered by a carburetor under low pressure. Today fuel pumps are electrically driven and usually located in your fuel tank, and they pump fuel at high pressure to an electronic fuel-injection system. Mechanical fuel pumps were located close to the engine, which when added to a hot climate sometimes made the gasoline boil. The vapor from the boiling liquid interfered with engine performance, causing the engine to cut out (cease running). Today fuel pumps are usually placed inside the fuel tank. The placement of fuel pumps inside fuel tanks allows the gas to stay cooler because it is in liquid and away from the hot engine.

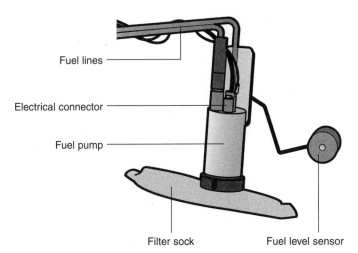

Fuel lines

Electrical connector

Fuel pump

Filter sock

Fuel level sensor

Putting the fuel pump inside the fuel tank keeps gasoline cooler, and that is good for engine performance.

Fuel Filter

A fuel filter is like a spam filter on your computer—it keeps the trash out. But in the case of a fuel filter there is literally a screen that keeps the dirt and rust from finding its way into your fuel. Check your owner's manual for the correct time to change your fuel filter.

Fuel-Injected Vehicles

Since today's vehicles are fuel-injected, let's take a look at how this system works.

The electronic fuel-injector system is regulated by a computer—the engine control unit, or ECU. The ECU is sent messages by sensors. These sensors tell the ECU when fuel is needed and how much fuel is needed. The injectors spray enough fuel to precisely match the amount of air let in when you step on the gas pedal. The ECU also gets messages from oxygen sensors. These sensors relay the percentage of unburned fuel in the exhaust. If there is unburned fuel in the exhaust, the ECU adjusts this problem by having the injectors spray less gas.

Cars sold in the United States have fuel-injection systems.

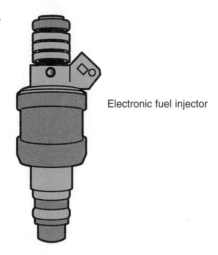

Electronic fuel injector

Engine Sensors

The ECU has a workforce of sensors that report back so that the needs of any driving conditions are met. These sensors are needed to make sure the air is less polluted by making sure the gas is burned and not sent out into the air. They also help to ensure your engine and transmission work efficiently. Here are just a few of your vehicle's hardworking sensors:

- The manifold air temperature (MAT) sensor sends the ECU an intake air density reading. The ECU uses this to balance the air/fuel mixture.

- Oxygen (O_2) sensors keep up with the oxygen in the exhaust and send that information to the ECU to see if the fuel mixture needs adjustments. Some cars have one oxygen sensor; some cars have two.

- The throttle position sensor sends a signal to the ECU regarding the position of the throttle (open or closed). The ECU uses this to regulate fuel flow.

- The coolant temperature sensor sends a signal to the ECU when the engine is running at the correct temperature.

- The manifold absolute pressure (MAP) sensor reports the pressure of the air in the intake manifold to the ECU. This information is used to balance spark timing to match fuel mixture timing.

As we talked about in the beginning of the chapter, the 1970s saw the automobile go through major changes in an effort to reduce emissions and make vehicles more fuel-efficient. Vehicles must meet a set requirement level for emissions for the first 100,000 miles. This requirement level is set by the Environmental Protection Agency (EPA).

> **Auto-Biography**
>
> The Environmental Protection Agency (EPA) came about during the 1970s. This office enforces laws in an effort to make sure vehicle fuel and fuel emissions become friendlier to our environment. For more information, check out the EPA website at www.epa.gov.

Throttle Body and Multiport Fuel-Injection Systems

Introduced in the mid-1980s, a throttle body fuel injection was the first injection system to replace the carburetor and featured a single injector or a pair of injectors. Because vehicle engines had not evolved much by then, this system was not much different than the carburetor.

Fuel-injector systems evolved, and now the multiport fuel injection system has a fuel-injector for each cylinder. Fuel injectors are attached to the fuel rail and intake port of the engine. This makes fuel metering more precise and allows your engine to perform better. The multiport (also called sequential-port) fuel injection has an electric fuel pump to pump the fuel. A fuel pressure regulator is normally located on the fuel rail. This device makes sure there is correct fuel pressure, and if there is excess fuel the regulator makes sure it goes back to your tank instead of out your exhaust.

The Least You Need to Know

- Make sure you know where your gas tank is before you purchase a vehicle—it should never be in a crush zone.
- All cars are now equipped with electronic fuel-injection systems instead of carburetors.
- The ECU (engine control unit) is a computer in your car that regulates vehicle functions.
- Today's multiport fuel-injection systems make fuel metering more precise and allow your engine to perform better and get better fuel mileage.

Fuel System: Troubleshooting and Maintenance

In This Chapter

- Safety first when dealing with your vehicle's fuel system
- What to know before you begin
- Replacing your fuel filter
- Troubleshooting your fuel pump, fuel tank, and fuel lines

Life is like an open road. It's smooth and clean, but every now and again you hit a pothole or some sort of debris. Owning a car is no different. You have long, straight, smooth times with no worries and then you have times when you must do either maintenance work or repair work. If you decide to work on your vehicle yourself, this involves a bit of study and some time. If you take your vehicle to a technician for professional service, you need to know enough about your problem to tell the technician and you need to know enough to help make a judgment about the repairs that will be made. A little knowledge will save you time, money, and aggravation. It might even save your life.

In Chapter 12, we told you about the parts of the fuel system. Now we'll tell you how to troubleshoot and fix some of those parts. You might feel more comfortable having your auto technician work on your vehicle's fuel-system repairs, but if you want to do it yourself, we'll tell you how to replace your fuel filter and how to troubleshoot some problems.

Fuel Filter Maintenance

Cars made after 1987 are equipped with electronic injection systems and have more expensive, longer-lasting fuel filters that are often mounted in hard-to-reach locations. (There are variations on this system, so check your owner's manual for specifics on your particular vehicle.) However, fuel filters still get clogged with rust, chipped paint, or debris from the pump and need replacing periodically. Prior generations of car owners were told to change their filters each year or at least every 15,000 miles. The good news is that today's fuel filters don't need to be changed as frequently (check your owner's manual for recommendations), but the bad news is when you do replace the filter, it costs more. Why? Well, fuel filters are built better and nowadays they are usually located in the fuel tank or along the fuel line, which makes replacing them harder. Another possible problem is some manufacturers' timetables for replacing fuel filters are lenient.

So what's a dedicated routine maintenance person to do? Check your owner's manual, and then talk to a recommended, ASE-certified technician at a dealership who frequently works on vehicles like yours. Tell him or her how much you drive your vehicle in a year's time and on what types of roads (that is, paved roads or dirt roads), and the make and model year of your vehicle; also, find out how often he or she thinks you should change your fuel filter. Usually if the car has some years on it, changing the filter once a year is a good plan to keep your engine running smoothly. You don't want trash clogging a fuel injector and causing your engine to perform poorly.

Speedbumps

It's important to take safety precautions when working on any part of your car, but it's especially true when working on the fuel system. Use extreme caution when working with a chemical as volatile as gasoline. Sparking is a hazard when working with the fuel system. Take off all jewelry before you begin, and place—don't throw!—tools in the toolbox, so that there is no chance of sparks. Wear safety glasses, and do not smoke or let anyone nearby smoke. Your work area should not have any gas appliances (fuel vapors are also extremely volatile), and you should not use a work light with a hot bare bulb. Gas spills can become a hazard if not cleaned up (or not cleaned up properly).

Before You Begin

Before you do any work on your car's fuel system, look up in your owner's manual where the fuel filter is located. If the information is not in your owner's manual, or you don't have one, get a model-specific service manual from your local parts store. Fuel filters can be located anyplace between the fuel tank and fuel injectors, and that includes places like the fuel tank, frame rail, and fuel lines. Some vehicles have more than one fuel filter in various locations—again, check your owner's or service manual. Most of us don't have a vehicle with a carburetor, but if you do, the fuel filter is usually located between the fuel pump and the carburetor.

It's a good idea to buy a vehicle-specific manual if you are going to attempt maintenance or repairs on your fuel system (see Appendix C for information on ordering one). Some manufacturers also offer online vehicle-specific information, so if you'd rather check your vehicle out online, do a search for your vehicle manufacturer and then the make and model vehicle and see what you can find. But make sure you use the information supplied by the manufacturer. Should you come across some interesting information from a layperson who owns a vehicle like yours, just think of it as research that needs confirming with the manufacturer and your technician.

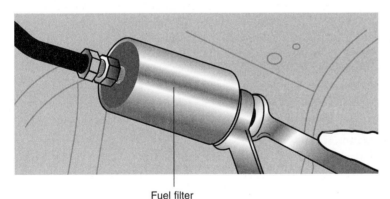

Check your owner's manual for the correct time to change the fuel filter.

Fuel filter

Before changing the fuel filter, read all the directions outlined in your owner's manual and let them soak in. If you are not certain you want to attempt this job, have your ASE-certified auto technician do it. If you change the fuel filter yourself, make sure you have all the tools needed before you begin. Here is a list of basic parts and tools needed (ask the salesperson at the auto-supply store whether your car requires additional parts):

- Filter
- Jack

◆ Jack stands

◆ Open-end wrenches

◆ Pliers

◆ Clean rags

◆ Safety glasses

◆ Gloves

◆ Drop cloth

◆ Pan to catch spilled fuel

◆ Container approved to hold gasoline

◆ Fire extinguisher

◆ Extra fittings

CarLogic

Your vehicle should have been sitting with the motor off for at least one hour before you attempt any maintenance or repairs under the hood. An added concern with a fuel-injected system is that this system is highly pressurized and can take many hours for the pressure in the fuel lines to abate. There are ways to relieve this pressure. Check your owner's manual or service manual for the best method for your vehicle. Never try to disconnect any fuel lines without first relieving fuel-system pressure.

Steps to Changing the Fuel Filter

Gather the parts, tools, and safety equipment (gloves, safety glasses, drop cloth, fire extinguisher) you will need, and then follow these steps:

1. Disconnect battery cables and cover battery posts.

2. **Very important!** Before you zero in on where your fuel filter is located, you'll need to release fuel-line pressure. (See CarLogic, above).

3. If necessary, use the floor jack to jack the car up to get to the fuel filter. Use jack stands to better support the vehicle. Wheel chocks are good to use as an extra safety precaution. (See Chapter 1 for more on how to use jack stands and wheel chocks.)

4. Put a pan under the filter. Have a clean mechanic's rag handy to wipe up any gas spills.

5. If your car's fuel pump is attached by bolts, use the wrench to work the bolts off that fasten the fuel filter to your vehicle.

6. If you have relieved pressure from the fuel lines, remove the inlet hose from the filter. These are usually metal lines with fittings that may require you to use two wrenches to loosen the connection.

7. Remove the outlet hose from the filter.

8. Install the fuel filter in the right direction. There should be an arrow that indicates the correct orientation. The arrow should point toward the engine. Put the filter back in place per specific vehicle—for example, if the filter was attached to the firewall, reattach it there.

9. Reattach the inlet and outlet hoses.

10. Reconnect the battery.

11. Turn the ignition key to ON for a few seconds to allow the fuel pump to build the system pressure back up to normal and then start your engine.

12. Check for leaks.

13. Make sure all fittings and parts are tightened correctly and back in their proper places.

14. Clean up! Properly dispose of all gas-soaked drop cloths, the old filter, and rags. Used petroleum products usually go to the solid waste collection center in your city. Check disposal policies with your county or city governments, or ask gas stations and auto-parts stores to see whether they dispose of used gas for customers.

Speedbumps

For your safety and the safety of the environment, certain laws dictate the kind of container to use for storing or transporting gasoline. The container needs to be made of sturdy (plastic or metal) material. Approved containers, which are red, display a warning about the volatile nature of gasoline. You can find these containers in automotive-supply stores, discount stores, and hardware stores.

Checking the Fuel Pump, Fuel Tank, and Fuel Lines

As we told you in Chapter 12, nowadays fuel pumps are usually located in the gas tank. However, placement is vehicle-specific, so you will have to check your owner's

CarLogic

If your engine won't turn over one morning, check the normal things first: the key is turning okay in the ignition without a clicking sound, and the battery connections are good—that is, the lights will come on and the horn will blow. If those things check out, the problem could be fuel related. You'll want to ask your technician to check the fuel pump, whether it is working properly, and whether you have a clogged fuel filter or fuel injector.

manual to find out where your pump is located. Repairing or replacing a fuel pump located in a gas tank will require you to read the vehicle-specific manual carefully so that you follow all safety rules, follow the procedure directions to the letter, and have the right parts and tools. Usually this repair involves removing the fuel tank, so you might want to have your ASE-certified technician do this repair as well as repairs to the fuel tank. Remember, if you have a fuel-injected vehicle, you will always have to relieve pressure in the lines before working on the system. Replacing a faulty fuel pump is more expensive than changing the fuel filter. Keeping the filter clean could keep the pump working longer.

You can hear your fuel pump cycle on when your vehicle is switched to On (usually a buzzing noise). If you do not hear that sound and the vehicle will not start, you probably have a fuel-pump problem. Gas tanks can become damaged over time. You usually have to replace a damaged plastic gas tank, but a qualified technician may be able to repair a metal tank. Fuel lines are usually made of metal and rubber and can become faulty over time. You should always replace fuel lines with the same type material as the original: steel and the appropriate rubber.

Many fuel-system problems can be avoided if you keep up your maintenance routine. One thing you might not think of as maintenance for the fuel system, but can work out that way, is to keep your fuel tank full as much as possible. This cuts down on any moisture accumulating at the top of the tank that could cause rust if you have a metal fuel tank.

Checking/Replacing the Air Filter

Changing an air filter is one of the simplest maintenance jobs and well within the abilities of the average driver. On older carburetor-equipped vehicles, the air filter is located in the housing on top of the engine. Replacement is a simple matter of removing a wing nut and the top of the air cleaner housing, and then replacing the circular element inside.

Most modern fuel-injected vehicles have the air cleaner mounted in a plastic box or housing located in the engine compartment. Check your owner's manual (or service manual) for the exact location, but it should be pretty obvious. These housings (and the filters inside them) are usually rectangular and have quick-release clips or plastic knurl nuts that you simply open by hand to split the housing and gain access to the air filter. The replacement process is designed to be easy.

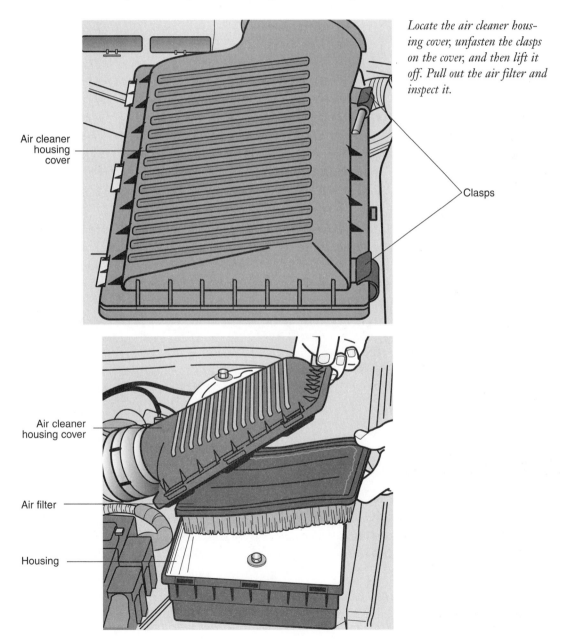

Locate the air cleaner housing cover, unfasten the clasps on the cover, and then lift it off. Pull out the air filter and inspect it.

Air cleaner housing cover

Clasps

Air cleaner housing cover

Air filter

Housing

An obviously dirty air filter should be replaced, but having your air filter checked or changed at least twice a year during your seasonal inspections is a good maintenance practice. A dirty air filter will cut down on engine performance and increase fuel consumption. Extremely dirty or clogged air filters can even cause the Check Engine light to illuminate.

Once you install the new air filter, make sure you get the housing back together properly. If it fails to seal correctly, it could affect your engine performance or cause the computer to turn on the Check Engine light on the dashboard.

Checking/Replacing the PCV Valve

On older vehicles, it was common practice to periodically remove the PCV (Positive Crankcase Ventilation) valve and clean it with a solvent bath. Check your owner's manual or service manual for the exact location for your particular vehicle and engine.

Most PCV valves are located on the intake manifold or valve cover and are readily visible. Their purpose is to extract crankcase vapors that can cause pollution and contaminate your engine oil. The PCV valve uses normal engine vacuum to collect and direct these vapors to the intake manifold, where they're drawn into the combustion chambers and burned with the fuel charge during normal engine operation.

Typical PCV system.

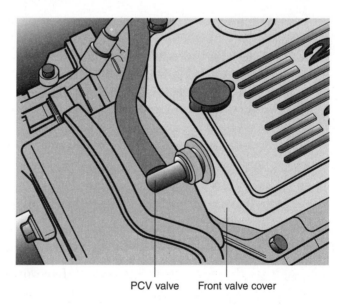

PCV valve   Front valve cover

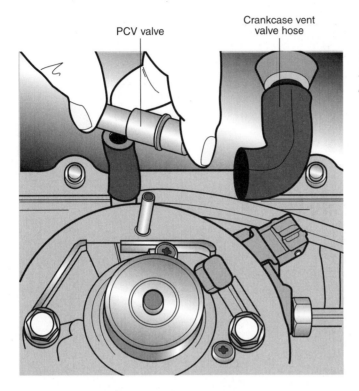

PCV valve

Crankcase vent valve hose

Test the PCV valve by shaking it and listening for a clicking noise.

A PCV valve is a simple device that will have a hose attached to one end and the other end inserted into a rubber grommet on the intake manifold or valve cover. Simply disconnect the rubber hose and pull the PCV valve out of the valve cover. To check it, shake the PCV valve and listen for a clicking noise that tells you the valve is not clogged and is moving freely. If so, you can simply wipe the valve clean and reuse it. If the valve doesn't click, or if you suspect it isn't working properly, replace it. It's a relatively inexpensive part that's easy to remove and replace.

The Least You Need to Know

◆ Working on the fuel system requires many safety precautions.

◆ Changing your fuel filter or having it changed yearly is a good practice for older cars; ask your technician when to change the filter in newer cars.

◆ You must relieve pressure in the fuel lines before working on the fuel system.

◆ Paying attention to your maintenance routine will keep your fuel system in good repair.

Chapter 14

Engine System

In This Chapter

- ◆ Ladies and gents, meet your car's internal combustion engine!
- ◆ What the number and layout of cylinders tell you about your car
- ◆ What's all this about four strokes?
- ◆ How the oil and water pumps work to keep your engine running
- ◆ How engines keep their balance

Finally, it's time to learn about that thingy under the hood that gets all the attention, the engine. We'll talk about how the engine works and get into sticker lingo, like what "4.0 liter V-8" and "dual overhead cams" mean. Vehicle engine descriptions can be confusing, but are worth the time to figure out. It can also be fun to go a step further and read about the evolution of engines for different model cars. For example, the Ford Mustang, born in 1964, has debuted at least sixteen notable engines.

Car-history buff or not, knowing what the words on the sticker mean when you buy a new or used car will help you know exactly what you are purchasing. I'll tell you the basics of how an internal combustion engine works, go into detail about the four-stroke engine, and define what a V-8 engine is.

Common Engine Parts

- Intake valve
- Valve cover
- Intake port
- Head
- Coolant

- Engine block
- Oil pan
- Camshaft
- Exhaust valve
- Spark plug

- Piston
- Connecting rod
- Crankshaft

The Engine System in Brief

You have probably heard engines referred to by different names. There are hemis, diesels, rotary, and gas, to name a few. But no matter the name, the engine's job is to convert heat into work or mechanical energy. These are all a type of internal combustion engine (ICE). The most common is the gas reciprocating internal engine, so that's where we'll spend most of our time.

Auto-Biography

Internal combustion engines can be classified in a variety of ways. One way is by the type of fuel they use, such as gasoline, diesel, or ethanol. Another is by their mechanical design, such as the traditional piston or the rotary, also known as a Wankel. Specific design characteristics, such as the shape of the combustion chamber and corresponding piston or cam location, define particular engines. Hemi, referring to the hemispherical shape of the combustion chamber, or overhead cam, referring to camshafts mounted on the head, are examples of these.

The typical internal combustion engine burns a highly combustible mixture of gasoline and air. This mixture is approximately 15 parts air to one part gasoline. The composition of this mixture is now controlled by electronic fuel-injection systems. When the gasoline is vaporized, mixed with the air, compressed, and ignited, it expands rapidly with great volume forcing the piston down and producing mechanical energy. This work is transferred to the crankshaft, which is connected to the rest of the drive train, eventually transferring that motion to the wheels.

External combustion engines such as steam engines use fuel to heat water to produce steam. The expanding steam is then used to drive pistons, converting the heat energy to mechanical energy. Internal combustion engines contain the combustion process inside rather than outside like the steam engine. That combustion process can be efficiently controlled within the cylinder of an internal combustion engine.

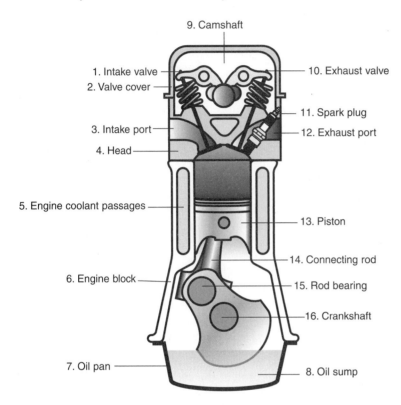

9. Camshaft

1. Intake valve
2. Valve cover

3. Intake port

4. Head

5. Engine coolant passages

6. Engine block

7. Oil pan

10. Exhaust valve

11. Spark plug
12. Exhaust port

13. Piston

14. Connecting rod

15. Rod bearing

16. Crankshaft

8. Oil sump

Here's where those major engine components are located.

Motor Sizes and Cylinder Configurations

Reciprocating piston engines are characterized by the number and arrangement of pistons and cylinders. Inline engines have anywhere from three to six cylinders arranged in a row. Four and six are the most common today, with a few fives. The familiar "V" arrangement uses two banks of cylinders set at an angle to each other like a V. The total number may be anywhere from 4 to 12, with V-6 and V-8 being the most common today. Another traditional configuration is the flat or pancake style, which also uses two banks of cylinders. These banks are directly opposed to each other, allowing an engine design that takes up less space. Flat fours and flat sixes are the common ones. The flat design or "boxer" engine is only used today by three manufacturers: Subaru, Porsche, and Ferrari; but it was also the engine design for the ubiquitous Volkswagen Beetle manufactured from just after World War II through the 1970s.

The most recent new design is called a W engine and uses three banks of four cylinders arranged in a W configuration to make a 12-cylinder engine, but this is currently only used by one manufacturer (Volkswagen) in a very limited number of high-end luxury vehicles.

Displacement is another way to categorize engines. As the piston travels from the bottom to the top of its stroke, it displaces a certain volume. The total volume of all the cylinders, measured in liters or cubic inches, gives you an indication of how powerful the engine is. The larger the displacement, the more fuel it can convert to mechanical energy. Car engine displacement today typically varies from about 1.5 liters to about 5 liters, with the larger engine being at least three times as powerful as the smaller. The largest V-10 and V-12 engines generally run about 7 liters.

The up-and-down motion of the pistons or the sideways motion in a flat engine is converted to rotary motion by the connecting rods, causing the crankshaft to spin below or between the pistons. This rotational power is modified by the transmission and eventually transferred to the drive wheels, making your car move.

Before we go into detail about each of the four strokes in the operation of the four-stroke internal combustion engine, we need to identify a few more important parts. We've mentioned the cylinders, the pistons, the connecting rods, and the crankshaft. The cylinder head completes the combustion chamber and contains *valves* and spark plugs. The intake valve opens at a precise time in the cycle to allow the fuel and air mixture to enter the cylinder. The exhaust valve also opens at a precise time to allow burned gasses to leave. The spark plug ignites the fuel and air mixture at a precise moment in the cycle. The valves are controlled by a camshaft, and the spark plugs are controlled by a distributor or an engine control computer.

> **Drive Time**
>
> **Valves** are needed to control the air and fuel mixture into your engine and the resulting burned gas out of the engine. The intake valve allows the mixture in and the export valve allows the burned gas out.

As engine manufacturers strive for increased performance and efficiency, many innovations have been incorporated into their engines. Overhead camshafts (OHC) are now being mounted directly in the cylinder heads. Some engines now have dual-overhead cams (DOHC), allowing each cam to control only the exhaust or the intake valves. These configurations require fewer moving parts than the older-style valve trains and make it easier to incorporate multiple valves and variable valve timing to increase power and efficiency.

Four-Stroke Engine

The four strokes of a four-stroke engine are intake, compression, power, and exhaust. Basically, this is what happens: a piston moves down on the intake stroke, goes up during compression, moves down on the power stroke, and goes up again during the exhaust stroke. Let's take a closer look at each part of the process.

Intake

The intake cycle begins with the piston at the top of its stroke, with the connecting rod centered over the crankshaft (hence the term Top Dead Center or TDC). This is the position where the piston is at the apex or highest point of its travel within the cylinder. During the lower stroke or intake stroke, as the piston moves down, the fuel-air mixture is taken into the cylinder through the intake valve. Now the intake valve closes.

Compression

The upward stroke (compression) compresses the fuel-air mixture. The fuel-air mixture is then ignited, usually by a spark plug for a gasoline engine, or by the heat and pressure of compression for a diesel engine.

Power

The expansion of burning gases forces the piston down for the third stroke, the power stroke. This happens when the spark plug fires, igniting the compressed fuel-air mixture, which causes the resulting fuel-air vapor to expand. This expansion sends the piston down the cylinder forcefully, which turns the crankshaft. Now your vehicle has the power to move.

Exhaust

The fourth stroke is the exhaust stroke, which removes burned vapor from the cylinder past the open exhaust valve or valves, through the exhaust port. The cylinder holds an immense amount of pressure. When the valve opens, gas is expelled with a violent force; this is why you need a muffler. So now the process starts again with the piston being sent back to the apex or Top Dead Center.

Engine Lubrication and Cooling

Your engine won't work without oil. Oil is needed to help cool the engine and keep all the moving parts lubricated. Without oil, your engine would weld itself together in a very short period of time. Oil is pumped through passages in the engine under pressure, and this is accomplished by your oil pump. The oil pump is located at the bottom of the engine in the oil pan. It's connected by a gear to either the crankshaft or the camshaft.

Whenever the engine is turning, oil is being pumped throughout the engine. An oil-pressure sensor is located in one of the oil channels and sends information to a warning light or pressure gauge on your dashboard. Should the light come on while driving or the needle fall into the low-pressure region, stop the car and try to find the cause. The most likely reason is low oil level that can be easily corrected by adding enough oil to bring the level back up to full. You are carrying an extra quart or two in your trunk, aren't you? If the needle doesn't return to the normal range or if the light doesn't go out, the problem needs to be more thoroughly diagnosed by a technician to determine why the pressure is low.

> **Speedbumps**
>
> Running an engine with low or no oil pressure will likely cause major damage, even seizure (the engine will not turn over).

While the major role of oil is lubrication, it also helps dissipate some of the heat produced in the engine. However, by itself it can't handle the enormous amount of heat created. That's why your engine needs a carefully designed cooling system. Engine coolant is circulated through channels in the engine block and cylinder head by the water pump. The coolant carrying that heat releases the heat in the radiator and returns to the engine to start the cycle over again.

Engine Balance

Reducing engine vibration contributes to a more comfortable ride. A well-balanced engine provides more power and causes less wear and stress on its parts.

Every revolution of your engine has from two to six power pulses. The flywheel, a heavy, well-balanced disc attached to one end of the crankshaft, smoothes out the resulting vibrations. Every rotating object wants to rotate about its own center of gravity. As long as the center of gravity of your engine's flywheel coincides with the center of rotation of the crankshaft, your engine should not vibrate. However, a heavy spot on the flywheel or an imbalance in the weights of the connecting rods and pistons attached to the crankshaft can create a problem. Since the pistons in inline and flat engines move in the same plane, balance can be achieved by carefully equalizing the weights of all components. In V-configuration engines, the pistons move in two planes, typically at 60 or 90 degrees apart. Balance is achieved by using counterweights on the crankshaft.

If you have a newer car with a four- or six-cylinder engine, your engine may contain balance shafts. These reverse rotating shafts help offset vibrations caused by the up-and-down motion of the pistons. The rotation of the balance shaft is carefully timed to the rotation of the crankshaft.

Your car may also have a harmonic balancer, also known as a vibration damper, attached to the crankshaft to reduce torsional vibration caused by the constant pushing of the pistons against the crankshaft. Engine mounts are also designed to absorb some of the vibration.

The Least You Need to Know

♦ A precise mixture of air and gasoline makes an engine purr.

♦ The four types of cylinder configuration are inline, V, W, and flat.

♦ The four strokes of a four-stroke engine are intake, compression, power, and exhaust.

♦ The oil pump keeps the engine lubricated with oil; the water pump and cooling system help the engine keep its cool. Both are necessary to keep your engine running smoothly.

♦ Vibrations are smoothed by flywheels and balance shafts.

Engine System: Troubleshooting and Maintenance

In This Chapter

◆ Keeping your engine lubricated

◆ Tools needed for an oil change

◆ How to change the oil

◆ Troubleshooting the engine system

In Chapter 14, we talked about the parts that make your engine work—what keeps it running smoothly and at a tolerable temperature. You learned that in order to work, your engine needs the proper fuel-air mixture, oil, water, and mechanisms that balance out vibrations. Now let's talk about how to maintain your engine and scope out possible problems you may encounter.

A Well-Oiled Machine

Lubrication keeps every moving part in the engine oiled so that it can move easily without creating more heat. There is plenty of heat already generated through compression, so it makes good sense to lubricate and not create any more. Pistons need oil so they can slide easily in their cylinders, and the bearings need to be well oiled to allow things like the crankshaft and camshafts to rotate freely. Oil flowing freely keeps heat-generating friction at bay. Here is how motor oil circulates: when you start the engine, the oil pump sucks oil from the oil pan, pushes it through the oil filter to remove dirt, and then delivers motor oil to various engine parts such as bearings and cylinder walls through oil channels in the engine. When you turn the engine off, pressure is reduced and the motor oil goes back down into the pan to await the next turn of the ignition key.

Changing Your Oil

Most manufacturers recommend changing your oil and oil filter once every 7,500 miles or once every six months. However, there are some conditions that make it a good idea to change your oil and oil filter sooner: your vehicle is used under dusty or off-road conditions, or your vehicle is frequently driven in stop-and-go traffic. Most auto technicians recommend changing your oil every 3,000 to 3,500 miles. A good rule of thumb: more often is better.

CarLogic

Some auto manufacturers recommend changing your oil filter with every *other* oil change. However, there is approximately one quart of dirty oil remaining in the old oil filter if it is not changed. Your engine prefers *clean* oil, so it's a good practice to change your oil filter whenever you change your oil.

Oil Change Tools

It's a good idea to go ahead and get all your tools and supplies out and lined up in the order of their use before you change the oil. That way you won't have to go in search of anything while focusing on the task at hand.

Here's what you'll need:

◆ An oil-filter wrench

◆ Combination wrench set

◆ A ⅜-drive (metric) socket set

◆ Oil container drain pan (at least six-quart capacity)

◆ Funnel

◆ Clean rags

◆ Newspaper

◆ The number of quarts of oil that your owner's manual recommends (buy one extra to keep in the trunk)

◆ New oil filter

◆ Wheel blocks or wheel chocks

◆ Safety glasses

◆ Gloves

◆ Empty milk jug or Gatorade jug, rinsed clean

◆ A jack and a pair of jack safety stands or a pair of car ramps

CarLogic

There are different types of oil-filter wrenches. A cup-style wrench cups the entire filter, or the cup fits on top of the filter and can be manipulated by a bar handle. The strap-type wrench fits around the body of the filter and will work on any filter but may be hard to manipulate. If you plan on doing all of your filter changes, we recommend you invest in the cup style for your filter.

Safety Check

No matter what job you are doing or how many times you've done the job, always follow safety guidelines before working on your car:

◆ Do you have on work clothes? Safety glasses? Gloves?

◆ Have you taken off all jewelry? Pulled your hair back?

◆ Is your car parked on level ground so it has no chance of rolling?

◆ Do you have jack safety stands?

◆ Have you let someone know you'll be working under the car?

> **Speedbumps** _____
>
> Watch out for hot oil. Be sure you have your safety glasses and gloves on. Prolonged or repeated contact with used motor oil can be harmful. Wash with soap and water if your skin comes into contact with used motor oil, and take off oil-soaked clothing as soon as possible. Also, throwing oily rags or clothes into your machine can damage your machine. .Wash them by hand (wearing gloves) or throw them away—unless you use a degreaser. Ask your auto-parts salesperson for the best product.

Getting Down to Business

Because warm oil is thinner and drains much easier than cold, start by letting the engine warm up for about 10 minutes (check the temperature gauge). After the engine has warmed up, turn off the ignition. Then follow these steps to change the oil:

1. Find a flat, level area to park your vehicle. Put your car in Park or out of gear, set the parking brake, and place blocks behind the rear wheels to prevent the car from rolling.

2. Jack up your car, allowing enough access to the underside of the engine so that you have room to move a wrench. Place your jack safety stands under the frame to support the vehicle. (Remember, never crawl under a car supported by the car jack alone—always use safety stands! The car could fall on you, causing injury or death.) Or if you have car ramps, carefully drive your car onto the ramps, set the parking brake, and chock the rear wheels.

3. Grab your drain pan and the wrench for the drain plug and crawl under the car. Locate the oil drain plug on the oil pan. It is usually at the lowest point on the oil pan. You can find the oil pan cover in the bottom of your engine.

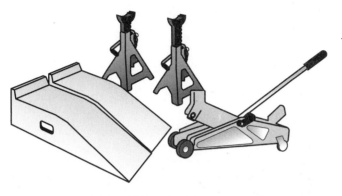

Use jacks and safety stands for the oil change.

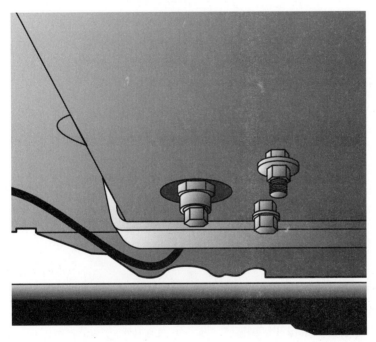

Find the drain plug.

4. Place your drain pan directly under the drain plug. You may want to put news-paper under the pan as well. (Check your owner's manual beforehand to make sure of oil pan placement so that you don't pull the transmission plug instead.) Completely unscrew the plug counterclockwise with the wrench. This may take some elbow grease. (Make sure you have the right wrench for the job—refer to Chapter 3 on how to use socket, open-end, and closed-end wrenches.) Try to dislodge the plug with a socket wrench first. Loosen it just enough so that you

can unscrew it the rest of the way with your fingers. If you take the plug completely off, oil will come out suddenly, so be prepared.

If the plug won't budge, get the proper size socket and ratchet or a box wrench. (The plug will mostly likely fall into the drain pan along with the oil. No problem. You can fish it out when all the oil has completely drained out.)

After placing the drain pan in place to catch old oil, loosen the drain plug with the socket wrench.

5. Give the oil a good hour to completely drain out unless you are in a big hurry. Allowing the oil to completely drain out will mean you got as much dirty oil to drip out as possible.

6. When all the oil has drained into the pan, retrieve the drain plug and put it back in place on the engine oil pan. Tighten it firmly, but not so firmly that you strip the threads.

CarLogic

How tight is just right? Finger tight. Use a combination wrench (the closed end) and use one finger to pull it tight—or if you have weak hands, use two fingers— but that's all the pressure you need. This should seal the drain plug and keep you from stripping the threads.

7. Move the drain pan to a point under the oil filter. Pick up the oil-filter wrench and rotate the filter counterclockwise to remove it. A couple of turns with the filter wrench, and the oil filter should come free from the engine. Now you can unscrew it with your hands and drop it into the pan beneath it. Oil will escape from the filter and drain down into the pan. This is okay.

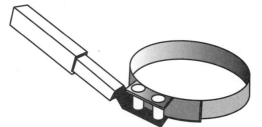

An oil-filter wrench (band type) helps loosen the oil filter.

8. Open the new filter. Notice it has a rubber gasket on the base. Take a little oil from one of the new quarts of engine oil and coat the rubber gasket thoroughly. This will make it easier to remove the filter next time. Without this lubrication, the rubber gasket will seal itself to the engine and cause a huge headache next filter change.

Lubricate the seal on the new filter.

9. Read your owner's manual for specific requirements for installing the filter. The general rule is to gently screw the filter on until the rubber gasket first makes contact. Then turn the filter an additional three quarters or a full revolution.

10. Okay, you are done under the car. Remove the drained oil. Carefully release the jack and whatever else (jack safety stands or ramp) you are using to hold up the car. Using a funnel, carefully pour the old oil into a clean milk or Gatorade jug so you'll have a capped container to transport for recycling without messy spills.

11. Find the engine-oil fill cap. (Most of the time it's on top of a valve cover and will say "Oil" or "Oil Fill" on it.) Unscrew the cap and pour in the proper amount and type of oil (check your owner's manual for amount and type of oil) recommended for your vehicle.

12. Put the cap back on the oil-fill hole, using a clean rag to wipe up any oil you have spilled.

13. Start the engine and let the vehicle run for about five minutes. Just let it idle; don't rev up the engine until the engine has built up oil pressure. Idling warms up the engine and lets oil circulate. It will also give you a chance to make sure the filter is not leaking. Check under the vehicle and make sure you are not leaking oil onto the pavement. If you have leaks, tighten the pan plug or filter carefully. Don't overtighten!

14. Turn off the engine. Check the dipstick on the engine; it should read "FULL." You should have no oil leaks under the engine.

Speedbumps

To keep the environment safe and keep you from being fined by the Environmental Protection Agency (EPA), make sure you dispose of dirty oil safely—and legally. Taking dirty oil to a dumpster or burying it is a violation of the law that carries hefty fines. Often, "quick oil change" shops will handle dirty oil disposal. Call your local city or county government to find out where to take your used oil, or ask your local quick oil change or auto-supply store.

Record your oil change in your maintenance log and schedule your next oil change. Congratulations, you did it!

Troubleshooting Possible Engine Problems

Sometimes your car may just feel a little sluggish, or it could be making odd noises, or the exhaust may be loud. Let's explore possible problematic scenarios. Sound intriguing? Trust us … your technician will love you for being able to tell him the variation that alerted you to the fact there might be a problem. (See Appendix A for a more detailed troubleshooting guide.)

Lack of Power

Maybe you are trying to pass someone and find your vehicle just does not have the get-up-and-go it used to have. You think back and know this isn't the first time your car has seemed to become anemic when you needed horsepower. Why? Here are some possible reasons:

- **You may have a dirty air filter.** Replace the air filter (see Chapter 4).

- **The spark plugs may be dirty or worn.** Clean and regap spark plugs; replace spark plugs (see Chapter 11).

- **Ignition wires may be bad.** Have your technician check and replace if necessary.

- **You may have water in the gasoline.** Have your technician drain the gas tank, flush it with fresh gas, and refill it.

- **If your car has a carburetor, you may have a bad accelerator pump or power circuit.** Have your technician replace the accelerator pump or carburetor.

- **The fuel filter may be clogged.** Replace the fuel filter (see Chapter 13) or have your technician do it.

- **The catalytic converter may be clogged.** Have your technician replace the catalytic converter.

Rough or Inconsistent Operation

If your engine seems to speed up and then "burps," one of the following might be the culprit:

♦ **Your engine may be overheating.** Check the coolant level (see Chapter 9).

♦ **The fuel pressure regulator may be operating at too low of a pressure.** Check the fuel pressure with a fuel pressure gauge. If necessary, have your technician replace the fuel pressure regulator.

♦ **The ignition timing may be set incorrectly.** Have your technician adjust the ignition timing.

♦ **It could be an ignition problem.** Check and replace the distributor cap (in older cars), rotor, ignition wires, and spark plugs.

♦ **There may be a fault in the computerized engine control system.** Have a technician check the engine control systems with a scan tool. Have the technician test circuits and repair or replace components as required.

♦ **The fuel filter may be partially clogged.** Replace the fuel filter (see Chapter 13) or have your technician do it.

♦ **The torque converter in the transmission may not be locking at the right time, or it may be slipping.** Have a technician check the lock up circuit or replace the torque converter.

♦ **There may be a vacuum leak.** Check or have your technician check and repair as needed.

♦ **There may be engine mechanical problems.** Check or have a technician check the compression to determine engine health. If you want to check the compression yourself, you'll need to buy a compression gauge. Checking compression involves removing each spark plug one at a time and installing the compression gauge into the spark plug hole. The gauge has an adapter on the end that screws into the spark plug hole in the cylinder head. You'll need to disable the ignition system so you can crank the engine over a few times without having it start. Check your model-specific service manual for the procedure to disable the ignition system. It can be as simple as disconnecting the coil wire at the distributor, but newer models may require that you remove one of the fuses from the fuse box under the hood. Install the compression gauge in each cylinder in turn, crank the engine over a few times, and record the highest pressure on the gauge. Check your service manual for the manufacturer's specifications on what the normal compression reading should be, but in general the cylinders should read about the same compression. If one cylinder is very high or very low, you may have an internal engine problem. It's time to call your technician.

Hissing Sound

The engine may not seem to run well. A hissing noise like air or steam can be heard coming from the engine. You may notice a drop in performance immediately after the noise begins. Check for one of these problems:

- ◆ **Your engine may be overheating.** Check the coolant level and make repairs as needed (refer to Chapters 4 and 9).

- ◆ **The exhaust system or catalytic converter is plugged.** Have your technician check and make needed repairs.

- ◆ **The vacuum line is leaking or disconnected.** Have your technician reconnect or replace the vacuum line.

- ◆ **The vacuum device is leaking.** Have your technician replace the vacuum device.

Auto-Biography

Any engine noise should be checked out by a technician. Possible causes may include ...

- ◆ Low power-steering fluid.
- ◆ A worn-out alternator.
- ◆ A problem with the water pump.
- ◆ A power-steering pump that needs replacing.
- ◆ A failing air-conditioning compressor.
- ◆ A burnt or broken valve, or a worn or broken camshaft.
- ◆ Spark plug wires on incorrect spark plugs.
- ◆ Valves that need adjusting.
- ◆ Low level of engine oil (you can check this yourself; see Chapter 4).
- ◆ An oil pump that doesn't provide enough pressure.
- ◆ Loose or damaged belts.
- ◆ An idler pulley problem.
- ◆ Internal mechanical problems.

Exhaust Noise or Smoke

Does your exhaust system sound like it's been on a diet of refried beans? Here are some possible culprits:

♦ **The muffler or exhaust pipe is worn out.** Have your technician replace the muffler or pipes as required.

♦ **The exhaust manifold is cracked or broken.** Have your technician replace the exhaust manifold.

♦ **The engine uses more oil than normal, and there is some smoke from the exhaust.** Check your oil level (see Chapter 4).

♦ **Gas mileage is way down.** You may have an engine-compression problem. Have your technician check the piston rings.

♦ **The car seems to be using more oil than normal.** Your engine's valve seals may be worn; have your technician check.

♦ **Gray smoke is coming from the exhaust.** The engine's piston rings may be worn; have your technician check.

♦ **White smoke or water vapor is coming from the exhaust.** Have your technician see whether water or antifreeze might be entering your exhaust and causing a white steam to escape. Overheating that caused a head-gasket failure might be the problem. This could be a serious repair problem, so when you see the smoke, go ahead and call your technician.

♦ **Black smoke is coming from the exhaust.** The fuel injectors may be leaking, or you may have a dirty air filter. Have technician clean or replace injectors and replace the air filter (refer to Chapter 4 on how to change the air filter).

♦ **You see blue or black smoke accompanied by a strong smell.** This may be from burning wires. Don't drive the car. A fire could be about to erupt. Have the car towed to a service center to be checked out.

♦ **Smoke is coming from under the hood and there's an oily smell.** You may have an oil leak. Find where the oil may be leaking on the exhaust system, and have the leak repaired.

♦ **Transmission fluid is entering the intake manifold through the vacuum modulator.** The cylinder head gaskets may be warped or cracked, or the engine block may be cracked. Have your technician check.

◆ **Engine is using more oil than normal.** The PCV system may not be working properly, the engine gasket and seals may be damaged, or the oil filter may not be tightened properly. You can check the oil filter, and you can check the PCV valve, but if this does not eliminate the problem, have your technician check it out. You can check the PCV valve by shaking it. It should rattle.

◆ **Your engine or oil light comes on while driving.** The engine light coming on can be caused by many problems; ask your technician. If the oil light comes on, it usually means low pressure due to low oil level. Have this checked out immediately. Oil pump failure is catastrophic—your engine will quit.

The Least You Need to Know

◆ Most cars today have a four-stroke engine that needs constant lubrication from clean oil.

◆ Change your oil every 3,000 to 3,500 miles. It's best to change the oil filter with every oil change.

◆ When changing oil, exercise all safety precautions and dispose of the old oil appropriately.

◆ Don't ignore noises or mediocre performance. Paying attention to developing problems now can save you time, money, and inconvenience later on.

Chapter 16

Drive Train System

In This Chapter

- ◆ Get on board the drive train
- ◆ A gearshift or not: manual and automatic transmissions
- ◆ Meet your drive train's private parts
- ◆ The different types of drive trains

Explaining the drive train is somewhat like explaining a root canal. Well, that's what some experts will tell you, but your dentist can always help a root canal along with a bit of nitrous oxide. And we are on hand to help you learn about this system with the same "this won't hurt a bit" mentality.

In this chapter, we'll look at the parts of the drive train system. Major car subsystems (the engine and transmission, for example) work together to apply the power and finesse needed for your vehicle to move and move smoothly. (In Chapter 17, we'll tell you how to perform routine maintenance and troubleshoot various problems on your drive train.)

The Drive Train Demystified

So what is the drive train? Because of the train analogy, you might think it's made of many parts coupled together, and that thought would be right on target. A straightforward definition of drive train is lots of parts put together for the purpose of sending engine RPMs (rotations per minute) to the pavement so your wheels can ease on down the road at different speeds and angles.

The drive train system relies heavily on gears. Gears are wheels with teeth cut into the edges. Because your car doesn't travel at just one speed, gears are needed to make the most of engine power. Normally the closest we may come to designing or building a car is with Lego bricks, so seeing the gears do their magic in our heads will have to suffice. But if you've ever ridden a bicycle on a straight road and encountered a hill, you know that when you have to pedal harder to make forward progress, gearing down is in order. The same concept applies to the transmission in your car. So like your bike, the car switches (either manually by you, or automatically) gears in order to use more engine power when needed just like a bicyclist gears down and uses more leg power. So the faster you go (higher gears), the less power is needed from the engine, but when moving from a stopped or slowed position, when heading up an incline, or when pulling heavy objects, you'll gear down and need more power from the engine.

CarLogic

Turn the music down and listen as your car goes through gear shifts. When you become familiar with the way your vehicle sounds as you go through gear shifts, it will be easy to tell if your vehicle is struggling and you need to gear up or down.

Major Parts of the Drive Train

- Differential
- Output shaft
- Planetary gear set
- Transaxle
- Engine
- Crankshaft

- Clutch disc
- Transmission input shaft
- Throw-out bearing
- Gears
- Pressure plate

- U-joints
- Axle
- Driveshaft
- Gearshift
- Clutch pedal
- Engine flywheel

Drive Train in Action

Let's go over how the drive train system works.

You use the gearshift to shift out of Park (automatic transmission) or into gear (manual transmission). The transmission is one part of the drive train. The transmission has gears and it sends engine power to the differential (another vital part of the drive train), which is in charge of moving your vehicle's wheels. The differential also has gears. First we'll look at one type of drive train that incorporates a manual transmission.

The drive train gets power from the engine. The engine sends power to the transmission crankshaft through the crankshaft. (The crankshaft is a twisting rod that sends power from the engine and it extends through the transmission, through to the differential, and finally to the wheels.) The crankshaft turns faster when the engine runs faster (more RPMs) and slower (fewer RPMs) when the engine runs slower.

This is where a bit of nitrous might come in handy, because there are many parts between the crankshaft and the wheels. We will just go over them quickly. The crankshaft is connected to the engine flywheel (wheel-shaped part that lessens engine reverberations), the engine flywheel is connected to the clutch disk, and the clutch disk and flywheel stick together (because of an asbestos-type backing). These two parts stay together until you get ready to manually change gears. When you step on the clutch pedal, this sends in another part, the clutch pressure plate. This part either keeps the engine flywheel and clutch disk together or lets them move away from each other when the clutch pedal is depressed. When the pedal is depressed, the clutch takes away the power from the engine so you can change gears. When you've shifted gears and remove your foot from the clutch, the flywheel and clutch disk go back together until you need to shift again.

Here is where it really gets deep. When we pass through the clutch assembly, the crankshaft has a name change. It is now called the input shaft. That's because it is inputting engine power into the transmission to gears of various sizes. Now moving on through the transmission and out—the shaft previously known as the input shaft is named the output shaft and sends engine power on to the driveshaft. Next we have the differential, which is another box of gears that takes the spinning driveshaft to the axle, which keeps the wheels in place.

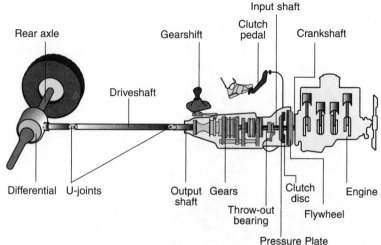

The typical rear-wheel-drive manual-transmission drive train.

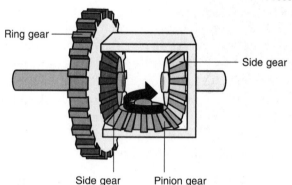

The rear differential has another gear set inside to transfer power to the rear wheels.

Transmissions

You've probably heard the word *transmission* and know every vehicle has one, and sometimes it is said to slip. Does that mean it needs therapy? Well, after seeing what is involved in this system, only your technician may know for sure; but in Chapter 17, we'll tell you what can go wrong. And since your drive train is the communications system of your car, always listening to your commands, it sounds like it already has some pretty good therapy skills.

Drive Time

A vehicle **transmission** is a box of gears of various sizes that accepts engine power from a twisting shaft and makes the engine run more efficiently at low and high speeds using gear selection.

Manual transmissions, which are also called standard transmissions, put you in the driver's seat. Manual transmission, as the name implies, means you change the gears manually. You shift into the proper gear at the proper time, which makes you feel like you're part of the process. Now with an automatic transmission, you sit back and the shifting is done for you. Not as much driving fun, but it is convenient in stop-and-go traffic. Both types of transmissions send power from the engine to your wheels.

Manual Transmission

With a manual transmission, you work the gearshift (with your hand) and clutch (with your foot). Some gearshifts are easy to manipulate, but some make you wish you'd eaten your Wheaties. Clutches are operated by either levers and cables or hydraulics.

A manual transmission usually works with four or five gears with fifth gear being overdrive. Oh, and unlike your bicycle, your vehicle can be shifted into reverse. An overdrive gear (located on the back side and attached to the transmission) is good to have for the following reason: imagine you're driving on the Autobahn (nice thought) or on an interstate for a sustained period of time and your speed remains high for that period—if you shift into overdrive, this gear allows you to keep that high speed without using more power from the engine. In fact, this gear lessens engine speed by approximately one third. (Great on the pocketbook and environment because the overdrive gear conserves gasoline!)

Your gearshift knob should have a simple diagram of route moves your hand needs to make to shift gears. It looks like an "H": first gear is in the top left of the H; second is straight down from first, in the bottom left; third is top right; and fourth is bottom right.

If you have never driven a manual-transmission car, learning how is a good idea. They are usually less expensive to purchase than cars with automatic transmission, and they get better gas mileage. They are also just plain fun to drive! Find a deserted parking lot, or a long stretch of road with little or no traffic, and practice.

Here is an approximation of gear-shifting speeds and when to use them:

- **First: 0 to 15 mph.** First gear is good for starting and stopping. (Manual transmissions do not have Park; instead, first gear is used for Park.)

- **Second: 5 mph to 25 mph.** Second gear can be used to start the vehicle and is good for gearing down in order to climb hills, pull heavy loads, or merge onto the interstate.

◆ **Third: 15 mph to 45 mph.** Third gear is a mid-gear that can help you merge onto the interstate and drive in stop-and-go traffic.

◆ **Fourth: 30 mph to 65 mph.** Fourth gear is an open-road gear in which you reach speeds up to 65 mph.

◆ **Fifth (overdrive): 45 mph and up.** Fifth gear is overdrive and is usually for interstate travel where speed limits are higher. The higher the number gear, the less the engine has to work.

Automatic Transmission

Cars that do not require you to change gears are referred to as automatic. Automatic-transmission vehicles still need a means to connect and then disconnect engine power from the transmission. In automatic transmissions, this work is accomplished by a torque converter, which uses an uncompressed fluid, transmission oil, to aid in changing gears.

> **Drive Time**
>
> A **transaxle** is used in front-wheel drive (FWD) vehicles. Transaxles wed the transmission and differential into one housing.

There are various kinds of automatic systems loaded into cars. You can have a system that looks much like a manual transmission in that the power comes out of the engine and heads to the rear wheels and is called a rear-wheel drive (RWD). And then there are the vehicles that are referred to as front-wheel drives (FWD). The setup in FWD vehicles usually incorporates a *transaxle*. The transaxle does not extend the length of the car but is located in the front of the vehicle. In this system, the differential and transmission are wed.

Front-wheel-drive vehicles use a transaxle, which combines the transmission and differential into one unit to deliver power to the front wheels.

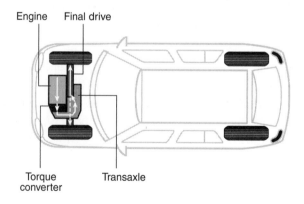

Engine   Final drive

Torque   Transaxle
converter

Here are the automatic transmission gears in action:

♦ **First gear** maxes *torque* (the engine is turning much faster than the wheels) and minimum speed. This is where you are when you start the engine and begin to take off.

♦ **Second gear** offers less torque than first gear (engine power) and is good for accelerating after starting off and for inclines. Your vehicle gears down upon noticing the engine will have to work harder to climb a hill or accelerate out onto the interstate, or it gears up to second upon moving out of the starting gear, first.

♦ **Third gear** lessens the work output needed from the engine while allowing wheels to turn faster. This gear is good for interstate travel.

♦ **Reverse gear**, of course, allows you to back out of a parking space, for example. It's used for when you need to reverse your direction.

♦ **Park** allows the car to be stationary.

Drive Time

Torque is the twisting force to an object and is measured in pound-feet. One pound-foot equals the twisting force produced when a one-pound force is applied to the end of a one-foot-long lever.

An automatic transmission is much easier to drive than a manual transmission because you don't have to shift gears, but sometimes it's not as much fun. Whether you want a manual or automatic transmission depends on many factors that are mechanical, practical, and personality based. If you'd just as soon not worry if you are gentle enough on your clutch, if you have to go up hills on your commute, if you have stop-and-go traffic, or you're a passive driver, then an automatic transmission is a good bet for you. If you want to feel you are more a part of the driving experience, a manual is a good bet. However, if your day-to-day drive is hectic, you might opt for a weekend vehicle that allows driving to be more than a means from point A to point B.

Here's how many automatic transmissions work: like the manual transmission, the automatic has an output shaft. The output shaft is regulated either by a governor or, in newer vehicles, by a sensor (electronic hydraulics). The governor or sensor commands the vehicle transmission fluid. This transmission fluid (uncompressed liquid) is sent to valves called shift valves. These valves do the transmission fluid's bidding because the fluid is pressurized and causes gears to shift up or down.

Cosmos Connection: Planetary Gears

The first automobile was the result of approximately 100,000 patents. Great minds worked diligently to bring the auto to life. Anyone thinking that the auto is heaven-made isn't completely off base, because the cosmos was used as a blueprint for some automatic transmissions. The automatic transmission works like our planetary system: gears called planetary gears revolve around a central "sun" gear. All automatic transmissions incorporate this same scheme with variations. Valves and sensors and other components know when to shift up or down automatically so you can enjoy the view.

CarLogic

While you are enjoying the view, be mindful of your speed. You can check it from time to time because of your vehicle's speedometer. This device may be operated by a cable if you own an older vehicle. Newer cars are computerized and the speedometer or odometer displays what is fed into the computer from a sensor (rotation) that is located in the transmission.

Types of Drive Trains

A two-wheel-drive vehicle means two wheels—rear or front, depending on whether you have rear-wheel drive (RWD) or front-wheel drive (FWD)—can take power from the engine at the same time. A four-wheel-drive (4WD) vehicle means all wheels can be driven by the engine simultaneously. Vehicle manufacturers have various names to describe drive trains. The old usage of 4×4 generally meant an off-road vehicle, but today the terms are not as specific. For example, we now have 4×4, 4WD, and all-wheel drive (AWD). Read your owner's manual to find out the definition of the drive train as provided by the manufacturer of the vehicle you purchased. AWD generally means a vehicle in which all wheels are powered by the engine at the same time and is used on a regular road or highway. These drive trains can aid you in snowy conditions. FWD is common in passenger cars. Pluses for FWD include good fuel economy; because it has fewer parts, it is lighter and provides good traction.

The Least You Need to Know

- ◆ Backing up is possible because of your drive train.

- ◆ The transmission allows you to drive at different speeds without taxing the engine.

- ◆ The differential allows your drive wheels to turn at different speeds.

- ◆ Manual transmissions usually have four to five speeds, with the fifth gear being overdrive.

- ◆ Automatic transmissions do not have a foot-operated clutch or gearshift but a torque converter.

- ◆ Front-wheel drive (FWD) is the most common drive train in passenger cars.

Chapter 17

Drive Train System: Troubleshooting and Maintenance

In This Chapter

+ How driving like a pro will save you money

+ Troubleshooting tips

+ Remember your maintenance routine

+ Adding fluid to a hydraulic clutch

+ Adjusting a clutch cable

In Chapter 16, we looked at the parts of the drive train, and you've probably gathered that repairing the drive train system is not conducive to the novice do-it-yourselfer. While you can always learn anything you'd like to learn, working on this system is tedious, and some components, such as the transmission, are computerized and serviceable only by an auto technician. However, knowing how to keep your car's systems maintained and repaired is what this book is about. This chapter will be a good ally when working to maintain and troubleshoot your drive train system.

Bear in mind, this system includes your engine. If your engine isn't performing at its optimal level, your vehicle's transmission won't function properly because it is receiving the wrong information from the engine. So, many times what is thought to be a transmission problem may be an engine problem. Keeping the engine maintained keeps the other systems running properly. If you do have a repair problem, an accurate diagnosis will get your vehicle back in top running form and will save you time and money as well.

Drive Well

One way to keep your drive train system in good shape is to drive like a pro. That means use your gears as they are intended to be used. If you have a manual transmission, don't drive in the wrong gear and don't ride the clutch. You can feel your vehicle's overexertion when you don't shift when you should. Automatic transmissions also have gears made especially for the type of driving you are doing. To avoid straining your automatic transmission, drop down into a lower gear when encountering a sharp incline, but use the higher gear when you level back out and increase speed. Your car usually tells you when it's struggling, so pay attention, read your owner's manual, and become a driving pro. (Refer to Chapter 16 for information on shifting gears.)

Simple Checks Come First

If you think you are having an automatic transmission problem and haven't changed your fluid and filter in a while, go ahead and have your technician do that maintenance work. This could fix a number of symptoms that may seem like a big problem but are caused by a clogged transmission filter. Be sure to use the correct automatic transmission fluid (ATF) as specified in your owner's manual. A different type of ATF can change the way a transmission shifts or cause it not to shift at all. Another relatively inexpensive repair is a band adjustment. When gears start slipping but the fluid is okay, often all you need to do is have a transmission specialist set the bands back to factory specifications. Fluid replacement and band adjustment are typically the only two maintenance procedures for automatic transmissions.

If you think you are having issues with your manual transmission, most often the clutch is responsible. Here are some common problems and their troubleshooting tips:

- **Clutch slips.** If you have a clutch cable with a manual adjustment instead of a hydraulic system, you may be able to adjust the cable length to eliminate the slippage. You will need to find the adjustment device, which is usually a locknut or wing nut with some type of retainer. It is usually located on the throw-out fork, which emerges from the bell housing behind or beside the transmission or transaxle. The cable should have some slack. If it is very tight, loosen it until there is about a half inch of free play at the clutch pedal. If this stopped the slipping, you should be okay for a while; otherwise, you will probably need a new clutch. (For more information, see the section "Clutch Maintenance" later in this chapter.)

◆ **Stiff clutch pedal.** This can be caused by several things. The most common cause is a cable hanging up in its housing. It may simply need some lubricant sprayed into the housing. Or the cable may be fraying and needs to be replaced. Other possible, but less probable, causes include stiff pivot points on the pedal arm and interference in the travel of the throw-out arm.

◆ **Clutch pedal sticks to the floor during speed shift.** Your clutch may be overcentering. You need to reduce the cable pull so the clutch pedal will only pull enough cable to disengage the clutch.

> **Speedbumps**
>
> Speed shifting is one of the most brutal techniques for a clutch. So remember: drive like a pro and go easy on your clutch!

◆ **Car makes grinding noises when shifting gears, in every gear.** First make sure the clutch cable is properly adjusted. If that doesn't cure the problem, have the technician check the pilot bearing or the throw-out bearing.

◆ **Transmission makes a rumbling or whirring sound.** If the sound disappears when the clutch pedal is pushed in, the input shaft bearing is probably wearing out. This usually indicates a transmission rebuild or replacement is necessary.

◆ **Oil spots.** If you find oil spots under your transmission, try to find the source of the leak. It could be coming from a seal or cover plate gasket.

 **Auto-Biography**

> Transmission cases seldom crack unless they are abused or strained like in auto racing.

◆ **Shifting feels stiff, especially in cold weather.** Your manual transmission fluid may be wearing out. Regular replacement of the fluid at the recommended intervals prevents shear down. The molecular structure of the lubricant is based on long polymer chains. Over time, constantly intermeshed in the gears, these chains break down and lose their lubricating properties. Use only lubricants recommended by the manufacturer when replacing your manual transmission fluid.

Speedbumps

When it comes to troubleshooting your transmission, try the simple, less expensive fixes first. Transmission work can be very expensive, and many times a quick fix is all that's needed. Do not be taken in by unscrupulous transmission shops. (Yes, they are out there!) Make sure the shop you choose has a good reputation with friends and relatives. Even then you will want to get several estimates. Ask for the worst-case-scenario estimate so you will be prepared. If they say they won't know until they get the transmission taken apart, tell them they must have some idea! If you decide to go ahead with the repair, ask for the old parts back. That way if there's any question about what was replaced, you'll have the old parts as evidence.

Remember Maintenance

With proper attention and responsible driving, the automatic transmission can last the life of your car. Check the level and condition of the fluid at the intervals recommended in your owner's manual. Transmission fluid out of the bottle or in good condition in your transmission will have a bright red, translucent appearance like cough syrup. As it ages and deteriorates, it changes color. The bright red darkens, turns purple, and then develops a darker shade of brown. Ideally you want it to be some shade of red. Older worn-out fluid will also have a burnt smell, and you may feel grit and small particles in the fluid as you rub some between your fingers.

Keep a check on your transmission fluid level. Should you need to add some fluid, add small amounts at a time. Never overfill, as this can cause damage to your transmission. (See Chapter 4 for a complete description on checking automatic transmission fluid.)

When it's time for a drain and fill for your transmission, the standard procedure replaces at best about 60 percent of the fluid. The rest of the fluid remains in components like the torque converter and valve body, along with a multitude of fluid passages. The transmission manufacturer has taken this into account when deciding on the replacement intervals. Should you go too long between fluid changes or other symptoms suggest a complete fluid change might be beneficial, a service center can do a complete change using a transmission flusher. This is more expensive, so try to keep to the suggested replacement schedule.

Manual Transmission Maintenance

Manual transmissions are simpler to maintain than automatic transmissions. Replace the fluid every 30,000 miles or when your owner's manual recommends. However, if the manual recommends replacing after 60,000 miles, ask your trusted auto technician for his opinion and why he suggests that time span. Check your owner's manual to see whether your car has front-wheel drive (FWD) or rear-wheel drive (RWD) and then decide whether you want to try replacing the fluid or give the job to your technician.

On RWD cars, getting to the fill plug and putting oil into the gearbox can be a little awkward. On FWD cars with transverse mounted engines, the fill and drain plugs are usually accessible. It isn't much different than changing engine oil.

CarLogic _____

To keep your drive train system healthy, have the entire system lubricated yearly.

Maintenance for Other Drive Train Components

If you have an FWD car, the engine and transaxle complete the drive train. If you have an RWD car, in addition to the engine and transmission, you have a driveshaft and differential/rear axle to complete the drive train. The driveshaft will have universal joints at each end that may be sealed with permanent lubrication or may have grease fittings that need periodic attention. The differential will require attention similar to a manual transmission. If you have an all-wheel or four-wheel-drive vehicle, you will have a second differential and transfer cases that again require attention similar to manual transmissions. Check your owner's manual for the maintenance guidelines for your car's drive train. Draining and filling any of these components is similar to changing the engine oil.

Clutch Maintenance

Cars with manual transmissions use either hydraulics (which use fluid) or a cable to operate the clutch from the clutch pedal. Check your owner's manual to see whether your vehicle has a hydraulic clutch. If it does, check that fluid monthly to ensure that the clutch reservoir is full and there aren't any leaks. Here's how:

1. Turn off the engine and raise the hood. Check for the clutch reservoir, a small plastic container located close to the back of the engine compartment. It looks like the brake-fluid reservoir, only smaller. It is usually mounted on top of the clutch master cylinder or remotely on the firewall on the driver's side. And remember before working under the hood to always observe safety rules: wear gloves and safety glasses.

2. After you find the clutch reservoir, check the fluid level. It should be filled to the top.

3. Add brake fluid if it's low and replace the cap. There is no such thing as clutch fluid. You use brake fluid in the clutch reservoir.

4. Check again in a week to make sure the fluid level hasn't dropped. If that is the case, check the master cylinder, slave cylinder (device that by hydraulic force disengages the clutch), and hydraulic line for leaks.

If you drive like a pro, making efficient shifts between gears, the clutch in your car will last 100,000 miles. It is a component that is designed to wear during use, so replacement should eventually be expected. If you engage in such driving behaviors as riding the clutch or speed shifting, you will need to replace your clutch much sooner. Most newer cars with clutch cables have self-adjusting mechanisms. They keep the cable at proper adjustment through normal use. You can check the adjustment by lifting the clutch pedal with your toe. If you hear a click, that's the ratchet mechanism in the self-adjuster. When the cable breaks or stretches beyond its functional length, replacement is often a simple matter of snapping one end of the cable housing assembly into the throw-out arm and snapping the other end into the adjuster.

> **Speedbumps**
>
> Moisture causes corrosion of the clutch hydraulic parts just like it does to your brake system, so keeping an eye on the fluid level is a good idea.

If you have an older car with a cable that requires manual adjustment, just follow the troubleshooting suggestions at the beginning of the chapter under "Simple Checks Come First."

The Least You Need to Know

◆ You may not be able to work on the drive train system, but knowing how it works will help you keep it healthy.

◆ Lubrication is good for this system.

◆ Checking the transmission fluid level and changing fluid and filter regularly could save you money.

◆ There are hydraulic and cable clutches; check your owner's manual to see which your car has.

◆ Get several estimates before you have your transmission repaired.

Chapter 18

Brake System

In This Chapter

- ◆ The most important safety system in your car
- ◆ The components of the brake system
- ◆ How your brakes work
- ◆ Easy does it!

Each system in your car needs to be monitored, but the brake system is unique. If it malfunctions, you are in serious trouble. That said, your car is a remarkable invention. Each year's models become safer and more high-tech. Computers will someday link car systems such as the engine system and brake system. Just imagine a virtual bumper that senses an object behind you—but out of your range of vision—and cuts the engine. Futuristic cars may very well be able to tell you when a system needs your attention. We aren't there yet, but today's cars are equipped with backup systems making total brake failure unlikely. Still, understanding how the brake system works and keeping it in good repair will help ensure your safety.

It's always a good idea to know what your car is trying to tell you. Usually your brakes give signs when something isn't quite right. And even the most distracted among us notice things like a difference in brake-pedal firmness or a chirping sound. But knowing what is causing the change or noise may be a mystery. In this chapter, we'll explain what makes up your brake

system and give you a tour of all its parts. (We'll cover troubleshooting and maintenance in Chapter 19, including a list of warning signs that indicate you need to have
your brakes checked.)

A Tour of Your Brake System

When Vyv first started driving, she, of course, knew all about the brake system in her
car. There was a pedal that she pushed down with her right foot and the car stopped!
Pretty strong legs, huh? But let's face it, not even power squats would grant enough
leg power to stop a 2,460-pound Mazda RX-7 at 60 mph. So grab a cup of coffee and
we'll tell you what really happens when you step on the brake pedal.

The parts that make up the modern brake system work according to a theory. They
turn motion into heat. Scientifically speaking, what happens is kinetic energy (motion)
is converted into thermal energy (heat). Heat is generated between the friction surfaces of your vehicle's brake pads and rotors (disc brakes) or brake shoes and drum
(drum brakes).

Most modern cars are equipped with dual-circuit hydraulic brakes. This system makes
total brake failure unlikely. Still, as car owners, knowing about this important system
is smart for at least two reasons: 1) unlikely doesn't mean never; and 2) knowledge will
help you know how to keep your brake system functioning correctly.

Dual-circuit hydraulic brakes are like having Plan B if Plan A fails. Most cars are
equipped with a brake warning light located on the dashboard. You'll notice all dashboard lights on when you start your car, but they should go off very shortly thereafter.
If the brake light doesn't come on, that's a bad sign, because it comes on to check
the brake system (you need to have this checked out by a technician ASAP). If the
light doesn't go off, that's an alert. First check to see whether your parking brake is
engaged. If not, the alert could mean you've lost brake pressure in half of your brake
system. If you are driving and the brake light comes on, you should still be able to
stop because of Plan B, but it is time to pull over and call for help.

Auto-Biography

Humankind learned the importance of halting a moving object shortly after
a caveman shoved a wheel down a hill and right into his cave, knocking over the missus' favorite mud vase. Was his explanation "Sorry, hon, no brakes!"?
Well, not quite, but you can imagine he found out somewhat painfully he'd have to find
a way to control forward momentum. The theory was to create enough friction against
the wheel to eventually cease motion. It was trial and error—and there were a good
many errors. The first recorded auto accident was in 1770 when an inventor named
Joseph Cugnot crashed his steam-powered car into a stone wall. Ouch!

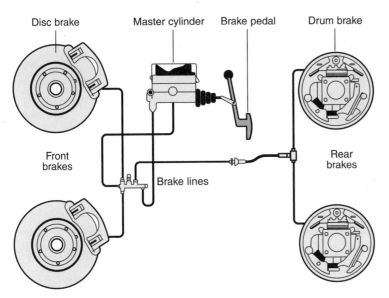

The three forces that work together to stop your car are leverage, hydraulics, and friction. Leverage comes into play when you depress the brake pedal. The master cylinder holds hydraulic fluid that sends fluid to the disc or drum brake. The fluid is forced into the caliper (disc brake) and wheel cylinder (drum brake) to create the friction that stops your car.

Major Components of the Brake System

- Master cylinder
- Hydraulic pressure
- Brake lines
- Brake fluid
- Brake shoes
- Brake pads

- Brake drums
- Rotor
- Disc brake
- Drum brake
- Power brake booster
- Backing plate

- Wheel cylinder
- Return springs
- Self-adjuster

Your Brake System in a Nutshell

Most cars today are outfitted with disc brakes on front wheels and either disc or drum brakes on rear wheels. (Some new high-end vehicles are equipped with front and rear disc brakes.) Disc brakes permit you to slow or stop your vehicle using hydraulic pressure to press frictional pads against a disc. Drum brakes slow or stop your car when brake shoes lined with frictional material are pressed, by hydraulic pressure, against the inside of a rotating drum.

The drum brake was invented in 1902. Do brakes wear shoes? Well, not exactly sling-backs, more like steel-toed work boots with asbestos-like inner soles, which were then mechanically operated with levers and cables. In the 1930s, mechanical systems gave way to the hydraulic system where brake shoes were activated by oil-pressured pistons. Inventive minds came to the rescue again when it became increasingly apparent that drum brakes had limitations: the shoes in drum brakes are subject to wear and need to be adjusted regularly. They also aren't good swimmers, losing most of their friction when linings become wet on a flooded road. So in the 1960s and 1970s, brake drums on the front wheels of cars were replaced with more expensive but less worrisome disc brakes.

Today's cars are also usually equipped with power-brake boosters. This mechanism, which works off engine vacuum or unused engine power, increases the force applied to the pistons in the master cylinder. This makes it easier to depress the brake pedal. Your brakes are linked by tubes and hoses that join the brake at each wheel of the four wheels on your car to the master cylinder. The master cylinder is a vital part of your brake system. It features a reservoir filled with brake fluid. Brake fluid is forced through brake lines when you press the brake pedal.

Still with me? Great.

When you step on the brake pedal, that pressure is like your index finger on the trigger of a squirt gun. You are pushing a plunger against the master cylinder. The master cylinder is located under the hood and is connected to the brake pedal. The plunger pushes brake fluid through steel tubes (to rear wheels) and rubber hoses (to front wheels) all the way to the brake on each wheel. Brake fluid is a liquid, so it can't be compressed, which makes for a smooth ride through all the nooks and crannies of the system.

How the Brake System Works: Parts with Visuals

Come closer and see how the brake system is put together. Can you even imagine all the patents and inventions it took throughout history to create the automobile? Well, the first automobile was the product of 100,000 patents. How cool is that!

Master Cylinder

Finding the main component of the brake system, the master cylinder, isn't difficult. You've probably already noticed it. It's close to the engine. Your master cylinder has a split personality. That is, two separate master cylinders abide in one unit. Each master cylinder handles two wheels, and that's great for you. Why? Well, because if one side fails, you can still stop the car. The brake warning light on the dash will light up if either side of the master cylinder fails, letting you know of a possible brake-fluid pressure problem.

Brake Fluid

The brake fluid reservoir is on top of the master cylinder. The reservoir will most likely be clear so you can see the fluid level.

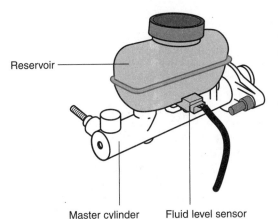

Reservoir

Master cylinder   Fluid level sensor

The plastic tank is a reservoir where the brake fluid is stored. The sensor, an electronic component, tells you when brake fluid is low by flashing a warning on your dashboard.

Brake Lines

Brake fluid travels on a journey from the master cylinder to the wheels through sturdy flexible hoses and steel tubes. The hoses and tubes are referred to as brake lines. Rubber hoses are used at the front wheels. Flexibility is needed for steering, so rubber hoses are needed there, but they're not needed for the entire journey. Steel tubes are incorporated in the remainder of the system.

Combination Valve

Your combination valve is a proportioning valve and a pressure differential valve combination. Confused? Well, let's see whether we can simplify that just a bit. A proportioning valve in a hydraulic system reduces pressure to the rear wheels. This allows a smoother stop. The pressure differential valve is used to turn on a dash warning light if the pressure drops in either part of the system.

Disc Brakes

Disc brakes give you fewer headaches than drum brakes. You don't have to replace them as often, and water immersion isn't much of a problem. The major parts on disc brakes are brake pads (made of metal with friction lining), rotors (which are also called discs and are made of iron), and calipers. You'll find two brake pads on each caliper. A caliper (as you can see in the following illustration) is not circular like the rotor (disc). Its job is to slow or stop your vehicle when you depress the brake pad. How? Well, it clips onto the disc with frictional pads on either side of the disc. You activate the hydraulic system by depressing the brake pedal. This causes brake fluid to move through brake lines and hoses until it reaches the wheel housing. The pressurized fluid then pushes a piston out (housed in the caliper) that causes the pads to press against the rotor. That friction slows or stops your vehicle.

Brake pads are situated in a caliper. The pads are pressed hydraulically against the disc. Friction causes the disc and wheel to slow or stop your vehicle.

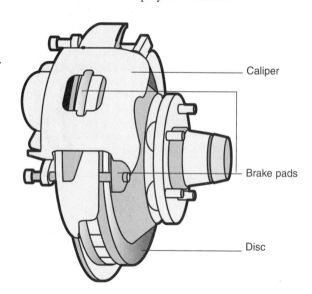

Caliper

Brake pads

Disc

Drum Brakes

The major players in your drum brakes are the backing plate (holds the drum brake together), brake shoes (a steel shoe with friction material lining), brake drum (made of iron with a machined surface where the shoes hit), and wheel cylinder (cylinder that has two pistons, one on each side). Drum brakes, like disc brakes, are engaged by hydraulics and work in a similar fashion except that drum brakes have shoes instead of calipers. When you depress the brake pedal, pressurized fluid goes through brake lines and forces pistons out, which press the shoe against the drum to slow or stop your car.

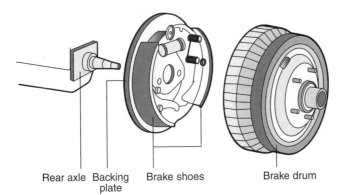

The friction caused by brake shoes pressing against a moving drum connected to the vehicle's wheel causes the car to slow or stop.

Rear axle Backing plate   Brake shoes   Brake drum

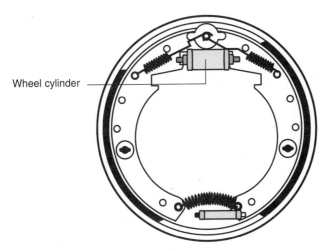

A wheel cylinder has two pistons. The pistons are forced out by brake fluid when you depress the brake pedal.

Wheel cylinder

Parking Brake

A parking brake is usually mechanical, not hydraulic. There is a lever or pedal in your vehicle which you pull or step on to engage the parking brake. The pedal or lever is connected to steel cables. This is good because in the event of brake failure, your vehicle can be brought to a stop by initiating the parking brake. Now that's an important bit of information to remember!

Speedbumps

Your parking brake (also referred to as emergency brake) needs regular attention. Even if you have an automatic transmission and never use the parking brake, you never know when you might need to use it as a backup to the hydraulic brake system. When the parking brake is seldom used, it may not release when applied because of stiff or corroded cables. Using the parking brake at least weekly helps keep the cables in good working condition.

Power-Brake Booster

The power-brake booster is situated on the part of your vehicle that separates the under-the-hood area from the passenger/driver area, or the firewall. Look directly behind the master cylinder. The power booster increases available foot pressure (when you depress the brake pedal) applied to the brake pedal so that the amount of pressure needed (by you) to stop your vehicle is much less. But that doesn't mean you can stop doing your power squats!

Antilock Brakes

When you must stop quickly to avoid hitting something, your wheels can lock and put you into a skid. This can be due to a mechanical problem or loss of traction, but either way, brake lockup is not a good thing. However, sometimes you brake hard, which can cause your wheels to lock and put your vehicle in a skid. And let's face it: we've all had those moments when we pressed the brake pedal almost six feet under. Panic will do that to a soul! When this happens, it takes longer to stop your vehicle. You have to take your foot off the brake pedal, and if you do you'll probably hit what made you tense up and brake heavily anyway, so you wind up losing control and in a skid. But antilock brakes help avoid this. You also lose control of steering when your brakes lock up; not to mention you leave rubber on the road, in the form of skid marks, that should still be on your tires.

The antilock brake system (ABS), which about 80 percent of today's cars have, was invented to help prevent brake lockup. This system has a microprocessor that knows the speed of each wheel. The microprocessor controls brake fluid pressure to each wheel. In other words, each wheel gets just the amount of fluid (pressure) it needs to stop without lockup. The system is not magic, however. It won't prevent every skid or lockup. You will need to learn how to use an ABS properly. You don't pump these brakes, but instead apply steady pressure to the brake pedal and keep driving. The microprocessor will do the rest. Practicing braking in an empty parking lot is not a bad idea until you get the hang of your car's ABS.

There are four main components in your ABS:

♦ **Speed sensors.** The antilock braking system needs some way of knowing when a wheel is about to lock up. The speed sensors, which are located at each wheel, or in some cases in the differential, provide this information.

♦ **Valves.** There is a valve in the brake line of each brake controlled by the ABS. On some systems, the valve has three positions. In position one, the valve is open; pressure from the master cylinder is passed right through to the brake. In position two, the valve blocks the line, isolating that brake from the master cylinder. This prevents the pressure from rising further should the driver push the brake pedal harder. In position three, the valve releases some of the pressure from the brake.

♦ **Pump.** Since the valve is able to release pressure from the brakes, there has to be some way to put that pressure back. That is what the pump does; when a valve reduces the pressure in a line, the pump is there to get the pressure back up.

♦ **Controller.** The controller is a computer in the car. It watches the speed sensors and controls the valves. When the ABS system is in operation, you will feel a pulsing in the brake pedal; this comes from the rapid opening and closing of the valves. Some ABS systems can cycle up to 15 times per second.

Auto-Biography

The theory behind antilock brakes is simple. A skidding wheel (where the tire contact patch is sliding relative to the road) has less traction than a nonskidding wheel. If you have ever been stuck on ice, you know that if your wheels are spinning, you have no traction. This is because the contact patch is sliding relative to the ice. By keeping the wheels from skidding while you slow down, antilock brakes benefit you in two ways: you'll stop faster, and you'll be able to steer while you stop.

Brake Easy

Learn to conserve your brake system like NASCAR's Tony Stewart. The 500-lap Martinsville track (the shortest track on the NASCAR circuit) has drivers braking hard twice a lap, which equals 1,000 times during a race. So braking easy during the first part of the race conserves the braking system for the end of the race, when Stewart is going for the win.

Although a passenger car won't be put through the stress of braking hard like a race car on a racetrack shorter than one mile in length, learning to brake easy is still a good lesson. Don't ride your brakes. Anticipate braking situations so you don't have to apply more pressure than is really needed. Being gentle to your brake system will keep it in good shape for the long haul.

The Least You Need to Know

- Your brake system is the most important safety system in your car.

- Become familiar with the major components of your brake system and learn to look for any warning signs to keep the system and yourself healthy.

- Most cars today either have disc brakes all around or disc brakes on the front wheels and drum brakes on the rear.

- Use your parking brake even if you have an automatic transmission. This keeps cables free of corrosion. It might come in handy one day should you have complete brake failure.

- Conserve your brakes by learning to brake easy.

Brake System: Troubleshooting and Maintenance

In This Chapter

♦ Reading the signs of trouble from your brake pedal

♦ Checking the brake system

♦ Checking the level of brake fluid

♦ Bleeding the hydraulic system

♦ Checking the drum and disc brakes

♦ Checking the wheel bearings, parking brake, and antilock brakes

In Chapter 18, we told you about the brake system in your car and why it is so important to keep it in good repair. We also discussed the different types of brake designs and the parts that make them work. Remember, even though your brakes have a dual master cylinder that works double time to keep your brakes from failing, you still need to keep eyes and ears on this very important vehicle system.

The fact is, even today's reliable brakes need occasional attention. It is always good to be prepared just in case something does go wrong with your braking system. Thinking out a scenario before it happens will help you in the event that "what if" becomes reality. In this chapter, we'll look at some maintenance checks you can do to maintain your brakes. Since your brake system is such an important part of your car and repairs have to be made perfectly to ensure your safety, we suggest brake-repair work be done by your technician.

Braking News: What Your Brake Pedal Is Trying to Tell You

Let's walk through some common "my brake pedal feels funny" scenarios, and the things you or your auto technician might need to check:

- **When you depress the brake pedal, the car slows but doesn't stop properly and then rolls a little.** Here are some things you can check: brake fluid—if it's low, fill to the marked level; master cylinder—if it leaks, replace master cylinder if necessary; air in the hydraulic system—bleed hydraulic system; brake pads or brake shoes—if they're worn, replace brake pads or shoes.

- **You find it is difficult to depress the brake pedal.** Look for the possible culprit here: bad power brake booster—replace; no vacuum to power brake booster—inspect and replace vacuum line; brake line is pinched—replace brake line; miscellaneous items that may have rolled or bunched up behind the brake pedal.

- **You have the dreaded brake pedal "fade."** When you depress the brake pedal, the pedal goes even farther down the more you depress the pedal, such as in heavy traffic with lots of starts and stops. Why? If you've just had your brakes redone, make sure they gave you the right kind and a reputable brand; brakes may have worn component parts—replace; restricted airflow may be caused by brake dust; you may have contaminated brake fluid—flush and replace; or you might have a leak in the brake hydraulic system—find and fix leak.

- **When you step on the brake pedal, the pedal goes too far down before the brakes apply.** Why? Brake fluid is very low—check fluid level in the master cylinder and fill to the Full level; brake fluid is contaminated with water, or has the wrong type of brake fluid—flush and replace; air in the hydraulic system—bleed hydraulic system; brake pads or brake shoes worn out—replace brake pads or shoes as required; bad power brake booster or booster check valve—replace power brake booster or check valve.

◆ **The parking brake won't release.** What's going on? As we mentioned in Chapter 18, you need to engage the parking brake weekly whether needed or not to keep the parts moving freely. The parking brake cables may be frozen—replace parking brake cables; parking brake linkage may need lubrication—lubricate; broken parking brake part inside rear brakes—repair or replace broken parts.

◆ **Your brake pedal feels soft or "mushy," not firm.** You could have a leak in a brake line or hose—replace; air bubbles in the hydraulic system—bleed hydraulic system; brake fluid is contaminated with water, or has the wrong type of brake fluid—flush and replace; brake pads or brake shoes are worn out—replace.

◆ **The brakes "grab," even when you brake lightly.** Does your car seem to drift to the left or right? Have you experienced a wheel lock-up? It usually happens suddenly but may get worse over time. Your parking brake may be on or stuck—release or check for damage; brake pads or brake shoes are worn out—replace the brake pads or shoes as required; bad front disc caliper or rear drum brake wheel cylinder—replace or rebuild both front calipers. Replace or rebuild both rear wheel cylinders.

◆ **The brake pedal begins to vibrate.** The brake rotors or brake drums, depending on what your car is equipped with, may be warped—machine (which is turning a drum or a rotor on a machine or lathe to cut away surface irregularities) or replace front-disc brake rotors or rear drums (most cars are equipped with disc brakes on the front and drum brakes on the rear); check for loose or broken front-end steering parts—replace any loose or broken parts; lug nuts loose—tighten all lug nuts (check owner's manual or ask how tight your lug nuts should be); wheels or tires are out of balance—have wheels/tires balanced; wheels are bent—replace; worn or defective tires—replace; loose or bad front wheel bearings—replace bad wheel bearings and repack and retighten loose wheel bearings.

CarLogic

If your car has antilock brakes (ABS), you may notice a pulsation in the brake pedal while you are braking during slippery road conditions. This is the electro-hydraulic control unit doing its job. It is controlling and adjusting brake-line pressure to each of the four wheels. Continue braking as usual and let the ABS optimize the braking conditions.

◆ **When you accelerate, it feels like you are being held back.** Do you smell something burning? First check to make sure your parking brake isn't engaged, or it may need adjusting if it is too tight. Then check for broken or loose parts inside your rear brakes—repair or replace.

◆ **Brakes are locking up.** A press of the brake pedal grants a vehicle that seems to turn sharply either left or right and without your permission. Brake pads or shoes may be loose or broken—replace; front disc caliper or rear drum brake wheel cylinder may be worn or defective—replace or rebuild both front calipers and replace or rebuild both rear wheel cylinders; loose or bad front wheel bearings—replace; repack and retighten loose wheel bearings.

◆ **When you step on the brakes, you hear a screeching or squealing or scraping noise.** This noise may come and go or remain constant. The car may or may not pull to one side when the brakes are applied. Dirt or brake dust may have gotten on the pads or shoes—clean and sand brake pads or shoes and rotors or drums; brake pads or shoes are worn out—replace; brake pads or shoes and rotors or drums are glazed due to overheating—clean and sand brake pads or shoes and rotors or drums; audible wear indicators are contacting the rotors letting you know it's time for a brake repair—replace.

Speedbumps

You can ride a horse, ride a motorcycle, or ride a train, but you cannot ride your brakes. Why? Because leaving your foot on your brake pedal will wear your brakes out prematurely. Another way to conserve your brakes is to anticipate stops. Jamming your foot down on the brake pedal is not good for your brakes. Also keep in mind that antilock brake systems have a unique personality. Read about them and get used to braking with them. Make sure you use a firm push down and not a pump, especially when the roads are slippery.

Let's Check Your Brake System

Estimations are great to kick around in your head. It is estimated that you should check your brake system every 10,000 to 20,000 miles. Then again, some experts give specific mileage milestones and others say there really isn't a specific timetable. However, by checking your fluid level you'll be one step ahead of leaks or low brake fluid–inspired problems.

Worn-out brake components are another matter. So what you might want to do is take that brake-check estimate and factor in the life your vehicle has led. If your vehicle has a checkered past—meaning if it has had a driver (drivers) who rides the brakes, or who brakes suddenly; if it's constantly in stop-and-go traffic; or if your vehicle is super-sized—these factors weigh heavily on how long your brakes will last. If your vehicle's brake system is put at a disadvantage with these driving habits or characteristics (you can change at least two of these), be more aware of any changes when braking and have the system checked out every 10,000 miles or upon noticeable differences.

It's time to have your brakes worked on when your brake linings are worn down to the minimum acceptable thickness. Your owner's manual and technician can tell you that number. Also, of course, you'll need to examine your brakes' parts if you are experiencing symptoms from your brake pedal. Usually the front brakes wear out before the ones on the rear, because the front brakes handle a higher percentage of the braking load.

Checking Brake Fluid Level

As noted in Chapter 18, brake fluid is stored in your master cylinder. Visualize your brake master cylinder. It's a small rectangular piece of metal with metal tubes running out of it. A plastic reservoir with a rubber cap sits on top of the metal housing. You'll find your vehicle's master cylinder located under the hood on the driver's side of the car. If you have a pre-1980s vehicle, the master cylinder may be made entirely of metal. Newer-model cars usually have plastic brake fluid containers. It's easier to check the fluid level in the plastic reservoirs, because you don't have to open the container. If you have the metal-type master cylinder, the top will probably be held on with metal clamps and you'll need a screwdriver to pop off the clamps and lift the lid.

The fluid should be up to the Full line. If you find this is not the case, buy brake fluid and replenish to the Full line, making sure you do not get any dirt, lint, or anything except brake fluid in the master cylinder. You will want to close the master cylinder container ASAP so moisture won't be allowed in either.

 CarLogic

While you are working around the master cylinder, be sure to check it for cracks or leaks. You should check the health of your master cylinder every two months.

Fill the brake reservoir with brake fluid. Check the fluid level in the reservoir after bleeding each wheel. Add fluid if necessary.

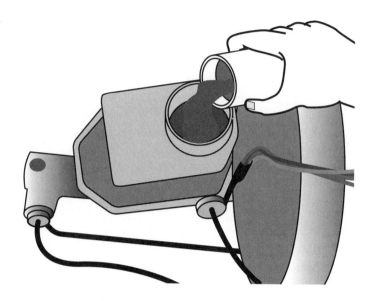

Bleeding the Brake System

Bleeding the hydraulic system is necessary to remove any air that may have entered the system during low fluid levels in the reservoir, or when the system was opened for repair or replacement of any brake component. Should air be entering through a leaky brake line, that line should be replaced before proceeding. Air is a compressible gas that contributes to a spongy feel in the brake pedal. Bleeding the brakes will purge the system of any air that has formed bubbles in the brake fluid. There are several techniques for bleeding brakes dependent on the design of the calipers and whether or not you have ABS. Refer to a repair manual written specifically for your car to find the correct procedure for your car. Unless you are a fairly advanced do-it-yourselfer, flushing and bleeding brake systems should be left to an ASE-certified professional.

Checking Drum and Disc Brakes

Brakes and tires are the most important parts of your car in terms of your and your passengers' safety. If you decide to work on your brakes, do so with the utmost diligence. Be aware that older and less-expensive pads and shoes can be lined with asbestos. The fine dust that coats the brake components at each wheel should not be inhaled. As soon as the drum is pulled or the rotor is exposed, all components should be soaked with brake cleaner to contain the dust. Be sure to observe all safety measures, including wearing a filter mask, goggles, and gloves.

While the designs of most drum brakes are similar, there are differences in attachment techniques and sequences of assembly and disassembly. When replacing shoes, you should also replace the springs and hardware. These parts are inexpensive and do suffer from metal fatigue caused by the heating and cooling cycles of normal operation.

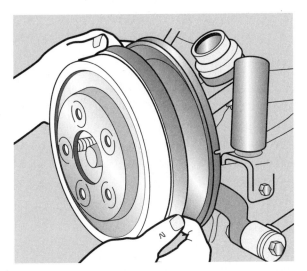

Removing the rear brake drum.

Checking Disc Brake Pads for Wear

Checking disc brake pads for wear is as easy as removing the wheel and looking into the inspection hole on the back of the caliper enough to determine how much brake lining is left. Just how much lining represents minimum recommended thickness varies with the manufacturer, but those states which have mandatory periodic safety inspections generally have their own minimum brake lining thickness specification to determine when the brake pads (or shoes) need to be replaced. You have to remove the brake pads and measure the lining thickness with a micrometer to be sure, but as a general rule of thumb, if you don't see at least $\frac{1}{32}$ inch (about 0.3 mm) of lining, it's time to replace the pads.

If you notice that one brake pad is worn more than the other, you could have a problem with the caliper that requires an overhaul or complete replacement. You may want to leave this job to your technician. However, replacing the brake pads in the caliper is relatively easy and usually doesn't require bleeding the system. Consult your model-specific service manual for the exact replacement procedure for your car.

Checking Drum Brake Shoes for Wear

Checking the rear drum brakes for wear is a bit more complicated. Again, jack up the vehicle, support it safely, and remove the rear wheel. Depending on your car model, removing the rear brake drum can be as easy as pulling the drum off with your hands. However, under most conditions, you'll have to turn a small wheel with a screwdriver or brake adjustment tool to retract the brake shoes slightly so the drum can be easily removed. Do not try to pry or beat the brake drum off with a hammer. If you look at the back of the drum brake assembly, you'll notice a small oval-shaped hole at the bottom. This is the brake adjustment port. It may have a rubber plug that has to be removed. Use a flashlight to look through this small hole and you'll see a toothed gear facing edge-on toward the hole. Use the tip of a flat blade screwdriver, or a brake adjustment tool that looks like a small crowbar, to rotate the wheel either up or down a notch at a time to back off the brake shoes. Rotate the brake drum while you're turning the adjustment gear. If you're turning it in the right direction, the drum will continue to turn freely and should slide off easily after a few turns of the adjusting wheel. If the drum appears to be held even more firmly, or feels like the brakes are being applied, reverse the adjustment direction.

Once you remove the brake drum, you'll see the whole brake shoe assembly. Again, look at the lining thickness on the front and rear shoes. If the shoes have rivets, that $\frac{1}{32}$-inch rule previously mentioned applies to the amount of brake shoe material left above the rivet hole. If the shoes are bonded (no rivets) then you should have at least $\frac{1}{32}$-inch thickness of brake material on the metal shoe. Again, both front and rear shoes should be about the same thickness if the brakes are working properly. Remember that the front and rear shoes have different lengths of brake material on them. This is perfectly normal.

Note that you'll get a lot more brake dust when you remove a drum brake. Avoid inhaling any of this dust and wash the assembly with brake cleaner or water to remove the dust. A particle mask is a good idea when doing this type of inspection. Once you replace the drum, you'll have to readjust the brake shoes. Turn the wheel until the brake drum just begins to drag on the shoes, and then back off one click on the adjuster. Again, consult your service manual for the specific procedure for your vehicle.

While the principle of operation is the same for all calipers, the design of the specific calipers varies greatly. When replacing pads, pay particular attention to lubrication points, retainer springs, and squeal-inhibiting procedures.

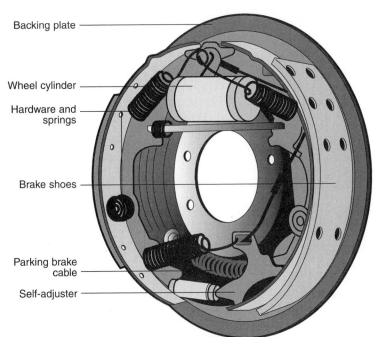

Backing plate

Wheel cylinder

Hardware and springs

Brake shoes

Parking brake cable

Self-adjuster

Typical drum brake assembly.

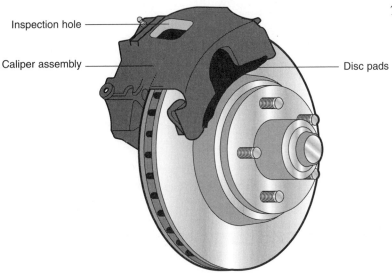

Inspection hole

Caliper assembly

Disc pads

Typical disc brake assembly.

CarLogic _____

If you have any reluctance or doubts about working on your brakes, leave the job to the professionals. If you decide to do the work yourself, before you attempt any repair on drum or disc brakes, get a repair manual specifically written for your car. The illustrations detailing all of the springs and the step-by-step procedures, as well as the caliper mounting bolts, guide pins, and lubrication points, will be invaluable.

Check Wheel Bearings

In most cases, wheel bearings will not need attention until the brakes are serviced. However, the bearings should be checked whenever the wheels are raised off the ground. With the vehicle securely supported on jack stands, spin each wheel, checking for noise, rolling resistance, and free play. Let the wheel come to a stop. Grab the top of the wheel with one hand and the bottom of the wheel with the other. Pull and push the wheel. If there is any noticeable movement, the bearings should be checked and repacked with grease or replaced.

The procedures for servicing wheel bearings vary by manufacturer and whether your car has front-wheel, rear-wheel, or all-wheel drive. Front and rear bearings have different techniques. There are many different procedures for the final torque of the axle nut. There are a few tools needed that may not be in your toolbox, and the procedure will probably take you a while, especially the first time. Use a repair manual like Haynes or Chilton for your car to see exactly what is involved (see Appendix C for information on ordering). You may decide this is best left to the technicians.

Wheel bearing.

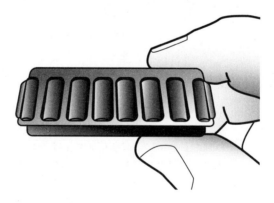

Adjust the Parking Brake

The parking brake or emergency brake is mechanically operated by cables and is independent of the hydraulic system. These brakes may be simply a mechanical operation of the rear shoes in drum brakes or they may have their own drums integrated into the rear rotors. Some cars use the front brakes or a drum incorporated about the drive shaft. There are a variety of configurations of cables and adjustment techniques. It's best to read a service or repair manual to find the proper technique for your car.

The cables and adjustment devices often sit under the car where they are constantly exposed to water and road grime. Use the parking brake regularly to keep it from seizing, and put some grease on the threads of the adjusters to keep them from seizing.

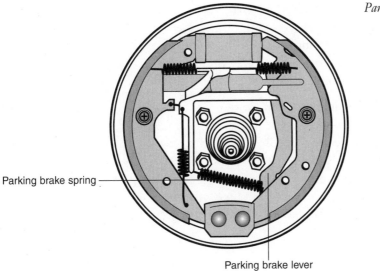

Parking brake.

Parking brake spring

Parking brake lever

Check Antilock Brakes

If the antilock brake (ABS) warning light comes on and stays on, first make sure the parking brake is released and then make sure there is no problem with the brake hydraulic system. If neither of these is the cause, the ABS system is probably malfunctioning. Although special equipment and test procedures are necessary to properly diagnose the problem, you can perform a few preliminary checks before taking the vehicle to a brake specialist:

♦ Make sure the brakes, including calipers and wheel cylinders, are in good condition.

♦ Check the electrical connections at the electro-hydraulic control unit.

♦ Check the fuses.

♦ Trace all wires to the speed sensors and to the brakelight switch, making sure that all connections are tight and there is no damage to the wiring.

If these steps do not resolve the problem, the vehicle should be checked by a brake specialist. The control unit constantly monitors the system, and a problem code will be stored that can be retrieved by the specialist.

Antilock-brake pump.

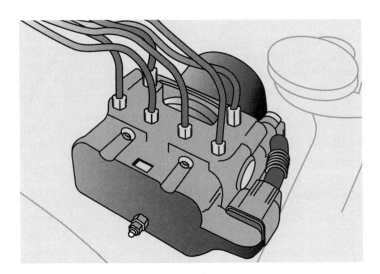

The Least You Need to Know

♦ When your brake pedal feels funny, pay close attention to the signs and tell your technician.

♦ Check your owner's manual for correct times to have your brake system checked, and then factor how large the vehicle is how and where it has been driven.

♦ Have wheel bearings checked anytime you raise your car completely off the ground.

♦ Most brake system repairs are best left to a skilled technician.

Part 3

Showing Off Your Vehicle

Ah, here's the really fun part: making that beautiful financial investment shine. Did you know that a quick peek in a book that lists values of used vehicles, like Kelley Blue Book, reveals that the difference between a vehicle in excellent condition and one in fair condition could finance a pretty wonderful vacation? This grants a bit of incentive to stick to a regular car-washing routine.

In Part 3, we'll tell you when to clean, explain why it's so important, and offer cleaning tips. we'll also tell you what products you'll need to keep around to clean your car. And yes, we'll talk about keeping your paint job sparkling when we chat about how often you should wax your car. In the next chapter, we'll discuss how to repair minor interior and exterior rips and dings. And have you ever wondered what those swirls are in your paint finish? We'll discuss that and tell you how to keep the swirls at bay. Did you know how important it is to keep your windshield clean? It's hard to drive safely when you can't see properly. A clean windshield is even more important when driving at night. And hopefully you won't be stranded often, but if you ever find yourself in that situation, you'll know what to do after reading the last chapter. So let's get started washing that car. And no fair squirting us with the water hose!

Chapter **20**

How and When to Clean

In This Chapter

- ◆ Why clean your vehicle?
- ◆ Cleaning basics and tips
- ◆ Cleaning the wheels and wheel covers
- ◆ How to clean your engine
- ◆ Waxing how-to's
- ◆ Don't forget the interior

A clean car is not only good for your psyche, it's also good for your wallet. An estimated $24 billion a year is spent battling corrosion damage. Not to mention how much more expensive it is to have a car professionally cleaned when it's too far gone to shine after a normal wash.

You don't have to spend grand amounts of time cleaning, but you do need to put cleaning your vehicle on your to-do list. Some experts recommend a once-a-week cleaning. Others say twice a month should be enough. If you can wash your car weekly, it won't be as dirty as it would be should you choose a two-week interval. So time-wise and effort-wise, once a week isn't really a lot more work than biweekly.

You can do it yourself or have it professionally done. Professional detailing jobs—expert cleaning inside and out that makes your car look like new—can run anywhere from $100 to $300—a bit pricey for weekly beauty treatments. But you can get a weekly cleaning for under $20 if you take your car to a do-it-yourself car wash. In this chapter, we'll tell you how spending Saturdays at the car wash or in your driveway is a great way to keep one of your biggest expenditures in great condition.

Why Clean?

A recent Shell survey found that most Americans are interested in how to keep their cars clean. But we aren't following up on that interest. Twenty-four percent of Americans perform some type of routine maintenance on their cars on a monthly basis, and only 18 percent clean approximately every two weeks. You can read more about our car-cleaning habits at www.shell.com/home/Framework?siteId=us-en&FC2=&FC3=/us-en/tailored/shell_for_motorists/fuels/optimax/power_tour_2707.html.

If you pay attention to celebrities who collect cars, you'll find that many times even though they could pay to have their cars cleaned (and repaired), they do those jobs themselves. Why? It may be that they aren't so sure anyone else will take care of their cars like them—for example, they use the right products and make sure the paint job is babied. And don't think for one moment mechanics don't appreciate a car that is kept in great condition and will go the extra mile to keep that car pristine. So, yes, there are many reasons to keep your car looking great!

CarLogic _____

For an eye-opener on why it's good for your bank account to keep your car clean, take a look at car pricing information from a company like National Automobile Dealers Association (NADA) or Kelley Blue Book. For example, if you were looking up a 2003 Chevrolet Tahoe (in Kelley Blue Book) with 50,000 miles described in excellent condition (good paint, pristine inside and out, and in great mechanical condition) this vehicle can be traded in for $17,800. The same Chevrolet Tahoe is valued at $14,525 in fair condition (when the paint and body need some repair, and there are minor mechanical problems).

Cleaning Basics for the Do-It-Yourselfer

It's a glorious Saturday and you're ready to wash the car. All you have to do today is turn on the faucet, because you did your homework and have all the products needed to do the job. For instance, you know you need a mild specially made car-wash soap. You bought it in the automotive department or in your local discount store's automotive department. You've read the directions and have just the right amount of soap in the bucket. And although it wasn't very expensive, you know that using too much isn't necessary to get the car clean. You cringe when you see your neighbor is just about to use regular household detergent on his brand-new shiny red sports car. There goes that beauty's waxed finish! Why don't you offer him some of your car-wash soap and tell him you've learned regular laundry soap is too harsh to use as a car wash? Maybe he'll offer you one of those beverages he has over in his cooler!

Here are the supplies you'll need to do an at-home car wash:

- Plastic wash bucket. Choose plastic over metal; if you trip over a metal bucket and it flies into your car, you've just chipped the paint—so plastic is best!

- Garden hose with a good nozzle.

- Clean cloths (such as old t-shirts), a mitt, or a sponge. Make sure the cloth, sponge, or mitt you are using is free of lint and powdered detergent residue. Rinse often. Three mitts or clean cloths are better. That way you have a cloth for the top of your car and glass (washing), a mitt for the bottom of your car, and one for tires.

- Microfiber cloth or sheepskin chamois cloth for drying.

- Commercially made car solvent for pre-wash.

- Commercially made car-wash soap (also referred to as car-wash shampoo).

- Brush for tires.

- Paint-safe brushes for between car sections and bug/tar removal.

- Polish for chrome.

- Lubricant for rubber parts.

- Protectant for leather parts.

Before you put water and soap to car, let's do a once-over of your car's surface. See any road tar? Dead bugs? It's elementary that you'll probably find road tar at the bottom of the car, but it can also splatter up, so give your paint job a good visual going-over. Look for dried bugs at the edge of hood, around headlights, and at the top of your windshield. If you find road tar, you can buy some solvent at the same place you bought your car-wash shampoo; that is, if you don't already have some. Dried bugs are common and can be removed with a well-dissolved baking soda and water mixture. (Make sure the mixture is liquid with no grittiness; otherwise you will scratch your paint finish. Try the mixture on the inside of your trunk first.) But remember, treating these areas with commercial solvents or baking soda will strip your wax, so you'll have to reapply wax to those areas after the wash.

> ### Speedbumps
>
> Read labels carefully before putting any cleaning product on your car. Your best bet is to test the product on a hidden place (trunk or door jamb) on your car before applying it to the outside.

Now, here is a bit of sad news if you are a sun worshipper. You really need to wash your car in the shade or at a time when the sun isn't so bright, like early morning or late afternoon. Why? The sun will dry your car too fast, and this can leave a soapy film or cause water spotting.

Here is a step-by-step guide to washing your car (for more in-depth information, go to autogeek.net/exterior.html):

1. Gather the supplies you'll need and park the car in a shaded area.

2. Wash the tires first. Use a product made to clean wheels and a brush or sponge just for the wheels. Do not use the same brush or sponge on the rest of the car, because it will most likely be gritty and the product you use for wheels may not be safe for your paint job. You can also use dishwasher detergent on tires, but apply a lubricant after washing to make them look great and maintain the rubber.

3. Apply solvent to remove tar, or a solution of baking soda and water to remove bugs, as needed.

4. Spray the entire car with water from top to bottom. This will remove some dirt and make the remaining grime easier to wash away.

5. Fill your bucket with less car-wash shampoo than recommended and fill the bucket with water. You will probably have to refill your bucket many times before you finish. Rule of thumb is when you are down to ¼ water in the bottom—refill. Having two plastic buckets with one containing just water for rinsing your soapy cloth each time will cut down on dirt in your soapy bucket.

6. Wash one section of the car at a time, beginning with the roof. Wash with a back-and-forth motion instead of a circular motion. (This keeps you from getting swirls in your clear-coat paint.)

7. Repeat for all areas until the entire car is washed.

8. Spray with water to rinse, including underneath your car.

9. Dry the car starting with the roof. Use a soft cloth that will not scratch your paint surface and turn the cloth many times (to find a clean section) in case the cloth picks up some dirt that will scratch your finish.

Auto-Biography

Microfiber fabric has a variety of uses today. One is drying vehicles after the wash job. Chamois is also used for this job. Professional detailers know both microfiber and chamois have common tendencies: they are soft and absorbent, and they don't leave lint. Microfiber is said to last longer than chamois. Both fabrics should be laundered according to the directions on the tag, because they are absorbent and powdered detergent can get caught in the fabric fibers, which will scratch your car's clear-coat surface. So read the laundering directions carefully.

Washing your car at home is fine if you follow certain criteria—you want to wash it on the grass so the dirty water doesn't run into storm drains. If that's not possible, the best place to wash your car is a car wash, because there, water running off your car winds up in a treatment plant. Remember, when you wash your car you are washing off chemicals that make your car run with chemicals to clean your car, and if you wash your car on your drive, all of this ends up in the storm drains, not treatment plants. So it's best to wash your vehicle at a car wash where the water goes directly to a treatment plant, or if you wash at home do so on grass.

Miscellaneous Wash Tips

Every job requires skill. And knowing the most time-efficient way to wash a car helps you do the job well and quickly. It's a good idea to check your owner's manual to see whether your car has any special finishes that require special treatment when cleaning. Here are a few more tips:

- Remember that the more often you clean your car, the easier it is and the less time it takes.

◆ If you live in an area that has hard winters, even if you can't clean your car as often as you'd like—clean it really well at the first sign of spring.

◆ Don't forget to clean the chrome and metal parts of your car. If you really want to make these parts of your car shine and keep them from rusting, check at the auto-supply store for specific polishes. Don't get polish on paint (this can cause your paint to dull), and always wax chrome and metal after cleaning it.

◆ Treat any rust spots you find using a product made for removing rust.

◆ Ragtops are not common nowadays, but if your car has one, a good vacuuming will keep the top looking good. Maintain raising and lowering mechanics by putting some lubricant on occasionally. Check the fabric for rips or tears and restitch or patch if necessary. Clean vinyl tops with mild soap and water, or pick up a commercial cleaner from your auto-supply store. Holes in vinyl can be repaired with a kit, also from the auto-supply store.

Wheels and Wheel Covers

If your car has front disc brakes, you may find your front wheels are dirtier than the back wheels. Why? Disc brakes are a little like the "Pigpen" character in the *Peanuts* comic strip who walks around in a cloud of dust. Disc brakes are constantly shedding dust particles.

Check your auto-supply store for a good wheel-cleaning product. Ask a salesperson for recommendations, and then read the directions carefully before using the product, because picking up just any product may not always be in your vehicle's best interest. For instance, some wheel-care products contain acid, so be careful not to get this product on any clear-coat surfaces. Basically, do a quick rinse—and this is where you'll want your nozzle on a higher pressure; wash your tires, rinse again, and then use the brake-dust cleaner. Next, apply a dressing to protect the rubber and make the tires look great!

Your owner's manual is not exactly a page-turner, but reading it will shed light on what you should or should not use on your car. It will tell you what kind of wheel covers you have so you can give that information to the salesperson and then you can buy a cleaner that won't harm your wheel covering (plastic wheel covers may be damaged by some cleaners).

Cleaning Your Engine

Why clean your engine? You aren't going to be showing your car at an auto show, right? Well, there are several reasons why cleaning your engine is a good idea. First of all, it's just easier to work on a clean engine, and doing your regular maintenance will be less aggravating when you aren't putting your hand in grease at every turn. Also, it's easier to identify fluid leaks on a clean engine. And if you take your car in for servicing, a mechanic can often be more thorough and accurate when working on a clean engine. Also, don't forget about the ever constant resale value. When a potential buyer pops the hood, the clean motor visual will most likely help you close the deal and at a higher price.

You can clean the engine yourself, but do your homework before you begin. If you're not comfortable about cleaning your engine, have it done professionally. Consult your owner's manual for any cleaning instructions and cautions that may apply specifically to your vehicle's engine. And remember safety rules: always wear eye protection (and a mask is not a bad idea) when using chemical cleaning agents.

Here is how you can clean your engine without damaging it, yourself, or the environment. Start by gathering the supplies you'll need. Regardless of what the label may proclaim, there are no magical cleaners that leave your engine sparkling after a spray-on and rinse-off. Choose one of the citrus-based, environmentally friendly cleaners or degreasers. Any cleaner or degreaser will require you to do some or a lot of scrubbing. Have your garden hose with fine mist nozzle ready to go.

> **Speedbumps**
>
> Never use a pressure washer to clean an engine. It can damage electrical connectors. Pressure washers like the ones at automatic car washes are not kind to your vehicle's finish. If you have a car you really want to baby, washing the vehicle at home is a good idea unless you select the gentle spray and know exactly what car-wash soap product the car wash offers.

You'll also need the following:

- ◆ Plastic drop cloth

- ◆ Large drip pan to protect your driveway and to keep the mess confined

- ◆ Narrow putty knife

- ◆ Flat blade screwdriver to scrape away the hardened grease, oil, and dirt

- Small wire brush

- Screwdriver to fit into the small recesses and tight areas

- Aluminum foil, tape, and rubber bands to cover and protect everything that should not come in contact with water

- Rubber gloves and safety goggles

Now let's prep the engine compartment for cleaning. Using the aluminum foil, cover the air filters, air inlet holes, breather caps on valve covers and oil filler tubes, and dipstick tubes for engine oil and transmission fluid. Secure the foil with the tape and rubber bands. Ignition system components and electrical components are especially vulnerable to water damage. Cover and secure the covering for the alternator, distributor, coil, electronic modules, fuse and relay boxes, connectors, and sensors. Since you will be introducing a significant amount of water around the electrical components, it would be wise to disconnect the negative battery cable. There may be a couple of minor inconveniences from disconnecting the battery. You may need to reset the security code for the radio, or the car may not run quite as it did before until the engine control module resets itself.

Now it's time to get down and dirty. Put on your safety goggles and rubber gloves. Place the plastic drop cloth under the engine or drive over it before you begin prepping the engine. Also use a large drip pan under the area you are cleaning. Start scraping away the large areas of grime, so that when you apply the degreaser it can penetrate down to the metal. After all the large thick sections have been scraped off, apply the degreaser liberally. Let it soak for a few minutes, but start scrubbing with the wire brush while it's still wet or reapply some degreaser. It will be slow, dirty, and tedious, but it is the only way to clean safely and thoroughly. When you think you've got it all, use your garden hose with the mist nozzle and rinse well. Be careful that the water and degreaser don't get splashed back at you. After rinsing off all of the dirt, you will probably find spots that you missed. Let the water dry, and repeat the process.

The drip pan under the car should have collected most of the water and grime, and the drop cloth should have caught everything else. Let the water evaporate from the pan for a few days, and you can recycle the remaining grime with the waste oil container that you use for oil changes. Let the drop cloth dry off, and you can dispose of it with your solid refuse.

Let everything dry off, and then remove the foil. Reconnect the negative cable to the battery, and you should be able to start the engine. If not, you need to search for water where it doesn't belong. Most likely it will be in the ignition system. If you took care in your protective covering, this shouldn't be a major problem. A little more drying and it should be fine.

A clean engine compartment will look better, be easier to work on, and make it easier to find leaks and other problems.

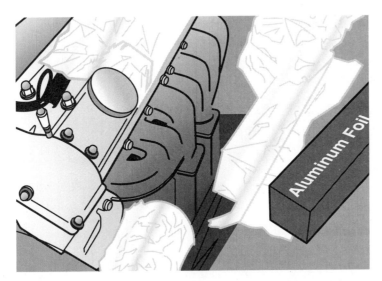

Use foil secured with tape and rubber bands to protect the alternator, distributor cap, fuse box, and wiring harnesses.

Rinse off dirt, repeating if necessary.

A paste of baking soda and water is great for cleaning battery terminals.

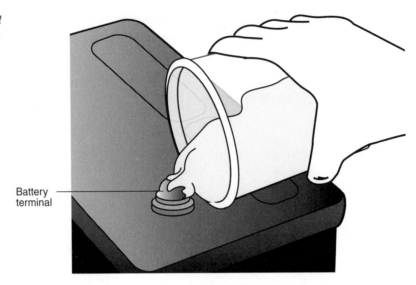

Battery terminal

Why Wax?

It's always good to know what kind of wax finish your car has. Today, approximately 97 percent of all cars, trucks, and SUVs coming out of the factory have a clear-coat finish. Clear-coats contain ultraviolet light blockers and UV light absorbers that help keep vehicle paints looking new longer by preventing oxidation.

So what does that mean in terms of cleaning your car? A clear-coat finish (also referred to as a two-stage paint system) is a layer of clear resin applied over the top of colored resin. The clear-coat finish protects the base coat. This finish needs to be regularly maintained. Weekly washings are best, and clear-coat finishes do need to be waxed at least twice a year.

Full sunlight and daily contaminants work together to rob your car of its beautiful shine. Waxing a couple times a year keeps the oil in the paint, which means it keeps the paint from oxidizing. Waxing can also remove minor surface scratches and give your car that "just off the showroom floor" look. As always, consult your owner's manual for your vehicle's precise finish and care recommendations. Ask around for the best wax product for your vehicle. Your local detailer or someone at a body shop should be able to help you.

Here are some waxing tips:

- Pick out the best wax for the job: spray, liquid, or paste (liquid or paste is recommended, with paste being the longer lasting). Park in the shade and make sure the body of your vehicle has cooled down before you begin the wax job.

- Make sure your vehicle is clean as a whistle before waxing.

- Avoid days with extreme temperatures: above 50°F and below 85°F is a good target to shoot for.

- Humid days can cause a vehicle to streak, so save the wax job for a crisp day. Scheduling spring and fall waxings might work in most parts of the United States.

- Read the directions on the wax before you begin to see how you need to apply and remove the wax. Organic waxes (like carnauba derived from a Brazilian tree) generally need to be removed rather than allowed to sit on the finish, because they harden quickly. If you do find the wax has gotten hard and not easy to wipe off, reapply a thin layer to that area and remove it quickly.

- Use the least amount of product that you possibly can. Thin layers are better, and you won't have to work so hard getting more wax off.

- Your wax can be applied by hand or by machine. A machine will give just the right amount of polish, but doesn't get into all areas—nooks and crannies—of the car. You don't have to have a machine polisher, but they are nice. However, you need to know how to use the machine so that you don't ruin your paint job. Just read the directions before using.

- Don't put water on your applicator pad. Just use wax.

- Don't apply in circular motions. Use long, straight, overlapping swipes.

- Wipe the wax off with clean microfiber cloths, terrycloth towels, or cloth diapers. Make sure any cloth you use is clean and free of lint, sand, or detergent residue.

- Wipe in both directions, turning the towels often. Have plenty of towels so if one gets caked up with wax you have another close by.

- When finished, wipe the entire vehicle again with a clean cloth, paying particular attention to the edges of trim pieces, doorjambs, and moldings where excess wax may have accumulated. Sometimes a *very* soft pastry brush and toothpicks (used with a steady, gentle hand) are needed to pick out wayward wax from small areas such as the car logo.

◆ For additional shine between wax jobs, several manufacturers offer spray-and-wipe products. Ask your trusted auto-parts salesperson.

How long your wax finish will last also depends on your car's existing paint condition. If it's not great, your best bet is to ask a professional detailer before you spend the time and money to wax your car. Also, the wax job will last longer if your vehicle isn't constantly exposed to the elements. UV exposure is a wax zapper. Keeping to a weekly cleaning schedule (done with care) will keep your wax job intact longer.

CarLogic

Organic carnauba waxes (from the Brazilian palm tree) come in paste and in liquid form. They give a deep, wet-look gloss. Carnauba wax lasts up to four months. Synthetic polymer waxes are usually liquids. In recent years polymer waxes have come a long way regarding the way they look. Polymer waxes are said to be more durable than organic carnauba waxes, but not all professional detailers agree that polymer waxes only need to be applied once a year. So waxing twice a year is still the best advice.

Cleaning Up the Interior

Now let's talk about the part of the car that you know intimately, the interior. First arm yourself with what you will need for the job. You'll need two garbage bags—one for the things you will keep that have accumulated in the car, and one for the actual garbage. If you have children, this makes sense; if not, all you may need is one garbage bag. Don't forget what may lurk under the seats.

Use lint-free towels and clear water for the dash area and seats. Cotton swabs are helpful for getting dust out of tight spots like air-conditioner vents. If you find stains on your upholstery or carpet, a stiff-bristled brush is indispensable. You may need to apply a carpet or upholstery cleaner. Ask at the auto-supply store what is best, and read the directions carefully before using. Don't spray too much—oversaturation of carpet may lead to rusting out the floor of your vehicle. For cleaning the windows, refer to Chapter 22. Now do a quick vacuum of your floor mats. Take them out and wash them if they're washable. If floor mats are carpeted, spot-clean with carpet cleaner as needed. Remember to clean under the mats as well. While the floor mats are drying, vacuum the floor, seats, and all nooks and crannies, being careful not to mark up plastic parts with the vacuum.

Using a protectant on your dash is fine and will make it look great, but if too shiny it may cause a glare. Also, protectants can make your steering wheel, accelerator, and brake pedal slippery, so it is not advisable to use protectants there.

The Least You Need to Know

♦ Keeping your car clean is like money in the bank—it enhances the value of the car.

♦ A weekly or biweekly cleaning schedule will keep your car happy and healthy.

♦ When cleaning front wheels, remember disc brakes shed dust particles and it may require a special cleaner to clean those dust particles off your wheel coverings.

♦ Take the proper precautions before cleaning your engine to protect both yourself and the electrical and mechanical components under the hood.

♦ Wax your clear-coat finish twice a year—spring and fall is best to avoid temperature extremes.

♦ For quick interior cleaning, arm yourself with basics: vacuum, carpet cleaner, brush, cotton swabs, soft cloths, trash bag(s), and protectant.

Chapter 21

Bodywork and Interior Repair

In This Chapter

- ◆ Repairing dangling trim
- ◆ Repairing damage to your clear-coat finish and restore shine
- ◆ Fixing dings and scratches
- ◆ Fixing a chip in the windshield
- ◆ Repairing interior damage
- ◆ Where to look for leaks

Your car has been around for a while and her dings are showing. Or you drove your new car to the mall and now have a banged door. (We know, we'd cry, too.) Or maybe the big orange bookmobile brushed your new silver sports car's bumper and now it's silver and orange. (Vyv *did* cry!) Did you drive your grandmother to her church-group meeting and she left her sewing scissors in the seat and then sat on them, leaving a huge rip in the vinyl? So what do you do now?

Let's face it, automobiles have to stand up to a lot of multitaskers (owners included) whose minds are on anything but whether your car's inner and outer beauty remains. And if you noticed, we haven't even begun to talk about the abuse your vehicle gets from children. No matter where you get auto beauty problems, take care of them ASAP so they don't become huge problems.

Tidying Up Trim

If you have dangling trim, you need to give it attention as soon as possible. Anything dangling from a car is hazardous when on the highway. First of all find out how the trim is affixed to your car. Generally trim is attached by either adhesives or screws. Usually dangling trim isn't a big deal to fix. If a screw has worked out, get out your screwdriver and replace it. If there is damage to your trim and you need a new piece, order one from the auto-parts store or the vehicle manufacturer. Price the trim at both places. You'll probably spend less at the auto-parts store, if they can get the trim. If the trim is applied by adhesive, you'll need a couple of products. Tell your trusted salesperson what you are doing and that you need some type of adhesive remover and two-sided mounting tape.

For trim attached by adhesives, you'll want to carefully, which means slowly (don't yank), peel the entire section off. Now that you have the trim off your vehicle, put it someplace safe where you won't trip over it. Next, clean the old adhesive off the trim with adhesive remover (you can get this at the auto-parts store). While you are in a cleaning mood, gently rub the area on your car where the trim was located with a cloth dampened with a little water. You should be able to tell from the way the trim was applied if you'll need one or two pieces of mounting tape. Check it out and use what is needed for the width of trim. Now you are ready to apply the two-sided mounting tape. Pull the backing off. Make sure you have the trim lined up with a piece of trim that is still intact on another section of your vehicle (for example, the trim may be coming off the rear door, so line the trim up with the trim on the front door or rear fender). Press the trim in place slowly so that you can make sure it is even.

Restoring Clear-Coat Finishes

With 97 percent of all cars rolling off the assembly line with clear-coat paint, it's a good idea to learn how to care for the new high-tech finishes. There are several different varieties of clear coat, and scientists continue to formulate durable yet beautiful finishes. Some types of clear coat include urethane, polyurethane, and polyester.

A clear-coat finish is more durable than yesterday's two-stage paint finishes—that is, primer layer and color (pigment) layer. Clear-coat covers the pigment layer so today's cars have, from the bottom up: primer, color paint, and clear coat. This finish keeps the color layer from fading and chipping, but it does need TLC; it requires weekly cleanings to keep it in pristine condition.

The finish is also vulnerable to small circular scratches or micro-marring. Micro-marring is also known as swirl marks or "swirly-ques." If you are meticulous about your washing routine, you can prevent small scratches and spider-web marks. So wash weekly to remove environmental dirt and grime, avoid big brushes at car washes, use the correct products (wash shampoo and clean mitts or cloths), and make sure you keep cleaning cloths devoid of any gritty substance, including powered detergents when laundered. Also remember when washing or waxing, use back-and-forth motions with clear-coat paint—not circular motions.

Should you get swirls anyway, there are ways to rid yourself of that problem. Your best course of action is to wash, polish, and wax. That should do the trick, but if not, there are products that will take swirl marks away. The product does, however, take away some of the clear-coat finish, so you can only use it a limited number of times.

To restore a clear-coat finish that is very dull, you'll need a different product. Clear coat is just like putting a clear coat of lip gloss over colored lipstick. Of course, you can't keep reapplying the clear coat like you do lip gloss (unless you do touch-ups or completely repaint your vehicle), but you can purchase a clear-coat polishing compound. When applying, use straight lines, not circular motions, and use a clean cloth that is lint-free. Here are two steps to make your dull paint shiny:

> **Speedbumps**
>
> Rubbing compounds are too abrasive for a clear-coat finish. Never put abrasive products on "healthy" clear coat. Make sure you buy a mild polishing product. And as always, if you aren't sure what to buy, ask before you buy and read the directions carefully before you apply it to your car. A compound would only be used if your next step would be to repaint your vehicle.

1. Wash and dry your car. Remember to use products with mild abrasives on your damaged clear-coat finish. Rubbing compound is good to revitalize paint that looks hazy. The compound takes the dull layer of paint off—the part that has oxidized. You only use rubbing compound when your paint appears to be dead as a doornail. When you've finished with the rubbing compound, wax to protect the new layer of paint.

2. Wax your vehicle to protect the new oils in the just-exposed layer of paint.

CarLogic _____

Whether your vehicle's finish is just-off-the-assembly-line shiny or dull, before apply-ing any product to your car's finish, educate yourself on what each product does and how to apply the product. If you are not sure you can apply the product according to label instructions, talk to a detailer and decide if you should attempt this job or if you should have it professionally done.

Dealing with Dings and Scratches

Yikes, how did that scratch get on your car? To fix it, you need to determine exactly what color paint is on your vehicle. You can find out that information by looking on the manufacturer's information slip. Usually you'll find this information on a metal decal under the hood, in the doorjamb, in the glove compartment, or in the trunk. In any event, when you find the metal decal it will tell you the specific paint color code for your car.

Now check out the scratch really well. Is there rust around it? If so, you'll also need to buy rust converter to take care of the rust. If your car has a clear-coat finish, you'll need to purchase some clear coat as well.

Now that you know the color paint you need, take a trip to your auto-supply store and get some paint in that color. If they don't have it, you may have to contact your car dealer; but nowadays you probably won't have to go any farther than the auto-parts store. Tell your trusted salesperson what you are doing and ask for the best products. Since scratches are common and the fix is quick and painless if you don't procrasti-nate, this small problem won't become a bigger rust problem later. You may find the (touch-up) paint color of your vehicle (pigment layer) and clear coat come packaged together.

Here are the general steps for repairing a scratch or ding:

1. Clean and dry the area.

2. Assess how far the scratch or ding penetrates. If the abrasion isn't very deep, applying a polish will most likely do the trick. You can also try a glaze (a glaze cleans, adds lubricating oils to the paint, and can also get rid of swirls and scratches). If the scratch goes all the way to the primer layer or covers a large area, you may want to have the repair done professionally.

3. If you want to attempt the fix, wet-sanding is probably your best choice for this repair. Using about a 1,500-grit sandpaper, carefully sand the damaged area. Use

a light hand out toward the edges of the scratch, gently touching on the undamaged finish to blend.

4. If the scratch is all the way to the primer, apply primer first and let dry before applying the touch-up paint. Shake the paint can or bottle before you open it until it is well blended, and then apply it according to the directions. Some kits come with applicators. This may take patience. You want to go slowly with the application, making sure it is level with the other paint.

5. After the paint dries, apply clear coat. If you had to apply primer (that is, the scratch went all the way to the primer), first you will just add another step to the process of painting and allow to dry.

6. After the clear coat dries completely (you may want to wait a few days), wet-sand to smooth the new paint in with the rest of the car finish.

7. Apply polishing compound to blend the area in with the rest of the finish.

8. Wash the area, let it dry, and then apply wax to protect the new paint.

If you have deep imperfections in your vehicle's paint job like deep scratches or marks made when another vehicle sideswiped your vehicle, you may need to have the scratch or scuff mark wet-sanded—that is have the mark sanded with wet sandpaper. If you try this yourself, know what you are doing or you will cause a more costly repair. Sandpaper used on clear coat should not be less than 1,000 grit (the lower the grit, the coarser the paper), and 1,500 to 3,000 is more in the range needed for this repair. Ask your auto-supply person for the supplies needed to wet-sand your vehicle. Some sandpaper (used for this purpose) comes pre-soaked and you just have to dip it in water to begin, while other sandpaper will need to be soaked. If you are not experienced in this type of repair, have a professional do it.

Windshield Chips

Windshields are targets for stones and other debris thrown up from other vehicles. If the chip or crack is small, the repair bill from a glass specialist probably won't be more than $40; long cracks can be double that if repairable at all. There are kits at the auto-repair store for the DIY, but because of the knowledge of glass and special tools needed, we suggest you have windshield work professionally done. You should repair the chip as soon as possible to keep out dirt and grime.

If the damage to your windshield is anything more than a small chip or crack, you'll probably need to have the entire windshield replaced. This can be expensive, but the expense is normally covered by your insurance after your deductible is paid.

> **Speedbumps**
>
> Although there are currently no set standards for when to repair or replace a windshield, many states cite drivers for driving with a safety hazard if their windshield is cracked. If the chip/ding is quarter-size to 3 inches, it is normally a repair job. However, certain variables come into play as well, such as where the ding or crack is located. If the imperfection is in the driver's line of vision, have a qualified glass technician replace the windshield as soon as possible. Be aware that although a crack won't cause the windshield to shatter, the crack can get worse. Driving with a cracked windshield, especially when the crack is in your line of vision or expanding, is hazardous.

Fixing Interior Woes

You had the no-smoking rule in your car until the cross-country trip to get Aunt Flo. Who knew Aunt Flo smoked and had anxiety attacks if not allowed to light up every 10 miles? Okay, so now you know. And just as you relax into the sentiment that being a good person has its rewards and punishments, Aunt Flo dozes off and drops the cigarette. What's that smell? You pull over. Even in your agitated condition, you manage to get far enough off the road to keep from being hurt by oncoming traffic. Aunt Flo's cigarette didn't land in her lap, so that's good. But it did land on your car's floor, where it burned a nice hole in your carpet. Oh joy! But not to worry, we'll tell you how to fix that hole. (Wish we could help with the rest of the trip. See whether Aunt Flo likes chocolate.)

In any event, here is how to fix cigarette burns to your carpet, ripped vinyl, and those aggravating hanging headliners. And remember, the auto-parts store will have kits for some of these repairs, too, so be sure to ask.

Carpet Burns

If the carpet burn isn't very deep, you can simply snip off the burned yarn tips. Another option: cut a section of good carpet with the backing attached, cut out the piece that is burned, and then attach the good piece with double-sided adhesive.

For areas with more extensive damage, try this method. You will need small scissors, a razor knife, clear adhesive, and tweezers. Then follow these steps:

1. Use the scissors to cut away the burned yarn pieces. If you've ever made a latch-hook rug or watched someone make one, you're familiar with yarn pieces or you can just brush your hand across the carpet and feel the individual yarn pieces. Now take a razor knife and scrape away the damaged darkened burned spot in your carpet.

2. Look for a place that is carpeted but not really noticeable, such as under your seat. Cut enough yarn fibers to fill up the burned spot.

3. Apply some clear adhesive to the burned spot. This is the part that takes patience. Take yarn, one piece at a time, and stand it up in position until you fill in the spot.

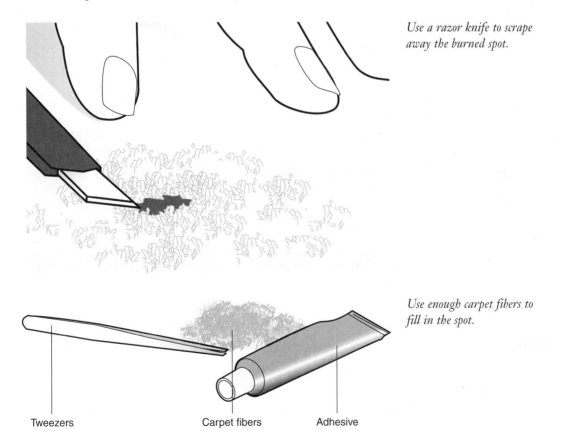

Use a razor knife to scrape away the burned spot.

Use enough carpet fibers to fill in the spot.

Tweezers   Carpet fibers   Adhesive

Use tweezers to put the fibers into place.

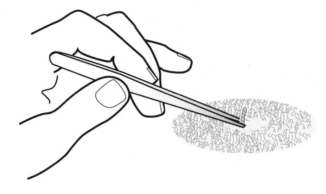

Rip in the Vinyl Seat

As we've emphasized, it's always a great idea to ask your trusted auto-parts salesperson about the best products for your particular situation. There are kits available to repair most interior problems. For a tear in a fabric seat, get out your sewing kit or borrow one. Make sure you have thread that matches the color of your seat. But for a rip in a leather or vinyl seat, you'll probably need to search out a kit at the auto-parts store or have the repair done professionally according to the severity of the damage. A repair kit will be sufficient for most simple rips, and the price starts at around $17.

Gauge the rip.

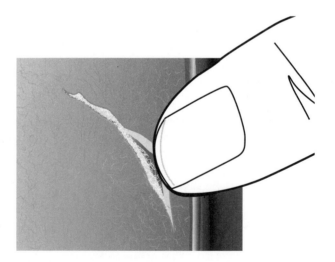

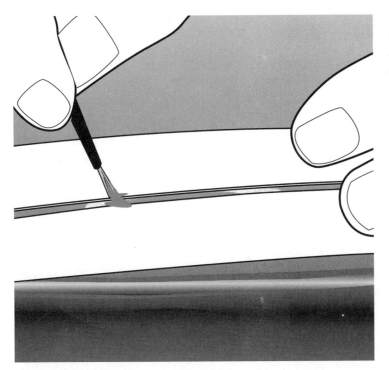

Using products from the kit to repair a vinyl rip. Make sure you keep the tape on until the adhesive dries.

Hanging Headliner

Ugh! Bad-hair days don't need any help from a sagging *headliner.* And not only is a sagging headliner aggravating, it's also dangerous because it can interfere with your view of the road. If your headliner is being unruly, the best option if you want to repair it yourself is to get a kit at the auto-parts store and follow the directions carefully. The kits we priced online listed at $50 for all the materials, including fabric needed to replace your headliner. If you'd rather have it done professionally, that's also a good option; but depending on where you have the repair done, you will pay at least double what it would take to fix the headliner yourself.

Drive Time

Your car's **headliner** is the fabric or vinyl covering your automobile's roof.

Finding and Fixing Leaks

You know your carpet is wet, but you don't know where the liquid is coming from. You look and look but still it's a mystery. It may be one of the following culprits:

- **Air conditioner.** After drying up the water, run the air conditioner for a few days and check the carpet again. If it's wet, the evaporator drain may be stopped up and sending the water into the interior of the car instead of outside. One way to check this is to see whether there is a puddle of water under your car when you park after you've had the A/C running. If there is no puddle and you have wet carpet, that's a good indication that it is the evaporator drain. Read your owner's manual to find placement of your evaporator drain. You can clean it out by carefully poking an unsharpened pencil up the tube. Be careful not to put a hole in the tube.

- **Coolant.** Coolant is usually colored and has a smell. If coolant is leaking inside your car, it's a good bet you have a leak in a heater hose or heat core. Fix this or have your mechanic repair this leak as soon as possible, because coolant is toxic.

If you have water leaking inside a window, check your car's weather-stripping. If you find tears and holes in the weather-stripping, you can fix them with an adhesive. Ask your auto-parts salesperson for the best one. Read the directions carefully, because you don't want adhesive on anything but the weather-stripping. And you should assess the job before you begin. Why? Well, if your vehicle has moldings you have to take off before you replace the rubber gasket, you may want to have this done by a professional. Whatever you decide, after you have the damaged weather-stripping repaired, keep it in good shape with a silicon protectant after each car wash.

After a leak in your car, you'll need to make sure your car is thoroughly dried out. If not, you'll end up with a mildew odor. If the carpet is ruined, replace it. (Replacement DIY carpet runs between $100 and $150, according to the size of your vehicle.) If you don't, your floor can rust through, not to mention you'll have the mildew smell and the possible health problems that can arise (such as allergies) after breathing in mildewed or coolant-soaked carpeting.

The Least You Need to Know

- ◆ Dangling trim can be distracting and hazardous when on the highway. Fixing it is easy.

- ◆ Clear-coat finishes can be revitalized. Remember to use long, straight strokes on clear-coat finishes, not circular strokes.

- ◆ Don't put off fixing small scratches or dings to the exterior of your car; they can become bigger problems later.

- ◆ You can use a kit to fix small chips or cracks in a windshield, but for more severe damage you might have to have the windshield replaced.

- ◆ Most interior damage such as carpet burns or small rips can be fixed with a trip to the auto-parts store.

- ◆ Wet carpet means something is leaking inside your car that shouldn't be—find out what as soon as possible.

Chapter 22

Line of Vision

In This Chapter

- A clean windshield makes safety sense
- What your windshield is made of
- How your wipers work
- A built-in cleaning system
- Cleaning your car's windows

Remember in Chapter 1 when Vyv waxed poetic about her dad's routine of checking out the car—even washing the windshield, headlights, and taillights before each trip? Well, we're about to go into more detail about that, along with some other maintenance jobs.

Think about it—you are driving directly into the sunlight. Not only is the sun blinding you, but also road grime that has accumulated for the past, oh, say … *how* long ago was it that it rained? Yikes, the windshield washer reservoir is empty. Well, it may not be that bad, but let's face it, we all are incredibly busy these days and some things, like washing the windshield, get left for a rainy day. And today as she writes this chapter, Vyv's son is celebrating his sixteenth birthday. Every aspect of making a car safe when on the road becomes even more important when you watch a child drive away for the first time. Let's make sure we can all see clearly!

Get to Know Your Windshield

We tend to be a bit vain about our cars—and that's a good thing. It's good to take pride in the appearance of your automobile. Keeping it clean keeps the paint and rubber in good shape. In the long run this will save you money. But a clean windshield also makes driving safer. This is especially important for nighttime and rainy-day driving, as well as driving in snowy conditions when salt has been put down on the roads. Every big automaker will tell you that cars can be designed to incorporate just about any convenience, but their *main* concern when designing an automobile is keeping the driver focused on the road. You can't focus on the road if you can't see it clearly.

Not only do you need to clean the outside of your windshield, but the inside as well. The inside glass in new cars generally will have a film resulting from vapors, also referred to as off-gassing, given off by things like stain-resistant upholstery and carpet treatments, plastic, and vinyl. We'll tell you how to clean your windshield and windows inside and out, whether your car is new or has a few years on it.

> **Speedbumps**
>
> Some cars have cabin air filters (common in Hondas and Toyotas) that are close to the windshield. These filters, if clogged, can make your windshield fog quickly, making it virtually impossible to see. If you are having a problem with windshield fogging, check your owner's manual to see whether you have a cabin air filter, find out where it is located, and learn how to replace it when it becomes clogged.

Cleaning glass such as a windshield isn't the easiest job. We know that from housework. But cleaning your car's windshield and windows will …

- Keep windows from fogging up as quickly or as often.
- Allow you to see better, especially at nighttime.
- Allow you to see better at difficult intersections.
- Allow you to see animals or debris in the road more clearly.

Most of us don't give much thought as to how a windshield is made. In case you're curious, here are some facts. Most windshields are static; that is, they stay in one position. They are made of laminated safety plate glass. This is a sheet of glass sandwiched between clear plastic. Laminated safety plate glass protects you from flying glass should the windshield be struck during a wreck. If that happens, usually the glass will shatter but remain intact so car occupants aren't cut. When rocks fly up and ding your windshield, only the outside layer is damaged. (See Chapter 21 for tips on dealing with windshield dings and cracks.)

Your windshield is held in place by rubber weather-stripping. The rubber weather-stripping has a groove on either side of the plate glass.

Windshield Wipers

Your car probably has an intermittent windshield wiper system. You've adjusted yours on many occasions according to the amount of rain and how quickly raindrops were hitting your windshield. Can you believe how lucky we are? Windshield wipers on the first cars were operated manually, by moving a lever back and forth. Today the swoosh of windshield wiper blades is somehow comforting inside a dry car.

When you turn the wipers to their highest speed, they move very quickly. Moving that quickly takes a lot of output power. This power is supplied by a worm gear attached to a motor. So those two parts explain the power behind the wipers, but do not tell us anything about how the wipers park themselves in their resting position or know how to sustain the intermittent cycle. The part responsible for that is called an electronic circuit or computer chip.

The more common repair in your visible windshield wiper system—which consists of the wiper arm, blade (houses wiper refills), and wiping element—is replacing the wiper blades that move the water off your windshield. This needs to be done at least every six months. The wiper blades are fragile and will only last for so long. Here are a few things that can go wrong with wiper blades:

 CarLogic

Although having to repair a windshield wiper motor is not common, replacing the motor is expensive. Before replacing a windshield wiper motor, check with your mechanic to be sure the problem part isn't the switch. You'll find the switch located on the wiper motor. Replacing it is more economical than replacing the entire motor. Also make sure every element of the wiper system is tested before the mechanic replaces the motor. Why? Again, because the motor will be the costliest repair.

♦ Streaking is usually caused by rubber that has become dried out. Clean the wiper blades each month or with each car wash, and more often if you regularly park under a tree that is dropping sap.

Windshield wiper motors are expensive to replace. If you do need to have yours replaced, ask your technician about options for finding a used motor. Auto salvage yards are good places to look for this part.

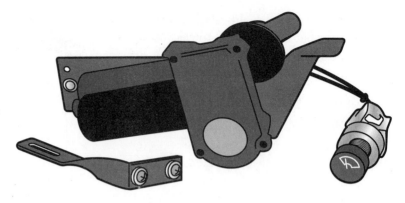

◆ High temperatures can cause the rubber to harden and lose its flexibility, resulting in chattering blades.

◆ Worn or rounded rubber happens sometimes during very cold temperatures.

◆ A damaged blade could be the result of scraping ice or a defective automotive car wash.

◆ Flapping can be a torn wiper that has become damaged from the environment.

There are products on the market that will cause rain to bead up on your windshield and roll off (RainX is one) so you won't need to run your wipers as often. Be sure to follow the directions carefully so the product will work as intended.

Windshields come in various sizes according to the design of the vehicle. Wiper blades are made to fit the angle of the glass. Check your owner's manual for the correct wiper blades and arms for your vehicle.

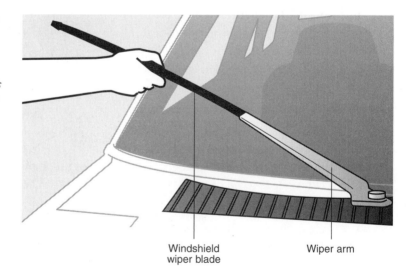

Windshield
wiper blade

Wiper arm

Many times all you will need to do is replace the wiper blades, but sometimes you'll have to replace the entire assembly. You can find blades and assemblies at your auto-parts store. Be sure to check your owner's manual for the correct size, or ask the salesperson at the auto-parts store to help you get the correct size, whether you are buying the entire assembly or just the wiper blades. You

Speedbumps

If your windshield is icy or has a large amount of snow or hail accumulation, don't start your wipers before you either manually clear your windshield or turn on the defroster.

shouldn't have any problem replacing just the blades or the entire assembly. However, make sure you know what size blades you need; if you don't get the correct size, you'll have the headache of another trip. Also, if your old blades are worn to the point that visibility is hampered, you may put yourself at risk.

Windshield Washer

Can you imagine not having your very own under-the-hood squirt bottle to clean your windshield? The electric pump–operated windshield washer reservoir connects with the windshield wipers. You will need to check the level of windshield washer fluid in the reservoir each month—more often if you live in a cold climate where salt is spread on the roads during the winter. If it's not full, fill it with an inexpensive washer fluid found at auto-parts stores and gas stations.

Reservoir lid

Windshield washer reservoirs come in various shapes and sizes, but normally have a photo on the lid that tells you what the reservoir is for.

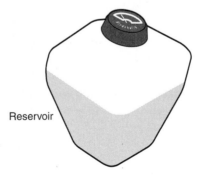

Reservoir

CarLogic

Before filling your windshield washer reservoir, make sure you read and follow the directions on the windshield washer fluid. The fluid may need to be diluted, but do so only if the manufacturer suggests it. Also, you want to make sure that you have the kind of windshield washer fluid that has antifreeze added so that it won't freeze in the winter.

Car Windows

Cars are as commonplace as our homes. We feel a certain comfort sliding inside them no matter what style or model. And just as we try to make sure our homes are safe, car designers work to make our vehicles as safe as humanly possible. One device that is meant to serve this purpose is window glass. It gives protection to those riding in a vehicle by warding off anything that could harm them from outside, like the natural elements. And we all know storms can sometimes be fierce. Side-window glass isn't made to endure as much trauma as your windshield, yet it still should be made out of high-quality material that will keep you safe if, let's say, a hawk flies slightly off course.

The windows of your car are made of tempered safety glass, which is a single piece of glass made by using a heating process that quickly cools the glass to harden it. This process increases the strength of the glass from 4 to 10 times that of regular glass. Tempered safety glass makes good safety sense because it breaks differently than regular clear glass. When tempered safety glass is struck, it does not break into sharp jagged pieces of shrapnel-like glass as normal window panes or mirrors do. Instead, it breaks into small pieces, without sharp edges.

Your rear window is also made out of tempered glass to protect you in case of a collision. But there is a fragile part to the rear window: the defroster grid. The defroster grid is silk-screened on your rear window. It is very fragile, meaning the only thing that should ever touch your rear window is a very soft cloth used for cleaning. Anytime you pack things in the rear and they rub against that window, you could be jeopardizing your rear defroster. So the best advice is be gentle with your rear-window defroster. Auto-repair stores may be able to help you replace a defective grid, but if the entire defroster grid becomes defective, replacing an entire rear window may be your only hope, and they are *not* cheap.

Time to Clean!

When it comes to cleaning your car windows, there are many cleaners to choose from. Ask friends or your auto-store salesperson for recommendations. You might want to leave the ammonia for household window cleaning. It can be harmful to other surfaces in your car (not to mention you!). You may want to follow the lead of many pros and use plain water for wiping and cleaning, and then dry the windows with newspaper. Newspaper is great for this job and works better than a cloth or paper towel, either of which will leave lint. The newspaper ink actually acts as a polish. You will, however, be wearing yesterday's news after you finish the job and will need to be careful not to touch your upholstery before you can wash up.

Speedbumps

Do not apply anything but water to clean tinted windows, or make sure the products you buy are okay to use on tinted windows (ask your trusted auto-parts salesperson). Tinted windows are made of Mylar and scratch easily. They can also be completely ruined if you use a product with ammonia.

Steps for Cleaning Windows

Now that you have your cleaning supplies at your fingertips, let's get ready to clean. Here is your step-by-step guide:

1. Begin cleaning the driver's side window, then the passenger window. Clean the outside mirrors as well.

2. Buff windows dry with newspaper.

3. Clean the inside of the windshield from the passenger side so you don't have the steering wheel to contend with.

4. Clean the rearview mirror gently, being careful not to bear down too hard and tear it off.

5. Clean the back windows and finally the rear window. Be very careful cleaning the rear window so as not to ruin your defroster grid. Clean with a good-quality microfiber cloth in the direction of the defroster grid.

6. Clean headlights and taillights.

7. Get rid of hard-water spots on windows (caused by mineral deposits) with distilled white vinegar. Vinegar is a versatile cleaner that won't damage your vehicle.

Use two parts vinegar to one part water to clean mild spots; to clean deeper spots, use undiluted vinegar. Hard-water spots need to be dealt with as soon as possible so that the spots don't become a permanent eyesore. Spots left for more than two weeks will etch into the glass. Should you have glass damage from hard water, ask your auto-supply store salesperson for a good glass polish. Polish and buff the area with a soft cloth.

8. Clean the front and, if applicable, the rear wiper blades when you wash your car and are working on the windshield glass. You'll need to use a damp cloth to wipe the rubber blades clean of all road slime and grime such as insects and accumulated road chemicals. Do not use products made to preserve rubber on other parts of your car on wiper blades, because the lubricant will leave a film on your windshield.

Try a microfiber cloth—smooth yet tough, this material allows you to clean windshields, wiper blades, and any part of the car that needs TLC—and clean with the cloth and water. Rule of thumb: keep a few microfiber cloths with you in the car for windshield cleaning when you stop to get gas.

The Least You Need to Know

- Dirty windshields are a definite driving hazard; always keep yours squeaky clean.

- Your windshield, windows, and rear window are made of protective glass designed to keep you safer during a collision.

- Use newspaper to buff windows dry; the ink acts as a polish and newspaper won't leave lint.

- Remember to check your windshield wiper reservoir during monthly maintenance and refill as needed.

- Clean windows make your car look like a million bucks!

Chapter 23

Roadside Emergencies

In This Chapter

- ◆ What to keep in your car—just in case
- ◆ Accidents happen
- ◆ Keeping cool if you're stranded
- ◆ Tips for staying safe
- ◆ Bad-weather driving tips

The American Automobile Association (AAA), the leading provider of automotive services to North American car owners, projected (from data taken for the same period one year previous, 2004) more than 7.4 million motorists would experience a vehicle breakdown during June, July, and August of 2005. That's a lot of breakdowns and during a time of year when tempers are affected by the heat.

Most breakdowns that happen on the roadside or away from home are caused by simple problems: flat tires, running out of gas, or battery problems. These are all problems that can be avoided. Hopefully, with a regular maintenance routine and the information we've given you in this book, you won't be sitting by the side of the road with a breakdown. However, should something unforeseen occur, you'll be ready. We'll also tell you how to cope with more serious problems (such as car accidents), how to stay safe if you are stranded, and how to keep your cool when driving in bad weather.

Be Prepared

If you've ever had to speak in front of an audience, you know the value of preparation. Preparation can't be overrated when it comes to arming yourself for a roadside emergency either. In case you have a breakdown or accident, you'll be glad you have the following items in your car:

◆ First-aid kit

◆ Phone book

◆ Little notebook and pen

◆ Extra coat or blanket (as climate dictates)

◆ Name and phone number of your insurance company and your insurance agent

◆ Your auto club telephone number or the telephone number of a towing company

◆ Charged cell phone and charger (your cell phone should be on and charging while you drive so that if you have to use it in case of an emergency, it's at your fingertips and ready for use)

> **Speedbumps**
>
> Don't talk on your cell phone while driving! In some states this is illegal and you can be fined. If you must make a call, pull into a safe place such as a parking lot.

◆ Quality (not plastic) flashlight (if you can get one with auto charger, great!) with a stash of alkaline batteries (keep a check on the expiration date)

◆ Quality jumper cables

◆ Toolbox items (refer to Chapter 3)

◆ Oil and funnels (remember to buy the motor oil recommended by your car's manufacturer—the appropriate kind is listed in your owner's manual)

◆ Two emergency triangles or two battery-operated flares

◆ Tire inflation product (nonflammable)

◆ Duct tape (for patching hoses or a multitude of other uses in emergencies)

◆ Road atlas or maps (state and city of your route and destination)

For long trips you will want to include some extra supplies:

◆ Safety matches (common household matches)

◆ New batteries for flashlight (check batteries for corrosion when you do your maintenance routine and replace if necessary; a good rule of thumb is to replace your "just in case" batteries with new ones before the expiration date and use them for other purposes)

◆ Thermal blanket or blankets (as climate dictates)

◆ Bottled water

◆ Umbrella or fold-up plastic raincoat with hood (plastic ponchos work well for this, too)

◆ Towelettes or wet wipes

◆ Night Owl or other reading light with batteries (or for a better light, carry a battery-operated LED fluorescent lantern)

◆ Spotlight

◆ Fire extinguisher (refer to Chapter 1 for type)

◆ Tire chains if applicable and legal in your state

◆ Small shovel to dig out of mud or snow

◆ Heavy-duty nylon rope for towing purposes

◆ Snacks that won't spoil without refrigeration

◆ Windshield de-icer and scraper (as climate dictates)

Most of these items can be found in an auto-supply store or the auto section of a discount store.

CarLogic

One way to make sure you always have access to some type of light is to buy a Forever flashlight. These flashlights do not need batteries or bulbs. Just shake the flashlight for about 20 seconds and you have light for approximately 5 minutes (when it stops shining, shake it again). Of course, you will still want a quality flashlight and extra batteries, but this makes a great backup.

In Case of an Accident

No one wants to think about auto accidents, and with good reason—the idea is frightening. But accidents do happen, and no matter whether your car hits another car, another car hits your car, or you stop to help someone else, there are commonsense steps you can take to keep a bad situation from becoming worse. Here's what you need to do in case of an accident:

1. If you are okay, the vehicle will run, and all passengers are still where you can see them (meaning inside the vehicle), move the car as far off the road as possible, bring it to a stop and turn off the ignition.

2. If there are injuries that require immediate action, take care of victims (administer CPR, apply pressure to a site where there is blood loss), but be extremely cautious not to make the injury worse. Don't move a victim unless not doing so puts the victim at great risk (for example, if the car is on fire).

3. Call 911 or the police. Usually if damages will likely exceed $500 or if there are injuries or a combination of the two—the police should be called. (Not many accidents occur with resulting damages of less than $500.)

4. If there are no injuries and everyone can safely exit the car without being in the line of oncoming traffic, clear out of the wrecked vehicle. Move as far away from traffic as possible.

5. Call your auto club or a towing service, and your insurance agent.

6. Write down the name of each driver, the driver's insurance company, agent, and the make and model of each car and its license plate number. Don't talk about who was at fault.

7. Ask witnesses what they saw and get their names and phone numbers.

8. When the police arrive, find out when you can get a copy of the police report. Also ask police whether the location where the accident occurred is a common spot for auto accidents.

9. If the police say it is safe for you to do so, use a disposable camera to take photos of the accident scene (see the following sidebar).

10. Make sure you are clearheaded and have read everything on any paperwork before signing it.

11. Do not leave the scene until the police tell you it is okay to leave. If the police were not called, make sure you get all contact information from the owner/owners of the other vehicle/vehicles.

    One exception to the rule of not leaving the scene of an accident is where your safety is concerned. Sometimes innocent drivers are rear-ended or bumped in secluded areas. Upon getting out of the car the innocent driver is harmed, robbed, and sometimes killed. Should you be the victim of a suspicious bump in a secluded area, don't get out of the car. Instead, put on your flashers and drive to the nearest police station.

12. Don't sign off on a claim until you are sure all repairs and medical bills are in and you are in agreement with repairs and medical treatment.

CarLogic

Always keep a disposable camera in your glove compartment (or use your cell phone, if it is a camera phone) to document an accident for your insurance agent. Make sure you don't step out into traffic while taking the photos. Here is what you need to document:

- Photos of your vehicle damage from various angles and distances
- Photos of other cars and the road or intersection where the accident occurred
- Skid marks (stay well clear of oncoming traffic)
- Close-ups of any injuries

What to Do if You're Stranded

The car you rode in as a child was more likely to strand you by the roadside than today's models. Today's cars are more reliable. And as we mentioned previously, if you perform routine maintenance, your odds of being stranded are less. But no matter, it's best to be prepared. A recent survey by the AAA of 1,500 motorists nationwide revealed that 28 percent of those responding had experienced at least one automotive breakdown during the prior 12-month period.

Cell phones are great, but get stranded where there is no service and you still have to fend for yourself. It's always good to have a backup plan. If your cell phone is working, but not your car's global positioning system (or if you don't have access to that type of service), pay attention to where you are by using landmarks or anything that will give your location, like highway numbers.

Being stranded on the roadside isn't something any of us want to think about long or often, but being prepared will make even this nightmare less frightening. It's a good idea to monitor your dashboard lights and gauges and listen for odd noises while driving so you can pull into a shop *before* you are stranded.

Here is a list of some common breakdowns and what to do to get back on the road ASAP:

- **Flat tire.** For a puncture that isn't too large, tire sealant will plug the hole and inflate the tire. But this can be messy for a technician (when he patches the tire) so only use sealant if there's no way to change the tire. Make sure you have a spare and the proper equipment to change the tire. Some higher-end autos are equipped with *run-flat tires.* These tires allow the driver to make it to the nearest gas station without damaging the rim.

Drive Time _____

> When regular tires lose air, you cannot continue driving safely. But if your car has **run-flat tires** you can drive to the nearest service station safely and without damaging your tire or wheel. This new technology adds sidewall stiffness to tires to allow the driver to continue at low speeds without air.

- **Overheating.** If your vehicle overheats, turn on your heater and see if the gauge responds. If the temperature gauge returns to normal, drive to a repair shop. If the temperature does not go down, safely pull off the road, turn off the vehicle, and call your auto club or a tow truck. Don't continue to drive a car that has overheated.

- **Running out of gas.** If you are a member of an auto club, many times you can call and they will bring you the gas you need to make it to a nearby gas station. Your other options include calling family or a tow truck.

- **Fluid leak.** Having your car's fluids (oil and coolant) and some funnels in the trunk will help you be on your way to the nearest service station for repair should your auto experience a leak.

- **Dead battery.** The average battery lasts between three and five years (it may be less than that if you live in a hot climate). If your battery is getting on in age, have it tested or replaced before you head out for a road trip. And while you are having your battery tested, go ahead and have the charging system tested. Overcharging can cause a battery to malfunction.

If your car breaks down and strands you along the side of the road, stay calm and put out your emergency triangles (in the front and rear of your vehicle) if you can do so safely, and then get back in the car if it is far enough off the shoulder to safely do so. If you are a victim of a carjacking, you may have to walk for help, but that is the only reason to get out of your vehicle until help arrives, unless your vehicle is on the highway. Don't accept a ride from a stranger. Call 911 or your auto club and relay your location. Ask how long it will take for help to arrive. When help does arrive, make sure it is the help sent by your auto club or 911 operator. Ask to look at the individuals' credentials!

Weather-Related Driving Emergencies

We all have to make the call of whether to drive in bad weather or when clear skies suddenly turn stormy. No matter what the scenario, weather happens, so it's best to arm yourself. If you have performed routine maintenance, all your equipment—windshield wipers, headlights, taillights, windshield, tires, and brakes—should be in good working order, which is really needed when driving in poor weather.

Here are some tips from the National Oceanic and Atmospheric Administration (NOAA) on what to do if you're driving in bad weather:

- When driving in wet, snowy, or icy conditions, slow stops and starts are best. It takes longer to stop on wet or icy roads, so leave at least two car lengths between you and the vehicle in front of you. Anticipate stops by braking gently. If you start to skid, steer in the direction of the skid until you feel your tires regain traction.

- Always leave earlier and drive slower than usual when you know you will be encountering bad-weather driving conditions.

- Focus intently on your driving with an ear to the radio for possible weather alerts.

- Keep your headlights on low beam when driving in fog.

- If visibility becomes a problem, pull over, but make sure you are well off the road and in a safe place. A nearby parking lot is safer than the shoulder of the road.

- Never use your cruise control on wet, slippery roads. The time it takes to disengage the cruise control could be the difference in avoiding a skid that turns into a spin.

◆ Do not drive in snow and ice unless there is no other way. The Weather Channel gives good tips on driving in snowy and icy conditions at www.weather.com/activities/driving/drivingsafetytips/snow.html.

◆ If you are driving in a thunderstorm with tornado alerts, be aware of weather alerts as well as changes in clouds as you drive. NOAA gives the following signs to watch for when in a threatening thunderstorm that may indicate a tornado:

1. Strong, persistent rotation in the cloud base.

2. Whirling dust or debris on the ground under a cloud base—tornadoes sometimes have no funnel!

3. Hail or heavy rain followed by either dead calm or a fast, intense wind shift. Many tornadoes are wrapped in heavy precipitation and can't be seen.

4. Loud, continuous roar or rumble, which doesn't fade in a few seconds like thunder.

5. At night, small, bright, blue-green to white flashes at ground level near a thunderstorm (as opposed to silvery lightning up in the clouds). These mean power lines are being snapped by very strong wind, maybe a tornado.

6. At night, persistent lowering from the cloud base, illuminated or silhouetted by lightning—especially if it is on the ground or there is a blue-green-white power flash underneath.

CarLogic

NOAA predicts the weather and issues bad-weather alerts. Whether you're going on a long trip or just making your daily commute, it's always a good idea to check the weather before setting out (consider buying a weather radio) and to make sure you listen to weather reports while driving. Even then, you may have to learn how to spot danger in storm clouds that could mean a tornado.

If you see a tornado, NOAA advises drivers to drive at right angles to the tornado to escape its path. If that's not possible, you should safely pull as far off the road as you can and get as far away from the vehicle as possible. If you can find a sturdy building, go inside and wait out the storm; but if not, stay clear of bridges and overpasses, lie down flat on your stomach in a ditch, and put your hands over your head. For more information on how to keep safe when driving during a tornado, go to NOAA's website: www.spc.noaa.gov/faq/tornado/safety.html.

The Least You Need to Know

- ◆ Having emergency supplies in your car will keep a bad situation from becoming worse.

- ◆ Should you be involved in an automobile accident, stay calm, pull off the road if possible, and call 911.

- ◆ If you are stranded by the roadside, call your auto club or 911 and family members; then stay put until help arrives.

- ◆ Stay safe by staying in the car, if possible, and waiting for help to arrive. Never accept a ride from a stranger.

- ◆ Don't drive during bad weather if possible, but if it's unavoidable, follow safety precautions as advised by NOAA and The Weather Channel.

A Troubleshooting Guide for Understanding Your Car

Your car is making a strange noise. You don't know why, but you know what it sounds like. All you need is a little musical accompaniment when you try to explain the sound to your mechanic. Or you may want to define the problem and fix it yourself. Perhaps you just need some tips on kid-proofing your car's interior, or help in figuring out what kind of car seat you need for your child. In any event, this guide will help you in deciphering and explaining what you need to know.

This appendix is divided into four sections:

1. "Common Problems" addresses those problems that often occur due to normal wear and tear on your car.

2. "Detailed Diagnosing and Solving" helps you evaluate and solve more complicated issues that are not as easy to diagnose.

3. "Computer High-Jinks" helps you determine what it means when your "Check Engine" light comes on, among other things.

4. "Troubleshooting Interior Problems and Safety Features" helps resolve those issues that come up on the interior of your vehicle, from kid-proofing the back seat to safety systems.

Common Problems

Many times your senses can help you or your technician decipher what is wrong with your vehicle. Let's take a look, sniff, and feel.

Leaks

♦ Red, green, brown, orange, or gold colors signal an antifreeze leak. (Colors vary according to the brand of antifreeze you use—and many times coloring is a marketing strategy by antifreeze manufacturers—so if unsure what type antifreeze your vehicle needs, ask your technician or someone at the auto-parts store. While you are asking, inquire about long-life or extended-life antifreeze, which usually last five years, instead of regular antifreeze, which lasts two years. Where is it coming from? Check the following until you find the leak: busted hose, water pump, leaking radiator, or overheated engine.

 CarLogic

Need to know if the leaking liquid is oil or antifreeze? Feel the consistency. If the leaking substance has a slightly oily feel, it is antifreeze. A very oily consistency signals—you guessed it—oil.

♦ If you see a dark brownish or black oily fluid leak, you will know it is probably an engine oil leak. The leak may be coming from valve covers, cam covers, engine oil pan gasket, or crankshaft seals at the front and rear of the engine.

♦ Red oily spots (the fluid may be a darker red to brown and smell burnt) signal that you may have a transmission leak from a faulty seal, while a lighter shade of red (a pinker color that doesn't smell burnt) indicates a power-steering fluid leak. This oil may be a pale red and is much thinner than motor oil. This leak may come from the power-steering pump, hoses, reservoir, or steering unit.

♦ Clear water (make sure it is clear) pooling under your car is most likely from condensation from your car's air conditioner and is usually a no-worry situation.

♦ If you find a golden oily liquid that could also appear almost clear, check for a brake-fluid leak. Get this checked out ASAP! The leak could be coming from brake lines, master cylinder, wheels, various joints, and fittings.

Smells

◆ A strong smell like that of burning toast often means an electrical short and burning insulation. A fire is possible. This possibility needs to be confirmed ASAP and fixed for your safety.

◆ A rotten-egg smell or a continuous burning-sulfur smell usually means a problem in the catalytic converter or other emission-control devices. This possibility needs to be confirmed and fixed as soon as possible.

◆ A burning-oil smell means exactly that. Look (following all safety rules) under the car for signs of an oil leak.

◆ A strong gasoline smell after a failed start may mean you have flooded the engine. Flooding is usually associated with cars with carburetors. Wait a few minutes. Try to start the car again. If the odor remains after you've determined the car is not flooded, you may have a leak in your fuel system. This is a dangerous situation and requires immediate attention.

◆ A burning-resin smell or a strong chemical odor may mean your brakes or clutch has overheated. Make sure your parking brake isn't on. If it is, disengage ASAP! Should you encounter this smell on a drive that has required a lot of braking, such as coming off a mountain, your brakes are hot and need to cool down. Try to avoid this situation by stopping periodically on the drive down to give your brake system a break!

◆ If you encounter a slight smoke coming from a wheel, you should pull over and call your auto club or a tow truck. This usually means you have a stuck brake.

◆ A sweet steamy odor probably means a coolant leak. If the temperature gauge or warning light does not indicate overheating, drive carefully to the nearest service station. Remember to keep an eye on your gauges. Overheating will kill your engine!

Speedbumps

If a sweet steamy odor is accompanied by a hot, metallic scent and steam from under the hood, your engine has overheated. Pull over as soon as you can do so safely and get a safe distance off the road. Continued driving could cause severe engine damage. Call your auto club or a towing service to tow your car to a shop.

Sounds

- ◆ Squeal—Sharp noise related to engine speed. Probable cause: loose or worn power-steering fan or air-conditioner belt.

- ◆ Click—Slight sharp noise, related to either engine speed or vehicle speed. Probable cause: loose wheel cover, loose or bent fan blade, stuck valve lifter, low engine oil, CV joint, or axle.

- ◆ Screech—High-pitched metallic sound; normally while the vehicle is in motion. Probable cause: the screech may be from brake-wear indicators giving you notice it's time to have the brake system checked out, but nowadays disc brakes have a tendency to screech even when there is no need for service. In any event, if you hear a screech, have your technician check out the cause just in case. Brake health is key to your safety!

- ◆ Rumble—Low-pitched sound like the gentleman who sings bass at church. Probable cause: faulty exhaust pipe, catalytic converter, or muffler; worn universal joint or other drive-line component. Also check the health of your tires.

- ◆ Ping—High-pitched metallic tapping sound associated with engine speed. Probable cause: using gas with a lower octane rating than recommended (always check your owner's manual to make sure you are using the correct fluids in your vehicle), or engine ignition timing.

- ◆ Heavy knock or pounding sound—Probable cause: worn crankshaft or connecting rod bearings, or loose transmission torque converter. Have it checked out ASAP.

- ◆ Clunk—Hit-or-miss thumping sound. Probable cause: loose shock absorber or other suspension component, or loose exhaust pipe or muffler.

- ◆ Car sounds like a tank—Check under your vehicle. You probably need to replace your muffler or exhaust pipe.

- ◆ Car backfires—Probable cause: incorrect ignition timing, faulty ignition, or leaking valves. Check or have your ignition and valves checked.

- ◆ Engine clatter—Probable cause: low engine oil or worn or badly adjusted valves. Check or have a mechanic check your oil and add more if needed. Valves the problem? Adjust or have them adjusted correctly.

- ◆ Engine whines or chatters—Possible cause: incorrectly tensioned camshaft drive belt. Diagnose or have the problem diagnosed as soon as possible.

- Clicking noise in your engine—Probable cause: dirty valve lifters. Try engine-oil additives first. Also check or have your technician check your oil and oil pressure. If that doesn't work, you may have to have the valves adjusted.

- Sounds like crickets under your hood—Probable cause: defective belts or wheel bearings. Check them now and replace if necessary to avoid a roadside breakdown.

Touch

- Having a hard time steering? Probable cause: misaligned front wheels or worn steering components, such as the idler or ball joint. Have this checked out and fixed ASAP.

- Car pulling to the left or right? Probable cause: first check to see whether you have underinflated tires. If that's not the case, you may have a damaged or misaligned front end. Have this investigated ASAP.

- Rough ride when going around corners? Probable causes: worn shock absorbers and improper tire inflation can contribute to poor cornering. Check air pressure first, and if that doesn't work check to see whether your shock absorbers are worn out.

- Car bounces too many times when you go over a railroad track? Probable causes: check your shock absorbers. There is no set time to replace shock absorbers and struts, but you definitely feel a difference in your ride when it's time to replace.

- One corner of your vehicle sits lower than the other? Probable causes: check the springs. They may have to be replaced. Try not to overload your vehicle again.

- Car seems to ride differently or vibrate? Probable causes: unbalanced or improperly balanced tires can cause a car to vibrate and may cause problems with steering and suspension.

Common Problems Demystified

- Have brakes checked if your vehicle pulls to one side when braking.

- Have brakes checked if your brake pedal sinks to the floor when pressure is applied and maintained.

- Have brakes checked if you hear or feel scraping or grinding during braking.

- ◆ Have brakes checked if the brake light on the instrument panel comes on.

- ◆ Check or schedule an engine check if you have trouble starting your engine.

- ◆ Check yourself or schedule a repair visit if the Check Engine light on your instrument panel stays on.

- ◆ Check yourself or schedule a repair if the engine runs rough while idling or stalls out.

- ◆ Check yourself or schedule a visit to the shop if you have poor acceleration.

- ◆ Check yourself or schedule a visit to the shop if you have poor fuel economy.

- ◆ Check yourself or schedule a visit to the shop if your car uses too much oil (more than one quart between changes).

- ◆ Check yourself or schedule a visit to the shop if your engine continues running after the key is removed.

- ◆ Check or have your transmission checked if you have uneven or hard shifts between gears.

- ◆ Check or have your transmission checked if there is a delay or no response when shifting from neutral to drive or reverse.

- ◆ Check or have your transmission checked if there is a failure to shift during normal acceleration.

- ◆ Check or have your transmission checked if you experience slippage during acceleration; that is, the engine speeds up but the vehicle does not respond.

- ◆ Check or have someone check for loose wiring if you experience alternator trouble. Wiring should be checked before you replace the alternator.

- ◆ Check or have someone check for corroded or loose battery terminals before replacing what appears to be a dead battery.

- ◆ Car won't start? Before replacing the starter, check to make sure you don't have a dead battery or poor battery connection.

- ◆ Does your car need a tune-up? Probably not. Newer cars have fewer parts that need to be replaced. Parts you will want to check as noted in your owner's manual are belts, spark plugs, hoses, and filters. Check your owner's manual and inquire at your shop when to schedule a tune-up for your particular vehicle.

Detailed Diagnosing and Solving

There's always something that can't be solved in one simple step. Some problems require a bit more investigative work, so put on your detective hat and check the following problems in a step-by-step manner. Pat yourself on the back when you so expertly figure out the cause of the problem.

Car Won't Start

There are many reasons why an engine may not start. Start by addressing the basics. Does your car have enough gas? Is your battery working properly? Are you trying to start the car with accessories turned on that should be turned off, like interior lights? Is compression taking place?

Try letting the car sit for a while before trying to start it again. Continually trying to start a car can result in flooding the engine.

 CarLogic

Put on your maintenance schedule (every three months) to lubricate your car's ignition switch and, while you are at it, don't forget all locking mechanisms. A little squirt of WD-40 with the easy-to-use Smart Straw is perfect for this job.

Problem: You try to start your car and hear nothing.

Solution: Before you call your technician, make sure you have your vehicle in Park. Your automatic-transmission vehicle will not start unless it is in Park. You know how to start your manual-transmission vehicle—depress both the clutch and the brake.

If it still won't start, inspect the battery for corrosion or loose cables; clean the battery and tighten cables as indicated. Don't forget all safety rules and put on those safety glasses. If you find you have left headlights or interior lights on in your vehicle, you will need to jump-start your battery (see Chapter 11 for how-to's). If your headlights come on but not at their brightest—or if they look like your house lights going dim during an ice storm—your battery may not be at full strength. Check the eye on your battery to see how much charge is left. If the battery is still able to be recharged, do so now.

Once you rule out a battery problem, check to see whether your starter is functioning. If the starter is not working correctly, you will need to have your technician replace it (or do the job yourself).

You may be able to tap on the back of a nonworking starter and get your car to start so you can get home or to the repair shop. Many times what goes wrong is the starter solenoid has stopped working correctly. The starter solenoid engages the gear with the flywheel. By tapping on the starter lightly with a wrench or hammer, you might have a chance to at least get to a repair shop. Remember to make sure your vehicle is not running, your car is in park, and you've set your parking brake before attempting this quick fix.

Problem: You hear a clicking noise when you try to start the car.

Solution: This could also indicate a problem with the battery. Check for corrosion and loose cables, and clean and tighten as needed. Another possibility is that a solenoid on the starter has jammed. Check or have your mechanic check the solenoid switch. A solenoid is a magnetic coil used to open and close a valve.

Problem: You hear a grating sound when you try to start the car.

Solution: Grating indicates a problem with the flywheel gear and starter drive gear. Don't continue trying to start your car when you hear this sound or it could result in more expensive repairs. The starter drive gear and the flywheel gear are probably not working correctly. You will need to have this problem fixed, so a call to a tow truck may be in order if you can't get the car to start.

Speedbumps

If you have a vehicle with a manual transmission, you could get a jump-start if the car still refuses to start. Jump-starting manual-transmission cars comes with some cautions. First, make sure the driver can handle the vehicle and has the vehicle in first, not reverse, if you are pushing from the back. If you are pushing off with another vehicle (don't exceed 3 to 5 mph), check the heights of both bumpers. If the bumpers are at different levels, body damage is possible. If the vehicles have compatible-height bumpers, have the driver depress the brake and clutch and turn the ignition on and put the car in gear. Driver should take foot off the brake and continue to hold the clutch pedal down. Then let out on the clutch slowly while being pushed. This should make the engine start up. (See Chapter 11 for a step-by-step description on jump-starting a vehicle.)

Problem: You hear a spinning noise when you try to start the car.

Solution: The starter drive gear and flywheel gear are probably not meshing, leaving the starter motor shaft to spin. You'll want to wait for the spinning to cease before trying to start your vehicle again. It is a good possibility that the gears will mesh after a little time, so leave the vehicle to sit for a bit.

Problem: You put the key in the ignition and there are no strange noises, but the car won't start or struggles to start.

Solution: Check the easiest to fix first and eliminate others until you find the culprit. Remember, fuel is one of the ingredients that starts your engine. If, after checking your spark plugs, you still have trouble, have your technician check out your fuel system. This system includes things like fuel filler, fuel tank, fuel pump, pump relay, fuel lines and filter to the fuel injectors, pressure regulator, fuel rail, and throttle body. And today's vehicles have computers and sensors that can throw the starting of your vehicle off, such as the PCM, oxygen sensor, coolant sensor, MAP sensor, throttle position sensor, and airflow sensor (if one is used). Another problem that can arise is bad gasoline that is tainted with water or debris.

If the vehicle starts on the next try, take it to the technician and have it checked. If you do the battery visual and discover it is clean and tight, then it is hard to determine whether you have a starter problem or a battery problem. If you have a battery with an eye, it will give you an idea of how much charge is left. Charge indicators are handy to have. Another thing to have checked is if combustion is taking place at the right time.

Car Starts, But Won't Move

Problem: Your engine starts up fine, but your vehicle won't budge.

Solution: If you are doing your maintenance, you should have the correct amount of transmission fluid unless there is a leak. You should never try to drive a vehicle without transmission fluid.

See whether you can shift into any gear. If you can manipulate it into gear, try to get it to a repair shop. If you are on the road, be very careful. Most cars will start off in second gear if need be. See whether your vehicle will go into second. If it just won't shift at all and you are in the road, carefully exit. If there is any way to put triangles out behind your vehicle, do so, but only if you can do so safely. Call for help. You will need a tow. If you found you could shift into a gear, it may be a worn transmission linkage. If it won't shift at all, it's probably the clutch.

Car Starts, Then Stalls

Problem: You start the engine in the normal way, but when you shift into gear, it stalls.

Solution: Cold days are hard on more than your internal thermostat. They call for more oomph from your car, too. More systems have to step up to the plate to get your vehicle's engine going. Parts like the air filter, fuel filter, alternator, fuel pump, fuel-pressure regulator, battery, starter motor, idle air control motor, fast-idle air valve, and engine-temperature sensor can cause a car to stall. And with today's cars becoming more computerized, if those things check out you may have a computer ECU problem.

If your car is quitting on you, see whether it will help to let the car warm up before you drive it; but stalling is not a normal occurrence in a fuel-injected vehicle that is running properly. Fuel-injected systems have anti-stall devices in place, so a stalling engine problem needs to be identified and fixed. Cars today have a powertrain control module (PCM), which knows (through sensors) what temperature the engine is running at—hot or cold. The PCM sends the correct amount of fuel enrichments to get the motor started and keep it going. So if it is a cold morning, the PCM takes that into consideration.

Key Won't Turn

Problem: Your key won't turn in the ignition.

Solution: This problem usually only affects older vehicles as the pins in the ignition switch become defective. Try the simplest solution first: make sure you did not pick up the wrong set of keys. If that is not the case, has your key become damaged? In any event, now get out your WD-40 and carefully, with the Smart Straw, spray the lubricant on your key and try to insert. You should always have a working spare key for your vehicle. You may have to order one from the manufacturer if you don't have an extra. Another thing to check if your key won't insert is whether you turned off your vehicle with your wheels cut too sharply. Turn the wheel slightly to the right or left to release the pressure on the switch. Get a little play in your steering wheel and try to insert the key again.

Here's a good rule of thumb: to keep your ignition lock cylinder in good condition, don't overload your keychain with keys. The excessive weight of the keys can cause premature wear on the cylinder, which leads to misalignment. The misaligned cylinder makes it impossible to get your key to work.

Can't Remove Key from Ignition

Problem: You can't get your key out of the ignition switch.

Solution: If your key gets stuck in the ignition, you will need to get a vehicle-specific repair book and find out the best way to get it out unless you decide to take it to a shop. Then, of course, the car will have to be towed. To avoid this situation, try to keep your locks lubricated. Also remember your car keys are easily damaged, so only use them to start your vehicle. Those pins that won't let you put your key in the ignition can also make your key hard to get out. Also try not to push your key too far when using accessories while the engine isn't running. It can get stuck if the pins are starting to wear.

Computer High Jinks

You are enjoying your leisurely commute home when you notice a light glowing on the dashboard that wasn't on yesterday. You silently hope it's the low-fuel light, but realize that's not the case. It's the Check Engine or Have Engine Serviced Soon light. What's wrong with your car, and how much is it going to cost you?

Let's take a step back and talk about that ominous Check Engine light. In 1986, cars became smarter. It was federally mandated that all cars be equipped with a means to monitor emissions. So what is in your car today, an OBD-II, monitors the engine and parts of the chassis and body, and may monitor accessory devices. What is OBD? OBD is a computer or on-board-diagnostic system. The first generation was called OBD-I. In 1995, the OBD-I system was updated with the current OBD-II. So what exactly does it mean that your car has an on-board-diagnostic system? Well, it means that when there is a problem with your engine and some other systems or devices as noted above, you'll get a Check Engine or Service Engine Soon alert. This dashboard Service Engine Soon alert is also referred to as the malfunction indicator lamp (MIL).

Diagnostic Trouble Codes

When the MIL comes on, something is wrong. The problem is noted in codes called diagnostic trouble codes (DTC). These codes are stored in the computer. In order to find out what those codes are, your technician uses a scan tool. You should always have the source of the problem checked out, but also remember that the light can come on for such problems as those we mentioned before in the book, such as not tightening the fuel cap completely. Sometimes the MIL will stay on for a cycle of time even after the problem has been resolved. What happens is the trouble code stays in the computer for a specified number of times you crank your vehicle. Also, sometimes the computer has a malfunction. Vyv's sister has a new-model SUV, in which the computer told her vehicle it was out of gas when it wasn't. So her vehicle stopped when it had plenty of fuel. The fuel sensor was faulty. So just as your computer at home can run smoothly the greater percentage of the time, when it does have a problem, normally the problem requires a call to technical service. When your Check Engine light comes on, you will need to call your favorite technician.

Scan Tools

Car owners can buy scan tools that hook into their vehicles. The scan tool reader plugs into a port located under the dashboard. (If you can't find the port, as always, check your owner's manual.)

There are several good reasons to buy a scan tool reader. If you live in a state that requires your vehicle to be inspected, this tool will give you an idea of whether your vehicle will pass inspection or not. If the reader detects a code, it will be identified on the screen of most readers. Some codes may not be serious enough to require a trip to your technician—for example, the loose fuel cap—but you should call and make sure. Also, it is nice to know what is wrong with your vehicle so you'll have an idea before you go into the shop. Knowing what is wrong helps you know whether you are getting the best repair for the money. Reputable technicians respect people who care enough about their vehicles to stay informed. Another plus is a reader can reset trouble codes. (But make sure you read the directions carefully before you reset anything relating to your OBD-II.) Your technician will probably charge for this service.

The diagnostic trouble code is a set list used industrywide. However, manufacturers do sometimes add codes to particular models that might not be covered in a scan tool reader. You might be able to retrieve translations of these codes on the manufacturer's website or in a factory service manual.

Prices for the tools start below $100 and can go up to $2,500 or more, but you can get a quality reader for $150 to $200. You will need to do your homework before you buy. A good place to get scan tool reader comparisons and recommendations is *Consumer Reports* magazine. Our recommendation is to get a reader that won't break the bank, but that has a screen so you can read the codes (not have to download the codes into a laptop), and it's great to have the code translated on screen as well.

Uncoding the Code

Here's an explanation of what the letters and numbers in a DTC (P0100) stand for:

◆ The first letter stands for the system the code is coming from: P is for powertrain; B for body; C for chassis, and U means unidentified system.

♦ The second character lets you know whether the code is from the standard OBD-II list or a manufacturer code. A "0" indicates a generic code; the number "1" one is from the manufacturer.

♦ The third character is a number and stands for the subsystem: 1 is for emission management (fuel and air); 2 is for injector circuit (fuel or air); 3 is for ignition or misfire; 4 is for emission control; 5 is for vehicle speed and idle control; 6 is for computer and output circuit; 7 is for transmission; 8 is for transmission; 9 is for SAE reserved; 0 is for SAE reserved.

♦ The fourth and fifth numbers stand for particular problems. These can vary.

So in our DTC number P0100, the P indicates that the problem originates in the powertrain system; the 0 indicates this is a generic code and not manufacturer-specific; the 1 indicates it is a fuel and air malfunction; and the last two numbers, 00, further specify where the problem originates.

Code List

Here is a partial list of standard diagnostic trouble codes from SAE publication J2012:

Code	Description
P0100	Mass or Volume Air Flow Circuit Malfunction
P0101	Mass or Volume Air Flow Circuit Range/Performance Problem
P0102	Mass or Volume Air Flow Circuit Low Input
P0103	Mass or Volume Air Flow Circuit High Input
P0104	Mass or Volume Air Flow Circuit Intermittent
P0105	Manifold Absolute Pressure/Barometric Pressure Circuit Malfunction
P0106	Manifold Absolute Pressure/Barometric Pressure Circuit Range/Performance Problem
P0107	Manifold Absolute Pressure/Barometric Pressure Circuit Low Input
P0108	Manifold Absolute Pressure/Barometric Pressure Circuit High Input
P0109	Manifold Absolute Pressure/Barometric Pressure Circuit Intermittent
P0110	Intake Air Temperature Circuit Malfunction

P0111	Intake Air Temperature Circuit Range/Performance Problem
P0112	Intake Air Temperature Circuit Low Input
P0113	Intake Air Temperature Circuit High Input
P0114	Intake Air Temperature Circuit Intermittent
P0115	Engine Coolant Temperature Circuit Malfunction
P0116	Engine Coolant Temperature Circuit Range/Performance Problem
P0117	Engine Coolant Temperature Circuit Low Input
P0118	Engine Coolant Temperature Circuit High Input
P0119	Engine Coolant Temperature Circuit Intermittent
P0120	Throttle/Petal Position Sensor/Switch A Circuit Malfunction
P0121	Throttle/Petal Position Sensor/Switch A Circuit Range/Performance Problem
P0122	Throttle/Petal Position Sensor/Switch A Circuit Low Input
P0123	Throttle/Petal Position Sensor/Switch A Circuit High Input
P0124	Throttle/Petal Position Sensor/Switch A Circuit Intermittent
P0125	Insufficient Coolant Temperature for Closed Loop Fuel Control
P0126	Insufficient Coolant Temperature for Stable Operation
P0130	O_2 Sensor Circuit Malfunction (Bank 1 Sensor 1)
P0131	O_2 Sensor Circuit Low Voltage (Bank 1 Sensor 1)
P0132	O_2 Sensor Circuit High Voltage (Bank 1 Sensor 1)
P0133	O_2 Sensor Circuit Slow Response (Bank 1 Sensor 1)
P0134	O_2 Sensor Circuit No Activity Detected (Bank 1 Sensor 1)
P0135	O_2 Sensor Heater Circuit Malfunction (Bank 1 Sensor 1)
P0136	O_2 Sensor Circuit Malfunction (Bank 1 Sensor 2)
P0137	O_2 Sensor Circuit Low Voltage (Bank 1 Sensor 2)
P0138	O_2 Sensor Circuit High Voltage (Bank 1 Sensor 2)
P0139	O_2 Sensor Circuit Slow Response (Bank 1 Sensor 2)

P0140 O_2 Sensor Circuit No Activity Detected (Bank 1 Sensor 2)

P0141 O_2 Sensor Heater Circuit Malfunction (Bank 1 Sensor 2)

P0142 O_2 Sensor Circuit Malfunction (Bank 1 Sensor 3)

P0143 O_2 Sensor Circuit Low Voltage (Bank 1 Sensor 3)

P0144 O_2 Sensor Circuit High Voltage (Bank 1 Sensor 3)

P0145 O_2 Sensor Circuit Slow Response (Bank 1 Sensor 3)

P0146 O_2 Sensor Circuit No Activity Detected (Bank 1 Sensor 3)

P0147 O_2 Sensor Heater Circuit Malfunction (Bank 1 Sensor 3)

P0150 O_2 Sensor Circuit Malfunction (Bank 2 Sensor 1)

P0151 O_2 Sensor Circuit Low Voltage (Bank 2 Sensor 1)

P0152 O_2 Sensor Circuit High Voltage (Bank 2 Sensor 1)

P0153 O_2 Sensor Circuit Slow Response (Bank 2 Sensor 1)

P0154 O_2 Sensor Circuit No Activity Detected (Bank 2 Sensor 1)

P0155 O_2 Sensor Heater Circuit Malfunction (Bank 2 Sensor 1)

P0156 O_2 Sensor Circuit Malfunction (Bank 2 Sensor 2)

P0157 O_2 Sensor Circuit Low Voltage (Bank 2 Sensor 2)

P0158 O_2 Sensor Circuit High Voltage (Bank 2 Sensor 2)

P0159 O_2 Sensor Circuit Slow Response (Bank 2 Sensor 2)

P0160 O_2 Sensor Circuit No Activity Detected (Bank 2 Sensor 2)

P0161 O_2 Sensor Heater Circuit Malfunction (Bank 2 Sensor 2)

P0162 O_2 Sensor Circuit Malfunction (Bank 2 Sensor 3)

P0163 O_2 Sensor Circuit Low Voltage (Bank 2 Sensor 3)

P0164 O_2 Sensor Circuit High Voltage (Bank 2 Sensor 3)

P0165 O_2 Sensor Circuit Slow Response (Bank 2 Sensor 3)

P0166 O_2 Sensor Circuit No Activity Detected (Bank 2 Sensor 3)

P0167 O_2 Sensor Heater Circuit Malfunction (Bank 2 Sensor 3)

P0170	Fuel Trim Malfunction (Bank 1)
P0171	System Too Lean (Bank 1)
P0172	System Too Rich (Bank 1)
P0173	Fuel Trim Malfunction (Bank 2)
P0174	System Too Lean (Bank 2)
P0175	System Too Rich (Bank 2)
P0176	Fuel Composition Sensor Circuit Malfunction
P0177	Fuel Composition Sensor Circuit Range/Performance
P0178	Fuel Composition Sensor Circuit Low Input
P0179	Fuel Composition Sensor Circuit High Input
P0180	Fuel Temperature Sensor A Circuit Malfunction
P0181	Fuel Temperature Sensor A Circuit Range/Performance
P0182	Fuel Temperature Sensor A Circuit Low Input
P0183	Fuel Temperature Sensor A Circuit High Input
P0184	Fuel Temperature Sensor A Circuit Intermittent
P0185	Fuel Temperature Sensor B Circuit Malfunction
P0186	Fuel Temperature Sensor B Circuit Range/Performance
P0187	Fuel Temperature Sensor B Circuit Low Input
P0188	Fuel Temperature Sensor B Circuit High Input
P0189	Fuel Temperature Sensor B Circuit Intermittent
P0190	Fuel Rail Pressure Sensor Circuit Malfunction
P0191	Fuel Rail Pressure Sensor Circuit Range/Performance
P0192	Fuel Rail Pressure Sensor Circuit Low Input
P0193	Fuel Rail Pressure Sensor Circuit High Input
P0194	Fuel Rail Pressure Sensor Circuit Intermittent
P0195	Engine Oil Temperature Sensor Malfunction

P0196	Engine Oil Temperature Sensor Range/Performance
P0197	Engine Oil Temperature Sensor Low
P0198	Engine Oil Temperature Sensor High
P0199	Engine Oil Temperature Sensor Intermittent
P0200	Injector Circuit Malfunction
P0201	Injector Circuit Malfunction—Cylinder 1
P0202	Injector Circuit Malfunction—Cylinder 2
P0203	Injector Circuit Malfunction—Cylinder 3
P0204	Injector Circuit Malfunction—Cylinder 4
P0205	Injector Circuit Malfunction—Cylinder 5
P0206	Injector Circuit Malfunction—Cylinder 6
P0207	Injector Circuit Malfunction—Cylinder 7
P0208	Injector Circuit Malfunction—Cylinder 8
P0209	Injector Circuit Malfunction—Cylinder 9
P0210	Injector Circuit Malfunction—Cylinder 10
P0211	Injector Circuit Malfunction—Cylinder 11
P0212	Injector Circuit Malfunction—Cylinder 12
P0213	Cold Start Injector 1 Malfunction
P0214	Cold Start Injector 2 Malfunction
P0215	Engine Shutoff Solenoid Malfunction
P0216	Injection Timing Control Circuit Malfunction
P0217	Engine Overtemp Condition
P0218	Transmission Over Temperature Condition
P0219	Engine Overspeed Condition
P0220	Throttle/Petal Position Sensor/Switch B Circuit Malfunction
P0221	Throttle/Petal Position Sensor/Switch B Circuit Range/Performance Problem

P0222	Throttle/Petal Position Sensor/Switch B Circuit Low Input
P0223	Throttle/Petal Position Sensor/Switch B Circuit High Input
P0224	Throttle/Petal Position Sensor/Switch B Circuit Intermittent
P0225	Throttle/Petal Position Sensor/Switch C Circuit Malfunction
P0226	Throttle/Petal Position Sensor/Switch C Circuit Range/Performance Problem
P0227	Throttle/Petal Position Sensor/Switch C Circuit Low Input
P0228	Throttle/Petal Position Sensor/Switch C Circuit High Input
P0229	Throttle/Petal Position Sensor/Switch C Circuit Intermittent
P0230	Fuel Pump Primary Circuit Malfunction
P0231	Fuel Pump Secondary Circuit Low
P0232	Fuel Pump Secondary Circuit High
P0233	Fuel Pump Secondary Circuit Intermittent
P0234	Engine Overboost Condition
P0235	Turbocharger Boost Sensor A Circuit Malfunction
P0236	Turbocharger Boost Sensor A Circuit Range/Performance
P0237	Turbocharger Boost Sensor A Circuit Low
P0238	Turbocharger Boost Sensor A Circuit High
P0239	Turbocharger Boost Sensor B Malfunction
P0240	Turbocharger Boost Sensor B Circuit Range/Performance
P0241	Turbocharger Boost Sensor B Circuit Low
P0242	Turbocharger Boost Sensor B Circuit High
P0243	Turbocharger Wastegate Solenoid A Malfunction
P0244	Turbocharger Wastegate Solenoid A Range/Performance
P0245	Turbocharger Wastegate Solenoid A Low
P0246	Turbocharger Wastegate Solenoid A High
P0247	Turbocharger Wastegate Solenoid B Malfunction

P0248	Turbocharger Wastegate Solenoid B Range/Performance
P0249	Turbocharger Wastegate Solenoid B Low
P0250	Turbocharger Wastegate Solenoid B High
P0251	Injection Pump Fuel Metering Control "A" Malfunction (Cam/Rotor/Injector)
P0252	Injection Pump Fuel Metering Control "A" Range/Performance (Cam/Rotor/Injector)
P0253	Injection Pump Fuel Metering Control "A" Low (Cam/Rotor/Injector)
P0254	Injection Pump Fuel Metering Control "A" High (Cam/Rotor/Injector)
P0255	Injection Pump Fuel Metering Control "A" Intermittent (Cam/Rotor/Injector)
P0256	Injection Pump Fuel Metering Control "B" Malfunction (Cam/Rotor/Injector)
P0257	Injection Pump Fuel Metering Control "B" Range/Performance (Cam/Rotor/Injector)
P0258	Injection Pump Fuel Metering Control "B" Low (Cam/Rotor/Injector)
P0259	Injection Pump Fuel Metering Control "B" High (Cam/Rotor/Injector)
P0260	Injection Pump Fuel Metering Control "B" Intermittent (Cam/Rotor/Injector)
P0261	Cylinder 1 Injector Circuit Low
P0262	Cylinder 1 Injector Circuit High
P0263	Cylinder 1 Contribution/Balance Fault
P0264	Cylinder 2 Injector Circuit Low
P0265	Cylinder 2 Injector Circuit High
P0266	Cylinder 2 Contribution/Balance Fault

P0267	Cylinder 3 Injector Circuit Low
P0268	Cylinder 3 Injector Circuit High
P0269	Cylinder 3 Contribution/Balance Fault
P0270	Cylinder 4 Injector Circuit Low
P0271	Cylinder 4 Injector Circuit High
P0272	Cylinder 4 Contribution/Balance Fault
P0273	Cylinder 5 Injector Circuit Low
P0274	Cylinder 5 Injector Circuit High
P0275	Cylinder 5 Contribution/Balance Fault
P0276	Cylinder 6 Injector Circuit Low
P0277	Cylinder 6 Injector Circuit High
P0278	Cylinder 6 Contribution/Balance Fault
P0279	Cylinder 7 Injector Circuit Low
P0280	Cylinder 7 Injector Circuit High
P0281	Cylinder 7 Contribution/Balance Fault
P0282	Cylinder 8 Injector Circuit Low
P0283	Cylinder 8 Injector Circuit High
P0284	Cylinder 8 Contribution/Balance Fault
P0285	Cylinder 9 Injector Circuit Low
P0286	Cylinder 9 Injector Circuit High
P0287	Cylinder 9 Contribution/Balance Fault
P0288	Cylinder 10 Injector Circuit Low
P0289	Cylinder 10 Injector Circuit High
P0290	Cylinder 10 Contribution/Balance Fault
P0291	Cylinder 11 Injector Circuit Low
P0292	Cylinder 11 Injector Circuit High

P0293	Cylinder 11 Contribution/Balance Fault
P0294	Cylinder 12 Injector Circuit Low
P0295	Cylinder 12 Injector Circuit High
P0296	Cylinder 12 Contribution/Range Fault
P0300	Random/Multiple Cylinder Misfire Detected
P0301	Cylinder 1 Misfire Detected
P0302	Cylinder 2 Misfire Detected
P0303	Cylinder 3 Misfire Detected
P0304	Cylinder 4 Misfire Detected
P0305	Cylinder 5 Misfire Detected
P0306	Cylinder 6 Misfire Detected
P0307	Cylinder 7 Misfire Detected
P0308	Cylinder 8 Misfire Detected
P0309	Cylinder 9 Misfire Detected
P0311	Cylinder 11 Misfire Detected
P0312	Cylinder 12 Misfire Detected
P0320	Ignition/Distributor Engine Speed Input Circuit Malfunction
P0321	Ignition/Distributor Engine Speed Input Circuit Range/Performance
P0322	Ignition/Distributor Engine Speed Input Circuit No Signal
P0323	Ignition/Distributor Engine Speed Input Circuit Intermittent
P0325	Knock Sensor 1 Circuit Malfunction (Bank 1 or Single Sensor)
P0326	Knock Sensor 1 Circuit Range/Performance (Bank 1 or Single Sensor)
P0327	Knock Sensor 1 Circuit Low Input (Bank 1 or Single Sensor)
P0328	Knock Sensor 1 Circuit High Input (Bank 1 or Single Sensor)
P0329	Knock Sensor 1 Circuit Intermittent (Bank 1 or Single Sensor)
P0330	Knock Sensor 2 Circuit Malfunction (Bank 2)

P0331	Knock Sensor 2 Circuit Range/Performance (Bank 2)
P0332	Knock Sensor 2 Circuit Low Input (Bank 2)
P0333	Knock Sensor 2 Circuit High Input (Bank 2)
P0334	Knock Sensor 2 Circuit Intermittent (Bank 2)
P0335	Crankshaft Position Sensor A Circuit Malfunction
P0336	Crankshaft Position Sensor A Circuit Range/Performance
P0337	Crankshaft Position Sensor A Circuit Low Input
P0338	Crankshaft Position Sensor A Circuit High Input
P0339	Crankshaft Position Sensor A Circuit Intermittent
P0340	Camshaft Position Sensor Circuit Malfunction
P0341	Camshaft Position Sensor Circuit Range/Performance
P0342	Camshaft Position Sensor Circuit Low Input
P0343	Camshaft Position Sensor Circuit High Input
P0344	Camshaft Position Sensor Circuit Intermittent
P0350	Ignition Coil Primary/Secondary Circuit Malfunction
P0351	Ignition Coil A Primary/Secondary Circuit Malfunction
P0352	Ignition Coil B Primary/Secondary Circuit Malfunction
P0353	Ignition Coil C Primary/Secondary Circuit Malfunction
P0354	Ignition Coil D Primary/Secondary Circuit Malfunction
P0355	Ignition Coil E Primary/Secondary Circuit Malfunction
P0356	Ignition Coil F Primary/Secondary Circuit Malfunction
P0357	Ignition Coil G Primary/Secondary Circuit Malfunction
P0358	Ignition Coil H Primary/Secondary Circuit Malfunction
P0359	Ignition Coil I Primary/Secondary Circuit Malfunction
P0360	Ignition Coil J Primary/Secondary Circuit Malfunction
P0361	Ignition Coil K Primary/Secondary Circuit Malfunction

P0362	Ignition Coil L Primary/Secondary Circuit Malfunction
P0370	Timing Reference High Resolution Signal A Malfunction
P0371	Timing Reference High Resolution Signal A Too Many Pulses
P0372	Timing Reference High Resolution Signal A Too Few Pulses
P0373	Timing Reference High Resolution Signal A Intermittent/Erratic Pulses
P0374	Timing Reference High Resolution Signal A No Pulses
P0375	Timing Reference High Resolution Signal B Malfunction
P0376	Timing Reference High Resolution Signal B Too Many Pulses
P0377	Timing Reference High Resolution Signal B Too Few Pulses
P0378	Timing Reference High Resolution Signal B Intermittent/Erratic Pulses
P0379	Timing Reference High Resolution Signal B No Pulses
P0380	Glow Plug/Heater Circuit "A" Malfunction
P0381	Glow Plug/Heater Indicator Circuit Malfunction
P0382	Exhaust Gas Recirculation Flow Malfunction
P0385	Crankshaft Position Sensor B Circuit Malfunction
P0386	Crankshaft Position Sensor B Circuit Range/Performance
P0387	Crankshaft Position Sensor B Circuit Low Input
P0388	Crankshaft Position Sensor B Circuit High Input
P0389	Crankshaft Position Sensor B Circuit Intermittent
P0400	Exhaust Gas Recirculation Flow Malfunction
P0401	Exhaust Gas Recirculation Flow Insufficient Detected
P0402	Exhaust Gas Recirculation Flow Excessive Detected
P0403	Exhaust Gas Recirculation Circuit Malfunction
P0404	Exhaust Gas Recirculation Circuit Range/Performance
P0405	Exhaust Gas Recirculation Sensor A Circuit Low

P0406	Exhaust Gas Recirculation Sensor A Circuit High
P0407	Exhaust Gas Recirculation Sensor B Circuit Low
P0408	Exhaust Gas Recirculation Sensor B Circuit High
P0410	Secondary Air Injection System Malfunction
P0411	Secondary Air Injection System Incorrect Flow Detected
P0412	Secondary Air Injection System Switching Valve A Circuit Malfunction
P0413	Secondary Air Injection System Switching Valve A Circuit Open
P0414	Secondary Air Injection System Switching Valve A Circuit Shorted
P0415	Secondary Air Injection System Switching Valve B Circuit Malfunction
P0416	Secondary Air Injection System Switching Valve B Circuit Open
P0417	Secondary Air Injection System Switching Valve B Circuit Shorted
P0418	Secondary Air Injection System Relay "A" Circuit Malfunction
P0419	Secondary Air Injection System Relay "B" Circuit Malfunction
P0420	Catalyst System Efficiency Below Threshold (Bank 1)
P0421	Warm Up Catalyst Efficiency Below Threshold (Bank 1)
P0422	Main Catalyst Efficiency Below Threshold (Bank 1)
P0423	Heated Catalyst Efficiency Below Threshold (Bank 1)
P0424	Heated Catalyst Temperature Below Threshold (Bank 1)
P0430	Catalyst System Efficiency Below Threshold (Bank 2)
P0431	Warm Up Catalyst Efficiency Below Threshold (Bank 2)
P0432	Main Catalyst Efficiency Below Threshold (Bank 2)
P0433	Heated Catalyst Efficiency Below Threshold (Bank 2)
P0434	Heated Catalyst Temperature Below Threshold (Bank 2)
P0440	Evaporative Emission Control System Malfunction
P0441	Evaporative Emission Control System Incorrect Purge Flow

P0442   Evaporative Emission Control System Leak Detected (small leak)

P0443   Evaporative Emission Control System Purge Control Valve Circuit Malfunction

P0444   Evaporative Emission Control System Purge Control Valve Circuit Open

P0445   Evaporative Emission Control System Purge Control Valve Circuit Shorted

P0446   Evaporative Emission Control System Vent Control Circuit Malfunction

P0447   Evaporative Emission Control System Vent Control Circuit Open

P0448   Evaporative Emission Control System Vent Control Circuit Shorted

P0449   Evaporative Emission Control System Vent Valve/Solenoid Circuit Malfunction

P0450   Evaporative Emission Control System Pressure Sensor Malfunction

P0451   Evaporative Emission Control System Pressure Sensor Range/Performance

P0452   Evaporative Emission Control System Pressure Sensor Low Input

P0453   Evaporative Emission Control System Pressure Sensor High Input

P0454   Evaporative Emission Control System Pressure Sensor Intermittent

P0455   Evaporative Emission Control System Leak Detected (gross leak)

P0460   Fuel Level Sensor Circuit Malfunction

P0461   Fuel Level Sensor Circuit Range/Performance

P0462   Fuel Level Sensor Circuit Low Input

P0463   Fuel Level Sensor Circuit High Input

P0464   Fuel Level Sensor Circuit Intermittent

P0465   Purge Flow Sensor Circuit Malfunction

P0466   Purge Flow Sensor Circuit Range/Performance

P0467   Purge Flow Sensor Circuit Low Input

P0468	Purge Flow Sensor Circuit High Input
P0469	Purge Flow Sensor Circuit Intermittent
P0470	Exhaust Pressure Sensor Malfunction
P0471	Exhaust Pressure Sensor Range/Performance
P0472	Exhaust Pressure Sensor Low
P0473	Exhaust Pressure Sensor High
P0474	Exhaust Pressure Sensor Intermittent
P0475	Exhaust Pressure Control Valve Malfunction
P0476	Exhaust Pressure Control Valve Range/Performance
P0477	Exhaust Pressure Control Valve Low
P0478	Exhaust Pressure Control Valve High
P0479	Exhaust Pressure Control Valve Intermittent
P0480	Cooling Fan 1 Control Circuit Malfunction
P0481	Cooling Fan 2 Control Circuit Malfunction
P0482	Cooling Fan 3 Control Circuit Malfunction
P0483	Cooling Fan Rationality Check Malfunction
P0484	Cooling Fan Circuit Over Current
P0485	Cooling Fan Power/Ground Circuit Malfunction
P0500	Vehicle Speed Sensor Malfunction
P0501	Vehicle Speed Sensor Range/Performance
P0502	Vehicle Speed Sensor Low Input
P0503	Vehicle Speed Sensor Intermittent/Erratic/High
P0505	Idle Control System Malfunction
P0506	Idle Control System RPM Lower Than Expected
P0507	Idle Control System RPM Higher Than Expected
P0510	Closed Throttle Position Switch Malfunction

P0520	Engine Oil Pressure Sensor/Switch Circuit Malfunction
P0521	Engine Oil Pressure Sensor/Switch Circuit Range/Performance
P0522	Engine Oil Pressure Sensor/Switch Circuit Low Voltage
P0523	Engine Oil Pressure Sensor/Switch Circuit High Voltage
P0530	A/C Refrigerant Pressure Sensor Circuit Malfunction
P0531	A/C Refrigerant Pressure Sensor Circuit Range/Performance
P0532	A/C Refrigerant Pressure Sensor Circuit Low Input
P0533	A/C Refrigerant Pressure Sensor Circuit High Input
P0534	A/C Refrigerant Charge Loss
P0550	Power Steering Pressure Sensor Circuit Malfunction
P0551	Power Steering Pressure Sensor Circuit Range/Performance
P0552	Power Steering Pressure Sensor Circuit Low Input
P0553	Power Steering Pressure Sensor Circuit High Input
P0554	Power Steering Pressure Sensor Circuit Intermittent
P0560	System Voltage Malfunction
P0561	System Voltage Unstable
P0562	System Voltage Low
P0563	System Voltage High
P0565	Cruise Control On Signal Malfunction
P0566	Cruise Control Off Signal Malfunction
P0567	Cruise Control Resume Signal Malfunction
P0568	Cruise Control Set Signal Malfunction
P0569	Cruise Control Coast Signal Malfunction
P0570	Cruise Control Accel Signal Malfunction
P0571	Cruise Control/Brake Switch A Circuit Malfunction
P0572	Cruise Control/Brake Switch A Circuit Low

P0573	Cruise Control/Brake Switch A Circuit High
P0574	Cruise Control Related Malfunction
P0575	Cruise Control Related Malfunction
P0576	Cruise Control Related Malfunction
P0577	Cruise Control Related Malfunction
P0578	Cruise Control Related Malfunction
P0579	Cruise Control Related Malfunction
P0580	Cruise Control Related Malfunction
P0600	Serial Communication Link Malfunction
P0601	Internal Control Module Memory Check Sum Error
P0602	Control Module Programming Error
P0603	Internal Control Module Keep Alive Memory (KAM) Error
P0604	Internal Control Module Random Access Memory (RAM) Error
P0605	Internal Control Module Read Only Memory (ROM) Error
P0606	PCM Processor Fault
P0608	Control Module VSS Output "A" Malfunction
P0609	Control Module VSS Output "B" Malfunction
P0620	Generator Control Circuit Malfunction
P0621	Generator Lamp "L" Control Circuit Malfunction
P0622	Generator Field "F" Control Circuit Malfunction
P0650	Malfunction Indicator Lamp (MIL) Control Circuit Malfunction
P0654	Engine RPM Output Circuit Malfunction
P0655	Engine Hot Lamp Output Control Circuit Malfunction
P0656	Fuel Level Output Circuit Malfunction
P0700	Transmission Control System Malfunction
P0701	Transmission Control System Range/Performance

P0702	Transmission Control System Electrical
P0703	Torque Converter/Brake Switch B Circuit Malfunction
P0704	Clutch Switch Input Circuit Malfunction
P0705	Transmission Range Sensor Circuit Malfunction (PRNDL Input)
P0706	Transmission Range Sensor Circuit Range/Performance
P0707	Transmission Range Sensor Circuit Low Input
P0708	Transmission Range Sensor Circuit High Input
P0709	Transmission Range Sensor Circuit Intermittent
P0710	Transmission Fluid Temperature Sensor Circuit Malfunction
P0711	Transmission Fluid Temperature Sensor Circuit Range/Performance
P0712	Transmission Fluid Temperature Sensor Circuit Low Input
P0713	Transmission Fluid Temperature Sensor Circuit High Input
P0714	Transmission Fluid Temperature Sensor Circuit Intermittent
P0715	Input/Turbine Speed Sensor Circuit Malfunction
P0716	Input/Turbine Speed Sensor Circuit Range/Performance
P0717	Input/Turbine Speed Sensor Circuit No Signal
P0718	Input/Turbine Speed Sensor Circuit Intermittent
P0719	Torque Converter/Brake Switch B Circuit Low
P0720	Output Speed Sensor Circuit Malfunction
P0721	Output Speed Sensor Range/Performance
P0722	Output Speed Sensor No Signal
P0723	Output Speed Sensor Intermittent
P0724	Torque Converter/Brake Switch B Circuit High
P0725	Engine Speed Input Circuit Malfunction
P0726	Engine Speed Input Circuit Range/Performance
P0727	Engine Speed Input Circuit No Signal

P0728	Engine Speed Input Circuit Intermittent
P0730	Incorrect Gear Ratio
P0731	Gear 1 Incorrect ratio
P0732	Gear 2 Incorrect ratio
P0733	Gear 3 Incorrect ratio
P0734	Gear 4 Incorrect ratio
P0735	Gear 5 Incorrect ratio
P0736	Reverse incorrect gear ratio
P0740	Torque Converter Clutch Circuit Malfunction
P0741	Torque Converter Clutch Circuit Performance or Stuck Off
P0742	Torque Converter Clutch Circuit Stuck On
P0743	Torque Converter Clutch Circuit Electrical
P0744	Torque Converter Clutch Circuit Intermittent
P0745	Pressure Control Solenoid Malfunction
P0746	Pressure Control Solenoid Performance or Stuck Off
P0747	Pressure Control Solenoid Stuck On
P0748	Pressure Control Solenoid Electrical
P0749	Pressure Control Solenoid Intermittent
P0750	Shift Solenoid A Malfunction
P0751	Shift Solenoid A Performance or Stuck Off
P0752	Shift Solenoid A Stuck On
P0753	Shift Solenoid A Electrical
P0754	Shift Solenoid A Intermittent
P0755	Shift Solenoid B Malfunction
P0756	Shift Solenoid B Performance or Stuck Off
P0757	Shift Solenoid B Stuck On

P0758	Shift Solenoid B Electrical
P0759	Shift Solenoid B Intermittent
P0760	Shift Solenoid C Malfunction
P0761	Shift Solenoid C Performance or Stuck Off
P0762	Shift Solenoid C Stuck On
P0763	Shift Solenoid C Electrical
P0764	Shift Solenoid C Intermittent
P0765	Shift Solenoid D Malfunction
P0766	Shift Solenoid D Performance or Stuck Off
P0767	Shift Solenoid D Stuck On
P0768	Shift Solenoid D Electrical
P0769	Shift Solenoid D Intermittent
P0770	Shift Solenoid E Malfunction
P0771	Shift Solenoid E Performance or Stuck Off
P0772	Shift Solenoid E Stuck On
P0773	Shift Solenoid E Electrical
P0774	Shift Solenoid E Intermittent
P0780	Shift Malfunction
P0781	1-2 Shift Malfunction
P0782	2-3 Shift Malfunction
P0783	3-4 Shift Malfunction
P0784	4-5 Shift Malfunction
P0785	Shift/Timing Solenoid Malfunction
P0786	Shift/Timing Solenoid Range/Performance
P0787	Shift/Timing Solenoid Low
P0788	Shift/Timing Solenoid High

P0789	Shift/Timing Solenoid Intermittent
P0790	Normal/Performance Switch Circuit Malfunction
P0801	Reverse Inhibit Control Circuit Malfunction
P0803	1-4 Upshift (Skip Shift) Solenoid Control Circuit Malfunction
P0804	1-4 Upshift (Skip Shift) Lamp Control Circuit Malfunction

Troubleshooting Interior Problems and Safety Features

Remember the days when the only accumulated matter in your vehicle was an umbrella and box of Kleenex? Why do our cars tend to become unbearably messy when we have children? Here are some ideas to help keep your car's interior in order:

- Always carry wet wipes and a roll of paper towels in the car to wipe smeared hands and faces and to clean up spills. It's also handy to keep a small package of Kleenex on your console for wiping a runny nose.

- For some reason, children love to raise their arms skyward while riding. Unfortunately the headliner sometimes gets the chocolate before you can get to the wipes. A good way to minimize or keep stains from happening is to go to your auto-supply store and purchase a spray-on protectant. You can get them for vinyl or fabric.

- Seat covers are available in all types of fabric, and they're great for preserving a new seat or hiding flaws in a seat that's already had some rough treatment. Some covers can be taken off and washed. If you don't want to cover your seats, opt for slip-on seat covers you can slide on quickly as needed. You can also ask your auto-supply salesperson for spray-on protectant for your seats, but your car may already have a protectant. Read your owner's manual to find out.

- Sippy cups for toddlers and cups with tight lids for everyone else is a good rule to have in your car. Cup holders are widely available if your vehicle doesn't come equipped with enough. Just remember not to slam a door closed that has a cup holder that is in use. Usually the cup will fly out and the contents will be all over your seats and carpet. (How do we know? Don't ask!)

- A backpack or diaper bag is a good way to carry toys from the car to the house and back again when you don't have enough hands and don't want to make several trips. Or look for organizers that fit on the back of front seats.

- Protect the floorboard with a molded plastic floor tray that covers the entire floor area. Or try regular floor mats, which come in carpeted, vinyl, plastic, etc. You can take these out and clean them as needed. A floor liner that covers the entire floorboard area is another possibility. Liners are also great for lining the trunk and back area of SUVs and minivans.

- Keeping your children occupied while they are riding in the car means less damage to your vehicle's interior. Consider buying a vehicle with a DVD entertainment system or buying an entertainment system and installing it yourself.

Infant and Booster Seats

It's very important to know specific rules about what to do and how to troubleshoot possible problems relating to child safety seats. Here is a guide to what the National Highway Traffic Safety Administration (NHTSA) advises you to do to keep your child safe in a moving vehicle. Information on car seat safety is constantly being updated, so it is best to check NHTSA's website (www.nhtsa.dot.gov) before you purchase a car seat. It's also a good idea to read your owner's manual to find out where and how to secure your child safely in your vehicle.

 CarLogic

Need help installing your child's car seat, or just want to make sure you've installed it correctly? Any fire department or police station can help you with this. Call to arrange to stop by for a quick visit.

1. Infants are categorized as birth to at least 1 year and at least 20 pounds. Your baby should ride in an infant-only seat. This seat should be in the backseat and be rear-facing, or you can purchase a "convertible" seat (this seat also is placed in the backseat) that also faces the rear. Your baby only sees where he's been, not where he's going, until he's past 1 year and weighs more than 20 pounds. Your child's car seat should be secured by a safety belt or by the LATCH system (explained in the following sidebar).

   How to use: the seat should never be used in a front seat where an airbag is present; you should make certain the seat is securely installed in the rear seat and facing the rear; the child seat should recline at approximately a 45° angle; the harness straps/slots should be at or below shoulder level (there should be a lower set of slots for convertible child safety seats); the harness straps should be close-fitting on your child; the harness clip needs to be at armpit level.

2. Infants less than 1 year old who are 20 to 35 pounds should use a convertible seat used facing the rear and placed in the backseat of your car. When you purchase, make sure the seat is for heavier infants. Secure with safety belt or LATCH system.

   How to use: same as above.

3. Preschoolers and toddlers refer to children 1 to 4 years weighing at least 20 pounds to 40 pounds. You should use a convertible/forward-facing seat; forward-facing-only seat, or high-back booster. Secure seat to vehicle by a safety belt or by the LATCH system.

   How to use: the seat should be correctly installed in the rear seat facing forward; the harness straps/slots should be at or above child's shoulders (this means you'll usually be using the top set of slots for convertible child safety seats); the harness straps should fit securely on your child with the harness clip at armpit level.

4. Young children are categorized as 4 to at least 8 years unless they are 4'9" (57") tall (then they can use a safety belt). The seats needed for these children are belt-positioning booster (no back, only) or high-back belt-positioning booster. Caution: you should not use with lap-only belts—belt-positioning boosters are used with lap and shoulder belts.

   How to use: the booster is to be used with an adult lap and shoulder belt and placed in the rear seat; the shoulder belt should rest securely across your child's chest and also rests on shoulder. Caution: the belt should never be placed under the arm or behind the back; the lap-belt should ride low, across the lap/upper thigh area—not across the stomach. It is very important to observe the rules of correct placement of seat belts. Should an accident occur, a seat belt riding on the stomach area can cause injury, as can a seat belt placed under the arm. These injuries can be serious.

CarLogic

LATCH, or lower anchors and tethers for children, grants two lower anchor attachments and a top tether (top strap). LATCH makes a car seat easier to install. They should be in vehicles from year 2003 on and in some 2001 and 2002 models. LATCH is no safer than a car seat that is properly installed with a seat belt, but therein lies the point of LATCH. It is easier to get a correct installation of a car seat if your vehicle is equipped with LATCH. Because of the ease of installation, a LATCH system makes life easier for parents and grandparents. As always, check your owner's manual to see what equipment comes on your vehicle and to make certain you know what type car seat/booster seats conform to LATCH criteria.

It is very important that your child is secured properly in a car seat, booster seat, or with a seat belt. Be sure to check NHTSA's website for valuable information for parents of children 0 to 16 on how to secure kids safely in vehicles.

Seat Belts

Your car's seat belts should never be cleaned with strong cleaners. A mild soap-and-water mixture is fine, or you can ask for a special cleaner at your auto-supply store. Remember to keep the metal part clean. It is very easy for sticky drinks and crumbs to accumulate on this part of the seat belt, so clean the buckle weekly as you clean the rest of the vehicle. Should you find your seat belt not working correctly, take your vehicle to your technician or dealership and remember it's best to replace a faulty seat belt rather than to have it repaired. This safety feature needs to be strong with all parts working correctly, so it's best to have the replacement done by a professional.

Just as we need to make sure our children are strapped in securely with belts positioned correctly, we need to strap ourselves in correctly as well. Here are a few tips to keep in mind:

- Always make sure the seat belt fits snugly; it should not be loose.
- Never place the shoulder belt under the arm or behind your back. The shoulder belt should rest across the chest.
- Never wear a lap belt across your stomach. The lap belt should rest low across a stronger part of your body, the hips.
- Pregnant women can and should wear lap and shoulder belts. Sit up straight and wear the lap belt low. Do not let it rest on your stomach, though! You need the belt to rest in a strong area of your body, not on soft tissue.

Airbags

Your airbag is the seat belt's helper. This safety equipment works together to keep you safe should you have a crash. The airbag does not take the place of a seat belt. Its job is to keep you from striking parts of the interior such as the steering wheel with your upper body and head. Airbags are usually good for 14 years, but check your owner's manual for sure. They cost around $500 should you have to replace one in a relatively new vehicle.

Airbags are used to protect the driver and passengers, but they can injure or even kill. Airbags deploy rapidly and violently. You should wear your safety belt and sit at least 10 inches away from the bag to avoid injury from the deployment of the airbag. Injuries like broken noses, arms, and facial bones, and head injuries have occurred. So remember: just as proper wearing of seat belts is important, so is staying the proper distance from your airbag. The NHTSA cautions that you (the driver) leave at least 10 inches between the center of your breastbone and the center of the steering wheel. Children under 12 should always be properly restrained in a rear seat. Modern cars include a switch to turn off the airbag system of the passenger seat, in which case a child-supporting seat must be installed. Another caution with side airbags is trying to help victims after an accident. The side-mounted airbags have been known to deploy after an accident, so keep this in mind when you come upon an accident scene.

Headrests

Did you know there is a reason for headrests? Headrests help your chances of getting out of a rear-ender without whiplash. Some vehicles today, such as those made by Volvo and Saab, have incorporated technology that tells the headrest to automatically adjust properly to support your neck in the event of a crash. But even if you don't have an automatically adjusting headrest, by making sure you manually adjust yours to just below the top of your head, you should be good to go!

B

Regular Maintenance Routine Checklists and Vehicle Fact Sheet

Before you check off any boxes on this checklist, make several copies: a copy for each car and more copies for several years of check-offs (for the period of time you think you'll keep each vehicle). For easy access, file the current year's checklist in your glove compartment.

Time intervals on some of the maintenance jobs may vary according to the make and model vehicle you have. Our recommendation is to check your owner's manual and see whether your manufacturer's recommendations go along with this list. In most cases they will, but if not, just pencil in the correct information for your specific make and model vehicle. For example, the times to change coolant vary according to type of coolant (how many years it is supposed to last) and whether your radiator, head, and block are made of aluminum. So checking your owner's manual is good practice. You can also buy test strips to check your coolant's alkalinity.

In this appendix, we also include a vehicle fact sheet. Your owner's manual will have answers to the questions on this list. It will only take a few minutes to fill out the fact sheet, and doing so will save you a lot of time and aggravation when you go to the auto-parts store or take your vehicle in to be serviced by your technician. Make sure you keep this fact sheet in your glove compartment as well.

Fill-Up Check

Make these checks weekly, if possible, and for sure every two weeks. To make these checks go as quickly as possible, most convenience stores have items needed to wipe dipsticks, wash windshields, inflate tires, and so on. Just put an air-pressure gauge for tire checks in your glove compartment and you'll be set.

Run your car through the car wash right after you fill up, and you'll have most of your car duties for the week done. (Wash your car at least every two weeks—every week is better!)

❑ Check engine oil.

❑ Check tires for cuts, wear, and bulges; check air pressure and inflate if necessary.

❑ Check windshield wiper fluid (check freezing point of fluid before cold weather months).

❑ Clean front and rear windshield and lights.

❑ Check antifreeze (coolant).

❑ Check Engine Light on (see Appendix A for more info).

Monthly Check

Continue your fill-up schedule and add the following:

❑ Check belts for slack and cracks.

❑ Check brake fluid and add as needed, being careful not to overfill.

❑ Check hoses for firmness and to spot bulges.

❑ Check power-steering fluid.

❑ Check transmission fluid.

❏ Check all lights and horn.

❏ Check for brake pulling on a straight traffic-free stretch of road. Rest hands lightly on steering wheel and make a gradual stop (don't slam on brakes). If the vehicle veers instead of stopping in a straight line, there is probably brake lining wear that needs checking out.

❏ Check tire alignment on a straight traffic-free stretch of road. Rest hands lightly on steering wheel (you can check tire alignment on the same trip as brake wear) and feel if the steering wheel is veering instead of going in a straight line. If there is veering, you have an alignment problem.

Three Months or 3,000-Mile Check

Do fill-up and monthly checks as usual and add the following:

❏ Check battery and cables when you have the oil changed.

❏ Check engine air filter.

❏ Change engine oil and filter.

❏ Check exhaust (visually inspect when car is not running).

Six Months or 6,000-Mile Check

Continue your fill-up and monthly checks as usual and add the following:

❏ Check chassis lubrication.

❏ Polish your vehicle.

❏ Check fuel filter.

❏ Check wiper blades for wear (probably need changing every six months).

12 Months or 12,000-Mile Check

Continue fill-up and monthly checks as usual and add the following:

❏ Emissions check (refer to Appendix A).

❏ Technician should check brakes.

❏ Check cabin air filter.

❏ Test coolant with test strip from auto-parts store.

Vehicle Fact Sheet

Make: _____

Model: _____

Year: _____

Type of transmission/fluid: _____

Horsepower: _____

How many cylinders: _____

Power-steering fluid: _____

Coolant brand: _____

Ratio of water to coolant: _____

Disc brakes: _____

Drum brakes: _____

Tire size/pressure: _____

Spark-plug gap/size: _____

Oil weight/capacity: _____

Oil-filter number: _____

Air-filter number: _____

Fuel-filter number: _____

Octane rating: _____

Type paint finish/color #: _____

Car-shampoo brand: _____

Car-wax brand: _____

Tire-cleaner brand: _____

Other info: _____

_____

_____

Appendix

Resources

It's always nice to have important information at your fingertips. Here are some resources that will help you in your search for an auto club or for organizations that give up-to-date information on all matters of vehicle safety. We've also included some great places to buy tools and purchase vehicle-specific auto-repair manuals.

Auto Club

A good auto club can be a great backup plan for on-the-road emergencies.

AAA Auto Club: www.aaa.com; 1-800-222-1134. Emergency road service covers you, as driver or passenger. Optional Plus coverage entitles members to up to 100 miles of free towing. When it's time to purchase a new or pre-owned car, find reduced member rates on insurance, financing, extended warranties, maintenance, or anything automotive. Check out their website for more information and to obtain a list of AAA-approved auto-repair facilities in your area.

Safety

Find the safest cars, cars with the best gas mileage, ways to help teen drivers become good drivers, and much more.

AAA Foundation for Traffic Safety: www.aaafoundation.org/home/. This site offers great information for safer driving, from infants (carrier seats) to elderly drivers. This not-for-profit, educational/research-heavy foundation works to make our roads safer through educating drivers. Check out their quizzes and articles.

Advocates for Highway and Auto Safety: www.saferoads.org/; 202-408-1711. This group is working to have state and federal laws passed that will make travel safer. The group consists of insurance companies, consumers, health and safety groups, and insurance agents. Look on this site to find out what is going on in Congress relating to safer travel, as well as information on automobile safety ranging from the latest news to special reports and fact sheets.

Federal Highway Administration: www.fhwa.dot.gov/; 202-366-0650. This organization is an agency of the U.S. Department of Transportation. Their objective is to ensure roads and highways are in good repair by offering financial and technological support. You will find interesting information about U.S. roads and highways on this site.

Insurance Institute for Highway Safety (IIHS): www.hwysafety.org/; 703-247-1500. The Insurance Institute for Highway Safety is supported by automobile insurers. The IIHS offers current educational information to help drivers of all ages reach their destinations safely. Look on this site for information on buying safer cars, how to help your teen drive smarter and safer, information on safety devices in your vehicle such as airbags, and just about anything relating to vehicle safety.

National Highway Traffic Safety Administration: www.nhtsa.dot.gov/. The site includes more than 1,000 informative safety articles on topics ranging from airbags to child-passenger safety to vehicle and equipment information.

National Oceanic and Atmospheric Administration (NOAA): www.spc. noaa.gov. Check this site for information on how to stay safe when driving during a tornado, storm forecasts, and more.

The Weather Channel: www.weather.com. This site offers good tips on driving in snowy and icy conditions, as well as travel forecasts.

Tools

Get out your tool wish-list and go shopping!

ALLDATA and AutoZone: www.autozone.com; 1-800-288-6966.
ALLDATA and AutoZone offer parts at stores and online. ALLDATA also offers vehicle-specific repair information and informative articles.

Craftsman Tools: www.craftsman.com; 1-800-349-4358. Craftsman Tools, sold at Sears stores, offer just about any tool you will need for routine maintenance and many repair jobs. A bonus to the convenience of shopping at Sears stores or at their online store is if a hand tool breaks you can return it for repair or replacement.

If you're a do-it-yourselfer, check out **Craftsman Club.** You'll receive an official club membership card that entitles you to additional savings on hundreds of Craftsman tools during Club Saver Days, a free subscription to the Craftsman Club newsletter (which includes coupons and special savings offers for club members only), projects, and even specials on tools just for kids. You'll also be able to take advantage of special members-only online features.

Mac Tools: www.mactools.com; 1-800-MAC-TOOLS. Mac Tools is a company that does sales through mobile distributors. To inquire about their 8,000-item product line, check their website. Their tool buyers are ever-vigilant about offering customers the most current and ergonomic tools available.

Shopping for a Vehicle and Car News

Edmunds: www.edmunds.com. This consumer-friendly site offers advice to consumers on how to buy a new or used car. It also offers an automated quote tool and has comprehensive coverage of car news from auto shows to NASCAR, plus much more.

Service Manuals

If you're looking for an auto-repair manual specific to your vehicle, here's where to buy!

RepairManual.com: www.repairmanuals.com; 1-800-426-4214. Offers Autodata, Bentley, Chilton, Clymer, Detroit Iron, Haynes, MBI, OEM, and Seloc repair manuals. They advise customers to check back daily because they are constantly adding inventory to their catalog. Their ambition is to offer any repair manual a customer might request. They also offer parts, parts books, owner's manuals, tools, brakes, gaskets, belts, and oil filters.

Glossary

air springs Computer solenoid-controlled springs that feature a chamber of trapped air that absorbs shock between the wheel and body of the car. What makes the air spring different from a metal spring is that an air spring does not vibrate more with an increased load like a metal spring does.

automatic transmission A gearbox that changes gear ratios without driver interference except for starting the vehicle and putting the vehicle in reverse.

backing plate A round plate found in the drum-brake system used as a mount for the wheel cylinder.

battery A cache of electrical energy for starting the engine. All cars and light trucks today have a 12-volt battery. Most are also maintenance-free, meaning you don't have to add water to them periodically. Some even have built-in charge indicators to tell you whether they need charging.

bead The part of the tire that is situated on the rim. It features a hoop of high-tensile steel wires. These wires secure the plies and fit the rim seat, which holds the tire onto the wheel.

bias ply Type of tire construction that uses plies that run side to side from one bead to the other at a right angle of 26 to 38 degrees. Sometimes called a cross-ply tire.

body controller A computer in your car. It is responsible for many qualities that make your car smarter and safer, such as alerting you to leaving your lights on, leaving your overhead light on, and telling you to take your keys out.

brake bleeding A procedure pertaining to hydraulic brake systems in which the brake lines (pipes and hoses containing the brake fluid) are purged of any air bubbles.

brake fluid Specially formulated liquid used in a hydraulic brake system. This liquid sends brake pedal pressure from the master cylinder to the wheel cylinders or calipers.

brake hoses Flexible tubes used to transmit fluid pressure.

brake lines Small tubes or hoses made of steel or rubber through which brake fluid runs.

brake pads In disc brakes, a lining made of friction material applied by the caliper to the disc that aids in stopping a vehicle.

brake shoes In a drum brake, the crescent-shaped metal part that is lined with a friction-type substance that when pressed against the drum the vehicle begins to slow and then stop.

camber A measure dealing with how a car corners. The tops of a car's wheels when on a flat surface tilt inward when the camber is negative, outward when it is positive. The difference in this number equals the vehicle's camber.

camshaft In an internal-combustion engine, a shaft with lobes that causes the intake and exhaust values to open and close at precise moments.

caster This is a measure to ascertain straight-line driving stability. It is the angle between the vehicle's steering axis and a vertical line and is viewed from the side of your vehicle.

coil Pertaining to the ignition, this is an electrical transformer that sends high voltage to the spark plugs.

coil spring A part of the suspension system, coil springs are made of a heavy-duty torsion bar that is coiled around an axis. The coil spring supports vehicle height and weight and extends and contracts to take on wheel road activity.

compression cycle One of the four steps in a four-stroke engine. Compression occurs as the piston moves downward, compressing the hydraulic fluid in the chamber below the piston.

connecting rod A part of the internal combustion engine, this metal rod connects piston to crankshaft—sends power—which employs the up-and-down motion of the spinning crankshaft.

coolant Used in the cooling system, coolant is a mixture of water and antifreeze (ethylene glycol). Coolant has many jobs: it lowers the freezing point of the water, prevents rust and corrosion, greases the water pump. Then coolant takes heat from the engine. This air is moved on through the radiator.

coolant recovery tank In the cooling system, an overflow storage tank in the engine compartment.

crankshaft Pertaining to the internal combustion engine, this is the main rotating shaft in the engine. It is part of a power transfer beginning as the connecting rods transmit power from the piston to the crankshaft; this transmits power to the transmission, then on to the driveshaft, and finally to the drive wheels.

cylinder In an internal combustion engine, the round, straight-sided cavity or chamber in the engine block where a piston resides.

cylinder block In an internal combustion engine, where the cylinders, crankshaft, and other principal parts are found.

cylinder head In an internal combustion engine, a removable part of the engine that covers cylinders and pistons. It contains most of the combustion chamber.

damper In the suspension system, this is a hydraulic device like a shock absorber. It is attached to the steering linkage. The damper absorbs road shock and steering problems.

diesel engines Feature an internal combustion engine in which the fuel is injected into the cylinder near the end of the compression stroke and is ignited by the heat of the compressed air in the cylinder. No spark plug or carburetor is needed.

diesel fuel Fuel that is run in vehicles with diesel engines.

differential In the drive-train system, a gearbox designed so that the power fed into it is split and delivered to two outputs that can turn at different speeds allowing wheels to turn at different speeds. This aids in cornering. In rear-wheel-drive vehicles, the differential is located in the rear of the vehicle. In front-wheel-drive vehicles, the differential is located in the transaxle.

disc brake A type of brake that slows or stops a vehicle using hydraulic pressure to apply pads against a rotor.

drum brake A type of brake that achieves stopping friction by shoes pressing against the inside of a rotating drum.

dynamic balancing Pertaining to your car's suspension system, this is a tire-balancing practice that requires spinning the wheel to identify the heavy spots on each side. If your tire is not balanced in this way, you will notice the car shimmy.

electronic ignition system This type of ignition system has an electronic control unit controlling the timing and firing of spark plugs instead of points and a condenser like the previous generation. It was born in the 1970s. Most cars today have computerized systems.

engine block *See* cylinder block.

exhaust valve This valve opens to allow the exhaust gases an exit from the combustion chamber to the exhaust manifold.

firewall A part of the car that separates the heat of the engine from the passenger compartment.

gapping A specific measured space between the spark plug electrodes or points. Most spark plugs come pre-gapped.

head gasket A seal located between the cylinder head and the engine block. The head gasket keeps the coolant out of the cylinder and also keeps it from becoming tainted by exhaust gases.

headliner The fabric or vinyl covering your automobile's roof.

hub The central part of a car wheel.

hydraulic pressure Pressure employed through liquid.

intake port The opening that allows the fuel-air mixture an entrance into the cylinder head.

intake valve In the internal combustion cycle, the valve that opens in order to allow the fuel-air mixture an entrance to the combustion chamber and then closes so the explosion can occur.

jacking up your car Lifting all or part of your car off ground level. There are many different kinds of jacks. Check your owner's manual to see what kind is in your car. Some common ones are different varieties of hydraulic jacks and the mechanical scissor jack.

leaf springs A part of the suspension system, these springs are layers of metal (called leaves) bound together to act as a single unit to absorb shocks.

lug nut A rounded nut that fits over a bolt used especially to attach a vehicle wheel to its axle.

lug wrench Used to remove lug nuts. Lug nuts secure the wheels to the vehicle. Some wrenches are L-shaped while others are X-shaped. They are usually found in the trunk of the car with the tire jack.

manual transmission (standard transmission) A part of the drive-train system, this transmission is one in which the driver changes gears using a hand-operated gearshift and a foot-operated clutch. A typical manual transmission has four or five speeds, with the final or highest gear being overdrive.

master cylinder A component of the brake system connected to the brake pedal and having a reservoir filled with hydraulic brake fluid. Pressure is developed when the driver depresses the brake pedal.

octane A part of gasoline that keeps internal combustion engines from knocking. An engine with high compression requires higher octane, but always check your owner's manual to make sure you are using the correct octane gasoline.

off-gassing The release of chemicals from treated components such as upholstery and carpet in a new car. These chemicals are responsible for the white film that occurs on the windows of new automobiles.

oil pan The place at the bottom of the crankcase that stores oil.

output shaft The main shaft in the transmission. It transfers power on toward the drive wheels.

penetrating oil Very low viscosity (thin) oil that can aid in the removal of stubborn or rusty nuts and bolts. *See also* viscosity.

piston A part of the internal combustion engine, this cylindrical part moves up and down inside the cylinder compressing the fuel-air mixture.

piston rings In the internal combustion engine, these rings seal the space between the piston and the cylinder wall and work to keep the fuel-air mixture in and oil out of the combustion chamber.

planetary gear set In the drive-train system, a set of gears that include several planet gears rotating around a central sun gear.

plies Part of the tire that is composed of layers of cord fabric and rubber that run from bead to bead and into the inner part of the tire. This provides a strong, flexible form to hold the air pressure your vehicle needs while being strong enough to ward off most road debris.

pound-feet The unit of measurement for torque. That is, one pound-foot is equal to the twisting force produced when a one-pound force is applied to the end of a one-foot-long lever.

power The rate or speed at which work is performed.

power brake booster In the brake system, a mechanism that uses engine vacuum to help you brake.

rack-and-pinion steering A steering system that works by turning the wheels with a small pinion gear meshing with a toothed bar or rack.

radial A type of tire construction that uses steel-cable belts that run from bead to bead or side to side and at a right angle to the center line of the tire. In this type of tire construction, a belt is needed to stabilize the tread and define the tire diameter. Most cars today are equipped with radial tires.

radiator In the cooling system, the part of the system that gets rid of engine heat.

recirculating-ball steering A steering mechanism in which the steering shaft turns a worm gear that, in turn, causes a toothed metal block, which houses recirculating-ball bearings, to move back and forth.

return springs Springs used on drum brakes to pull the brake shoes away from the drums when the brakes are released.

rotor A disc-shaped component that revolves with hub and wheel. Also called disc.

run-flat tires When regular tires lose air, you cannot continue driving safely. But with run-flat tires you can drive to the nearest service station safely and without damaging your tire or wheel. This new technology adds sidewall stiffness to tires to allow the driver to continue at low speeds without air. Newer technology has produced designs that incorporate a liner around the wheel inside the tire to add support if air pressure is lost.

self-adjuster A device on a drum brake that counterbalances brake lining wear by keeping the shoe close to the drum.

serpentine belt A single continuous belt used to drive multiple devices, such as alternators, power-steering pumps, coolant pumps, and A/C compressors.

sidewall The part of the tire between the bead and the tread. The sidewall is made to be pliable to take bumps yet stiff to avoid buckling. This is also the part of the tire with all the vital information written on it.

solenoid A coil used to produce a magnetic field. It can be made to open and close electric circuits, and to open and close valves.

spark plug This is a part in the combustion chamber of an internal combustion engine. It is made of conductive core inside of a ceramic insulator.

specific gravity The weight of a liquid.

speed sensors In the braking system, the antilock braking system needs some way of knowing when a wheel is about to lock up. Speed sensors that are located either at each wheel or in the differential relay this information.

springs In the suspension system, springs have many jobs, such as supporting the vehicle's weight and absorbing shocks from bumps and dips in the road.

standard transmission *See* manual transmission.

static balancing Pertaining to your suspension, a process of wheel balance that depends on the equal distribution of weight evenly around the axle. A vehicle that has not been balanced in this way may shake.

steering linkage The steering linkage connects the steering wheel to the front wheels.

steering system A system that enables the driver to guide and direct the vehicle.

struts A structural suspension member that resists compression. It is also the shock absorber shaft.

sump Part of the engine system, it surrounds the crankshaft and holds some oil, which collects in the bottom of the sump (the oil pan).

suspension system A system that carries weight, sustains and regulates shock, and helps maintain tire contact.

sway bar Used in a suspension system to control vehicle body roll. Helps to keep the vehicle flat as it rounds a corner.

thermostat A part of the cooling system, this device controls how long it takes the engine to get warm. It does not open to allow coolant into the system until the engine is warm enough. Then the valve opens and coolant begins to circulate.

tire-wear indicator bars Strips of rubber on your tire that will tell you when it's time to buy new tires.

toe-in Pertaining to the suspension system, an alignment that allows for appropriate steering and balanced tire wear.

torque Turning or twisting force.

transaxle The transmission in a front-wheel drive vehicle. It combines both transmission and differential into one assembly.

transmission In the drive-train system, the gearbox that multiplies engine torque via gear reduction or torque conversion.

tread The part of a tire designed to contact the ground. Tread is made of rubber tough enough to live up to starts, stops, and cornering. A good tread grants high traction and low wear.

tread pattern The pattern in the part of the tire that makes contact with the road. This design helps the vehicle keep contact with the road when it rains and reduces the chance for hydroplaning.

unsprung mass In the suspension system, unsprung mass is the mass between the road and the suspension springs.

valve A device that controls pressure by opening or closing.

valve cover These relate to cars with overhead cams. The cover is made of thin sheet metal and covers the valve train.

valve train The valve train consist of rocker arms, valve springs, push rods, lifters, and cam.

vapors Particles floating in your new car that form fog, mist, or steam.

viscosity Used to describe your motor oil's thickness.

water pump A device in the cooling system used to pump antifreeze or coolant through the cooling system. The water pump is belt-driven and begins working when you start the engine.

wheel cylinder A disc that turns hydraulic pressure from the master cylinder into mechanical force that initiates the brake shoes to engage.

Index